Chinese Stardom in Participatory Cyberculture

International Film Stars

Series Editors: R. Barton Palmer and Homer B. Pettey

This series is devoted to the artistic and commercial influence of performers who shaped major genres and movements in international film history. Books in the series will:

- Reveal performative features that defined signature cinematic styles
- Demonstrate how the global market relied upon performers' generic contributions
- Analyse specific film productions as case studies that transformed cinema acting
- Construct models for redefining international star studies that emphasise materialist approaches
- Provide accounts of stars' influences in the international cinema marketplace

Titles available:

Close-Up: Great Cinematic Performances Volume 1: America
edited by Murray Pomerance and Kyle Stevens

Close-Up: Great Cinematic Performances Volume 2: International
edited by Murray Pomerance and Kyle Stevens

Chinese Stardom in Participatory Cyberculture
by Dorothy Wai Sim Lau

edinburghuniversitypress.com/series/ifs

Chinese Stardom in Participatory Cyberculture

Dorothy Wai Sim Lau

EDINBURGH
University Press

Edinburgh University Press is one of the leading university presses in the UK. We publish academic books and journals in our selected subject areas across the humanities and social sciences, combining cutting-edge scholarship with high editorial and production values to produce academic works of lasting importance. For more information visit our website: edinburghuniversitypress.com

© Dorothy Wai Sim Lau, 2019

Edinburgh University Press Ltd
The Tun – Holyrood Road
12 (2f) Jackson's Entry
Edinburgh EH8 8PJ

Typeset in 12/14 Arno and Myriad by
IDSUK (Dataconnection) Ltd,
and printed and bound in Great Britain

A CIP record for this book is available from the British Library

ISBN 978 1 4744 3033 3 (hardback)
ISBN 978 1 4744 3035 7 (webready PDF)
ISBN 978 1 4744 3036 4 (epub)

The right of Dorothy Wai Sim Lau to be identified as author of this work has been asserted in accordance with the Copyright, Designs and Patents Act 1988 and the Copyright and Related Rights Regulations 2003 (SI No. 2498).

Contents

List of figures   vi
Acknowledgements   viii
Notes on the text   ix

Introduction: a phenomenon after cinema – the Chinese
    stardom goes 'cyber'   1

1   Blogging Donnie Yen: remaking the martial arts body as a
    cyber-intertext   29

2   'Flickering' Jackie Chan: the actor-ambassadorial persona
    on photo-sharing sites   57

3   'Friending' Jet Li on Facebook: the celebrity-philanthropist
    persona in online social networks   84

4   YouTubing Zhang Ziyi: Chinese female stardom in fan
    videos on video-sharing sites   107

5   Discussing Takeshi Kaneshiro: the pan-Asian star image on
    fan forums   130

Conclusion: reimagining Chineseness in the global cyberculture   163

Bibliography   171
Filmography   194
Index   201

Figures

I.1 Two female warriors in *Crouching Tiger, Hidden Dragon*
fighting with 'Star Wars' lightsabers   3

I.2 Gong Li and Chow Yun-fat in the Chinese epic drama,
Curse of the Golden Flower   10

I.3 Jet Li's Wong Fei-hung in *Once Upon a Time in China* is
exemplary to the national allegory of China   17

1.1 A movie still of *Ip Man* included in a blog entry of
'The Fightland Blog'   36

1.2 The cinematic personality of Bruce Lee in *Enter the Dragon*
in the entry entitled 'Everyone was kung fu fighting:
the story of Ip Man'   43

1.3 The blogger poaches and posts an archival picture of Bruce
Lee and the Wing Chun master Ip Man   44

1.4 An online image of Donnie Yen's son dressed as Chirrut
Îmwe and his daughter as a Stormtrooper as part of the
family's Halloween celebration   50

2.1 'Jackie Chan's Star' – the title of a tourist's photograph
posted on Flickr   60

2.2 Lu Yan in *The Forbidden Kingdom*: showing Jackie Chan's
acrobatic performativity   71

2.3 'Jackie Chan feeling the love of his country'   78

2.4 As a UNICEF ambassador, Jackie Chan displays his paternal
power in front of the press in Myanmar   81

3.1 A Facebook picture shows Jet Li lending a shoulder to a
weeping victim during the relief work of the Yushu earthquake   92

3.2 An online game launched by the One Foundation as part of
     the fundraising for the relief work of Sichuan earthquake in
     China in 2008   95
3.3 A video post celebrates Jet Li's birthday yet promotes the
     actor-philanthropist's Buddhist-based image   100
4.1 'Ziyi Zhang and Michelle Yeoh talk about *Memoirs of A
     Geisha* on NBC's *Today* show'   116
4.2 The YouTube video encompassing images of Zhang Ziyi's
     'sex photo-gate' copied from the video-sharing site
     www.ku6.com   120
5.1 Takeshi Kaneshiro as the subject of celebrity endorsement
     of CITIZEN in 2012   131
5.2 The camera focuses on the 'beautiful' faces of Takeshi
     Kaneshiro and Gigi Leung in *Tempting Heart*   138
5.3 Creative work themed on 'Help for Japan: Hope' by Internet
     user 'mikomi'   157
5.4 'mikomi''s the other painting called 'Fukushima' as a means
     to solicit help from the Internet public to help Japan's
     recovery from the catastrophe   159

Acknowledgements

I would like to express my gratitude to Edinburgh University Press (EUP) for publishing my book. I very much appreciate my editors Gillian Leslie and Richard Strachan for their efficient work and timely help that made the publication of this book possible.

This book is developed from my PhD project. I owe Professor Esther Yau, my PhD supervisor and my mentor, for her advice, guidance, and confidence, given to me in my academic pursuit. Her intellectual vision and experience are always the source of inspiration to me. Moreover, I am indebted to the examiners of my PhD thesis – Professor Gina Marchetti, Professor Stephen Chu, and Professor Sze-wei Ang – for the useful comments they provided on various occasions.

I am wholeheartedly grateful for the emotional and practical support given by my family, especially my husband Alfred Yuen (阮立秋) and my son Pat-ngo Yuen (阮不我). The unfailing love, patience, and support Alfred offers me in my intellectual quest and in my life journey are always most valued. Special thanks to Pat-ngo who was born during the time I worked on this book project. As many people perceive, his arrival makes my writing as well as my role as a scholar-mother challenging, yet also incredibly rewarding.

Lastly, my thanks go to the publishers and editors who have granted permission for republishing the materials in my previous writings. A small portion of Chapter 2 is published in *Continuum: Journal of Media & Cultural Studies*, March 2014. Part of Chapter 3 appears in *Journal of Asian Cinema* 26:2, 2016. Chapter 4 is derived, in part, from my published essay in *Journal of Chinese Cinemas* 11:3, 2017. An earlier version of Chapter 5 has been accepted by *positions: asia critique* (to be published) and is reproduced here with its permission.

Notes on the text

This book examines Chinese stardom in participatory cyberculture. It uses the English names of the stars for the keyword-searches on the web to indicate the transnational capacity of the personalities. With the consideration of the fact that this method generates results not only in English but also in Chinese, accordingly, a translation of the Chinese-language materials, including fan-written texts, magazines, and online videos, is necessary. All the translations from Chinese to English have been done by the author, unless otherwise indicated.

The names of the Chinese stars will be primarily translated into the versions that are most popular in the Western or English-language world for easy reference, regardless of the origin of the celebrities, for example, Jet Li (from mainland China) not Li Lianjie, Jackie Chan (from Hong Kong) not Shing Lone, and Michelle Yeoh (from Malaysia) not Yeoh Choo-Kheng. For other names, which are often the well-circulated ones in media and fan discourses, this book primarily employs two streams of the Romanisation system for addressing stars from mainland China and stars from Hong Kong. For the former, the book adopts the pinyin system, which is the standard transliteration based on Mandarin pronunciation, for instance, Zhang Ziyi and Gong Li. For the latter, the book uses the Cantonese pinyin system, such as Chow Yun-fat, rather than Zhou Runfa. For both cases, the book follows the Chinese tradition of enunciating names by putting surnames prior to the given names.

Another aspect about the use of language to note refers to quotes of online texts. In order to keep the authenticity of the texts, this book will retain the original version, even though they may include incorrect spellings or grammatical errors.

Introduction

A phenomenon after cinema – the Chinese stardom goes 'cyber'

Stardom in participatory cyberspace

The success of Ang Lee's *Crouching Tiger, Hidden Dragon* (2000) is a phenomenal cinematic and cultural occurrence: a Mandarin-language, martial–arts–romance crossover hit, starring a highly celebrated Chinese cast became the highest-grossing foreign-language film ever in America in 2000 (Wu and Chan 2007: 196). It has also broken the box-office record for foreign-language films in England, Germany, France, Australia, and New Zealand (ibid.). In addition to the commercial acclaim, the film has nearly every component necessary to make it an 'authentically' Chinese production, for example, an iconic Chinese setting, period costume, and the Mandarin language the film adopts, assisting the film's market success of 'repackaging an ethnic story for a global audience' (Wang and Yeh 2005: 179). Among all these components, what thrilled viewers most was the magnificent martial arts action – leaps and bounds, fights and flights – in the film. A favourite scene features megastar Chow Yun-fat and then-newcomer Zhang Ziyi duelling while standing on slender, bending branches in the bamboo forest. Under the coaching given by renowned Hong Kong choreographer Yuen Woo-ping, the stars display acrobatic agility and dexterity, which is far from the result of mere wire-work. Their kinetic, dance-like movements carry the reinvented art of a longstanding tradition that is both captivating and mystifying. Some years after the release of *Crouching Tiger, Hidden Dragon*, scenes from the movie continue to circulate among the audience on the Internet. On YouTube, a platform that makes possible the virtually instantaneous broadcasting of moving images recreated by anybody, approximately 6,000 entries show up with the search words and the tags marked by the English film title. Some movie clips are directly cut from the movie's digital video disc (DVD) version; some others are the remix of elements from other films. Among the 'remix' entries, a constellation of videos feature the swordfight between Jen (Zhang Ziyi) and Shu Lien (Michelle Yeoh), with the heroines' swords turning into the lightsabers in Hollywood's all-time classic *Star Wars* (1977)[1] (Figure I.1). Shu Lien's sword glows red whereas Jen's glows green, alluding to the 'Green Destiny' as the plot reveals. All of a sudden, Zhang Ziyi and Michelle Yeoh have become 'Star Wars' female warriors, fighting in a digital realm combining martial arts acrobatics. The authentic kinetic choreography is infused with virtual effects to engender a new martial arts representation.

The cluster of 'fan-made' images on YouTube works to threaten the 'hegemony' of professional image-makers and propels screen performers into a situation where the image bite can replace the integrated performance (Pomerance 2012: 3). Such a kind of new representation becomes equally phenomenal in the sequel *Crouching Tiger, Hidden Dragon: Sword of Destiny* (2016), which was first released at Netflix, as part of the streaming texts (Robinson 2016). Different from its predecessor, the sequel is all English-language, which is an obvious offer for commercial appeal globally. This time the movie re-stars Michelle Yeoh, who is coupled with Donnie Yen, the most prominent martial arts star, to perform the action under the choreographic direction of Yuen Woo-ping again. Notwithstanding the presence of the martial arts talents, the physical prowess of the performers is put under question while the visuals are supplemented by computer-generated imagery (CGI) effects. The digitally reworked images of these two movies typify the display of the epic's action on screens other than the celluloid ones, evident in the emergence of 'multiply networked, distributed forms of cinematic production and exhibition' (Grusin 2016: 66). They also call into question the traditional manner in which globally known Chinese personalities are approached, explored, and contended with the arrival of cyberculture.

Cyberculture, which expresses key components involved in developing digital culture, provides an entry point of enquiry of this book. Pierre Lévy (2001), a prominent French philosopher and sociologist, defines cyberculture as a set of material and intellectual techniques: practices, modes of thinking, values, and attitudes that evolve alongside the growth of cyberspace. The term 'cyberspace' was coined by William Gibson in 1984 in his science-fiction novel entitled *Neuromancer*. It refers to the universe of digital networks, which becomes the battlefield of multi-nationals of global conflicts, cultural frontiers, and the new economics.

Figure I.1 Two female warriors in *Crouching Tiger, Hidden Dragon* fighting with 'Star Wars' lightsabers

Gibson's notion of cyberspace calls for consciousness with respect to the geographic movement of information, which is often invisible. As a global and dynamic domain synonymous to 'network', cyberspace offers a new medium for communication, akin to 'an immense heterogeneous virtual metaworld' (Lévy 2001: 25) undergoing relentless makeover and evolution.

The World Wide Web, a manifestation of cyberculture, is increasingly pervaded by crossover film talents who reside in a publicity atmosphere subdued by computer-based imagery as much as by cinema itself (Pomerance 2012: 8). The twenty-first century witnesses the convergence of popular film and the Internet, which in Julian Stringer's (2003) fancy phrase, 'appea[r] to be a match made in heaven' (276). As a portion and extension of the Internet, the World Wide Web is an information-sharing model utilising browsers to access web pages that are joined with one another via hyperlinks. As a vast 'territory' that expands at an ever-accelerating rate (Lévy 2001: 67), it is a twenty-four-hour global network developed as a new means of proliferating popular construction. Whereas the star system on the web shows continuities of the previous mode of star discourse, it generates new ways of understanding, discussing, and consuming fame. News, photographs, and videos about personalities can be publicised and relayed on promotional websites, entertainment sites, fan sites, and online clubs with unprecedented speed and spread.

Furthermore, dynamic configuration of stars in cyberspace suggests an absence of centre in the star-making process. Cyberspace is a transparent, navigable communication terrain in which one perceives the computer as not the centre but a knot or component of the calculating network. This is what Lévy means when Lévy characterises cyberspace as 'universal without totality' (2001: 91–102). Without centre or guideline, texts are produced in a manner that they can be connected to any point in any context, regardless of the significance of any related entities. Cyberspace is universal because it enables anybody in the world, irrespective of time and space, to be part of it. This is echoed by Paul McDonald's (2000) observation, which reads, 'If the World Wide Web has done anything to change the star system, it is through decentering the production of star discourses' (114–15). It points to the cultural circumstance in which the democratisation of the star-making process began to burgeon.

While the World Wide Web has already spawned a new genre of star texts, the emergence of Web 2.0 in the mid-2000s has pushed the change further, redefining star-making at the more forefront edge of digital technologies (Lévy 2001: 14). In the Internet culture earlier than the '2.0' era, fan sites replace the traditional circuits such as fan magazines and fan clubs, permitting the followers to circulate texts and resources about their idols. However, the hosts of the sites are often leaders in the fan groups. Web 2.0 has further advanced the fan-oriented expression and exchange, not inclined to privileged members in the group while allowing ordinary fans to be the agents of producing and distributing star-related texts. The term Web 2.0 was popularised by Tim O'Reilly, a data scientist, in 2004, alongside the proliferation of communications technologies and the growth of fan culture. The emphasis on user-generated content (UGC) endorses users to write, edit, organise, and post their own texts and to comment on or share those posted by others. A range of Web 2.0 sites such as photo-sharing sites, video-sharing sites, social networking sites, and blogs is marked by the 'architecture of participation', in O'Reilly's (2004) phrase, granting immense space for users' voice. The buzzwords of Web 2.0 like 'blogging', 'flickering', 'friending', and 'YouTubing' have become the key tropes that reshape the interplay of screen stardom and cyber stardom. These terms refer to a set of fan-based practices and logics that take roots from the earlier forms of star construction while they involve novel ways to create the personalities. The emergent mode of star discourse apprehends the fan autonomy and agency, making fans become full participants in cultural production.

As a domain basically without hierarchical orders and principles, Web 2.0 is the technical expression of a movement that begins from the bottom and that counteracts the top–down mode of conventional star-making. User participation fundamentally operates beyond the control of studios and agents, destabilising the monopoly over star construction by institutional forces like studios and star agents. Even though once film stardom was intertexual and multi-faceted that encompasses filmmakers, marketers, reviewers, fans, and the stars themselves, it appears to be a 'shared, but never equal, venture' (Austin 2003: 25) in which producers seem to possess privileges over the stakeholders in the star discourse. Differently, cyberspace has recognised that every user is a potential writer. Audiences are not mere consumers or users but also producers of cultural texts. The new breed of 'pro-sumer' (Toffler 1980: 5) and 'prod-user' (Bruns 2005: 23, 315–16) subverts the hierarchy of the star system, emancipating fan power with an unparalleled prevalence and magnitude.

The advanced form of fans' communication networks in cyberculture enables a heightened public scrutiny of stars by permitting an 'informal' variety of materials. Gossip, rumour, sexualised, or nude images hold more appeal for users than the institutionalised personae. Revelations of the 'hidden truths' of famed figures make star narratives more intriguing and controversial than previous modes of star knowledge, derived from professional identities. Stars and their personnel often closely monitor the materials that may not be 'legitimate' or even 'transgressive' yet of public curiosity, to give timely responses and take measures to remedy or salvage the reputation.

Furthermore, because participatory websites are open to everyone, stars and their personal assistants can launch 'fan' accounts at various sites to post 'desirable' news and photographs as part of the fame management and marketing. While professional journalism and studio propaganda monopolise and manipulate the publicity, participatory sites proffer 'a new context in which movie stars could peddle their "monopoly personalities"' (Pomerance 2012: 3). Through deploying a grassroots media conduit, celebrities and media companies conceal their continued hold on persona manipulation, presenting themselves as part of the fan community. A star can join Facebook and 'friend' numerous users, keeping fans updated on his or her work and attracting a broad following by forging social links and networks with other users. The marketing team can post movie stills and 'behind-the-scenes' photographs on Flickr, or make images available for purchase online. This advertising strategy achieves two results: first, a favourable image can be retained or an undesirable one redressed; second, media institutions can make money through the Web 2.0 sites, tapping into the networked public to generate part of the income for the movie project. This exemplifies the merge of industry logic and grassroots intensity, which resourcefully shapes the star construction in the current epoch.

Chinese movie stars in the global cyber setting

In view of the flourishing star construction in cyberspace, this book chooses to locate the analysis within the debates on Chinese film stars. Chinese stardom has been an expanding but under-explored area in recent scholarship. Call to mind that *Newsweek* in 2005 made a prediction about a return of international stardom in which Chinese personalities have earned prominence by participating in Hollywood productions and exhibitions as well as winning recognition in major international film festivals. The star phenomenon not only signifies a shift in the flow of global media capital, but also this gives their performers broad exposure outside China, bridging their names to audiences worldwide. Critical works such as Mary Farquhar and Yingjin Zhang's *Chinese Film Stars* (2010), the first anthology of the object of enquiry, show an effort of intervening in the field of star studies that has prosperously developed in the West. It encompasses a cluster of 'historically, geographically and aesthetically multifaceted star phenomena' studied through different approaches. Recent monographs devoted to individual stars such as Jet Li (Yu 2012) and Chow Yun-fat (Feng 2017) are informative additions to the scholarship. Two volumes explore Li and Chow in terms of how the territory of their stardom is expanded from Hong Kong cinema to trans-national cinema. Yu's book explores the star image of Jet Li who evolves from a Chinese wuxia hero to a transnational kung fu icon. Feng's study on Chow Yun-fat examines the role of Chow in mediating Hong Kong and Chinese identities in the dialectics of traditional and modern, East and West, and local and global. Whereas Yu's and Feng's books contribute to the current intellectual discourse of Chinese stardom, nonetheless, book-length studies of the subject are still in sheer paucity.

The Chinese personalities that formulate the scene of transnational stardom attracts critical attention. Existent literature, generally speaking, positions the Chinese stars who enjoy global presence along two vectors: first, the successful border-crossing of the Chinese martial arts or martial arts-inspired genres, and, second, the worldwide reception of Chinese films produced by fifth-generation directors in the 1990s and 2000s, of which the two vectors may contain some overlaps over each other. Hollywood's co-opting of Hong Kong film talents in the 1980s and 1990s vitally constitutes the scene of global film culture and raises Hong Kong/Chinese martial arts action to the international audiences. The three clusters of émigrés designated to various phases of the influx include: first, directors like John Woo, Tsui Hark, Ronny Yu, Stanley Tong, and Kirk Wong; second, performers including Jackie Chan, Jet Li, and Chow Yun-fat; and, third, choreographers such as Yuen Woo-ping Yuen, Yuen Cheung-yan, and Corey Yuen. In view of the second phase of the influx, literature discusses Hong Kong film stars such as Jackie Chan (Fore 1997; Gallagher 2004; Farquhar 2010), Jet Li (Stringer 2003; Yu 2012), Chow Yun-fat (Feng 2011), Michelle Yeoh (Funnell 2013a), and Donnie Yen (Funnel 2013b; Hunt 2014) with respect to the themes like transnational Hong Kong action and Chinese masculinity. While the screen spectacle impresses Hong Kong audiences, the stars have established the action fighter image for an audience beyond Hong Kong as the result of distribution in Southeast Asia and overseas Chinese communities. Soon being discovered by American cinephiles and distributors, their kinetic personae elevate them to superstardom as representatives of Hong Kong cinema on American and European screens.

Whereas fans hail the death-defying stunts and martial prowess, such fan fascination does not come from nowhere and bears certain historical traces. It can be considered as an extension of the 'kung fu craze' in the United States approximately a decade ago that shows the initial clues of the border-crossing occurrence. In the 1970s, Warner Brothers built the wave with enthusiasm that surpassed other studios in producing and distributing martial arts movies (Desser 2000: 24). A couple of television series named *Kung Fu* and *Enter the Dragon* produced by Warner Brothers serve as evidence of the marketability of the genre. Yet one could not find an apparent icon of the genre that could stand in the American arena until the emergence of Bruce Lee. Lee was the first and foremost figure who facilitated international Chinese stardom. Before Lee, Chinese actors and actresses of the cinemas of Hong Kong and Taiwan were known mainly within the regions. With his stardom rooted in Hong Kong cinema and the Mandarin-language movie circuit, Lee became famous to foreign audiences through his kung fu features circulated in the United States and Europe. His fans in different regions established diverse communication channels to circulate the news and images of Lee in their networks. For instance, 'Bruce Lee Fanzine', as an unofficial and non-professional publication, was launched in 1973 alongside the release of *Fist of Fury* in the same year. Evolved from mimeographed fanzines and self-published slash fiction that originated in the 1930s and was popularised in the 1940s, fanzines themed on Bruce Lee cover a wide range of materials, such as news, movie reviews, interviews, or even gossip about the megastar. The popularity of Bruce Lee in the West paves the way for Hollywood's subsequent import of Hong Kong film talents and the worldwide cult following of the icons.

Whereas the Chinese stars appear compelling and exotic in Hollywood narratives, the Chineseness is in part ethnicised or racialised while being globalised. Gina Marchetti's study, *The Chinese Diaspora on American Screens: Race, Sex, and Cinema* (2012), positions Jackie Chan and Jet Li in the dynamics between the African and Chinese diasporas as played out in Hollywood star vehicles. She probes the black connection in *The Karate Kid* (2010) and the interracial romance in *Romeo Must Die* (2000) within the framework of the martial arts genre. In her *Jet Li: Chinese Masculinity and Transnational Film Stardom* (2012), Sabrina Yu emphasises Jet Li's films in Hollywood, framing the actor as a crossover star and entangling the issues of transnational action and Chinese masculinity. Lisa Funnell's monograph entitled *Warrior Women: Gender, Race, and the Transnational Chinese Action Star* (2014) explores a range of female stars from Michelle Yeoh and Zhang Ziyi to Maggie Q and the Yuan sisters (Eugenia Yuan and Marsha Yuan) in the context of the Hong Kong–Hollywood connection. Analysis of the screen identities of the action heroines is tied to the racial stereotyping of Asian in Hollywood. While the border-crossing capacity of these transnational stars largely relies on the success of being cast in English-speaking Hollywood motion pictures, the star image evolves and confronts the polemics of the national and transnational, the local and the global, the 'Chinese' and the cosmopolitan.

In addition to the transnational Hong Kong action, the Fifth Generation directors' films from mainland China unpack a more recent mainstay of transnational Chinese stardom. Zhang Yimou and Chen Kaige, two leading figures of this movement, are famous for a cinematic expressivity and visual aesthetic that has impressed critics, scholars, and viewers across the globe. Zhang Yimou's early films – namely *Red Sorghum* (1987), *Ju Dou* (1990), and *Raise the Red Lantern* (1991) – all starring Gong Li as the lead actress, have received major awards at prestigious Berlin,

Venice, and Cannes film festivals. As equally notable as Chen Kaige's *Farewell My Concubine* (1993), which also stars Gong Li as well as Hong Kong pop singer Leslie Cheung, and that won the Cannes Palme d'Or for that year. These achievements were important milestones in the quest of international stardom of Chinese performers in the non-Hollywood-based circuitry.

Following the success of these films, the proliferation of pan-Chinese filmmaking extends the access of the charisma of Chinese stars in the milieu of global capitalism. The decade of 2000s witnesses the state-owned studios merge or rebuild themselves as vast entertainment conglomerates, becoming part of the process of 'industrializing Chinese cinema' (Zhang 2008: 104). A highly commercialised mode of production and cutting-edge technology – the core elements of the 'blockbuster' outlook – spawns the pervasiveness of the allure of the performers. Colliding with the emergence of the 'corporate era', Zhang Yimou, after several years of relative dormancy in the latter half of the 1990s, revitalises his filmmaking career with two martial arts epics: *Hero* (2002) and *House of Flying Daggers* (2004). Pursuing the trend of creating multi-starrer co-productions (Willis and Leung 2014: 7) purported by *Crouching Tiger, Hidden Dragon* (2000), *Hero* is the first global blockbuster produced in mainland China that has attracted audiences both in and outside China and has set a model for the transnational mode of production (Rawnsley and Rawnsley 2010: 1, 4; Khoo 2010: 123). Zhang Yimou's *House of Flying Daggers* (2004) and *Curse of the Golden Flower* (2006), Chen Kaige's *The Promise* (2005), Feng Xiaogang's *The Banquet* (2006), John Woo's *Red Cliff* (2008), and Jiang Wen's *Let the Bullet Fly* (2010) follow such a model and formulate a 'pan-Chinese', or 'pan-Asian', creative-productive network.[2] These productions received satisfactory box-office returns in North America and worldwide, capitalising on the Orientalist imagination as part of the marketised discourse (Figure I.2). They employ high-powered casts from Hong Kong (Donnie Yen, Tony Leung Chiu-wai, Chow Yun-fat, Maggie Cheung, Andy Lau, Daniel Wu, Nicholas Tse, Cecilia Cheung) the PRC (Jet Li, Zhang Ziyi, Gong Li, Zhao Wei, Zhou Xun, Liu Ye), and Taiwan (Takeshi Kaneshiro, Chang Chen, Jay Chou). The list includes the key action stars who have been filmed in Hollywood films and those who are better known in festival and art-house circuitry chiefly through the films of Wong Kar-wai. Literature explores personalities like those of Maggie Cheung (Williams 2003; Hudson 2006; Wang 2012; Chan 2014), Tony Chiu-wai Leung (Gallagher 2015, 2016), and Leslie Cheung (Stringer 2010; Chan

2010) as polysemic, multi-dimensional, and hybridised, not lying in the paradigm of the Orientalised image as their action counterparts whose transnational profile was more Hollywood-oriented. Their star presence embodies 'mutating currencies of transnationality' (Lee 2011: 1), which seems more complex and unstable than the outcome of mere 'Hollywoodisation' or 'Americanisation'. It coincides with Lisa Funnell's (2013b) argument that it is necessary for transnational Chinese stardom to move beyond the Hollywood crossover and to consider the stars within Chinese industrial contexts (118). It also prompts us to reevaluate the transnational Chinese image without presuming that globalisation is always 'Western'. These famed figures present a cultural critique of the West, particularly Western modernity, and introduce change and complexity in hegemonic dynamics. Whereas the tension between Chinese-speaking stars and the Anglo-American system is often the critical focus, such tension was not set up as solely between the oft-cited dichotomy of 'East' and 'West'. Rather, it is established in a network for connecting new visualities and communities, which emerged as a result of global capitalism (Yue and Khoo 2014: 4), reimagining Chineseness in the milieu of contemporary border-crossing stardom.

Figure I.2 Gong Li and Chow Yun-fat are in the main cast of the Chinese epic drama, *Curse of the Golden Flower* (2006), which exhibits the appeal to the global film market

A shift of emphasis in the dialectics of East–West film industries is further evident in the Chinese icons who persistently shuttle between various film industries. Many transnational Chinese stars succeed in gaining popularity in the global cinematic arena and many of them have returned to Hong Kong, China, or Asia to continue their film careers. Since the mid-decade of the 2000s, Jackie Chan has travelled between the borders of Asia and Hollywood for movies. His 'homecoming' works include *New Police Story* (2004), *The Myth* (2005) – on which he collaborated with director Stanley Tong who also made his return after his stay in Hollywood, *Shinjuku Incident* (2009), *Shaolin* and *1911* (both 2011). Chow Yun-fat, subsequent to his famous appearance in *Crouching Tiger, Hidden Dragon* (2000), came back to China for movies such as Zhang Yimou's *Curse of the Golden Flower* (2006), the biographical drama *Confucius* (2010), Jiang Wen's noir action comedy *Let the Bullets Fly* (2010), and Wong Jing's crime drama *The Last Tycoon* (2012). Zhang Ziyi, after her performance in *Memoirs of a Geisha* (2005) as a member of the main cast, participates in an array of pan-Asian productions directed by the well-known Chinese or Hong Kong filmmakers, for example, Feng Xiaogang's costume drama *The Banquet* (2006), Chen Kaige's biographical picture *Forever Enthralled* (2008), and Wong Kar-wai's 'Ip Man movie' *The Grandmasters* (2013). John Woo, the foremost successful Hong Kong director in Hollywood, also has returned to China to make the historical epic *Red Cliff* (2008 and 2009). All these instances are solid evidence of the trend of global cinema turning to Asia, or China in particular, for new markets. This, moreover, suggests that 'global' Chinese stars have shifted their attention back to the mainland Chinese or Asian markets. The occurrence entails the intricate interplay of the Hong Kong, Chinese, and Hollywood film industries by replotting the border-crossing contours of Chinese martial arts imagery in global capitalism, complicating the transnational dynamics of institutions, representations, and identities.

At the juncture of cinematic culture and cyberculture, transnational Chinese stars become available to the global audience with the entertainment fodder in web-based channels. They are extensively discussed, followed, and tweeted on the web, proving their global fame not only in the Chinese-speaking world but in other language communities as well. Levelled to popular Hollywood stars like Brat Pitt, Robert Downey Jr, Angelina Jolie, Johnny Depp, and Leonardo DiCaprio, the Chinese personalties' presence in televised interviews, online entertainment tabloid news, viral video advertisements, and downloadable movie trailers universalises their crossover image and Orientalist allure.

The visibility of Chinese stars in the cyber setting, furthermore, advances the erudite discussions of the topic. Three studies offer an analysis of online discourse, enquiring into the elaborate interplay of star construction and reception – with each study embracing its own focus. Julian Stringer (2003) offers a critical account of Asian American culture by analysing how the ambivalence of Asian American fans has shaped Jet Li's star image. As Stringer posits, whereas some fans relish Jet Li's 'perfect' Chineseness as embodied in his Hollywood roles, others highlight his limitations as an ethnic actor. Stringer accordingly suggests a need for continual interrogation of Li's image in the Asian American viewing circle. In addition, the two monographs written by Sabrina Yu and Lin Feng on particular Chinese stars, namely Jet Li and Chow Yun-fat, have devoted one chapter of their books on the star appeal in the online context, validating the growing importance of cyberspace as a new means of exploring Chinese personalities. Sabrina Yu (2010) evinces duality of star image by engaging with Jet Li's star construction through his publicity at The Official Jet Li Website. By investigating the three key aspects of Jet Li's offscreen persona – ordinary hero, moral model, and sexy icon – which contradict the screen images manifested on the website, Yu finds that both stars and fans play important roles in the star-making process. Lin Feng (2017) analyses the 'glocalised' star image of Chow Yun-fat by emphasising the online marketing campaign of the Hollywood franchise *Pirates of the Caribbean* of which the third instalment *At World's End* (2007) has starred Chow as a pirate captain, Sao Fung. The analysis relies on the empirical online results, arguing that the circulation of a transnational image exhibits multiplicity rather than universality of a star's publicity. Although these articles show a rising effort of studying Chinese stars in new space, the effort is far from being sufficient to catch up with the escalating visibility of the personalities on cyber screens.

In response to the intellectual gap, this book aims at examining the star phenomenon lying at the crossroads of Chinese stardom and cyberculture. This book is the first academic monograph that investigates Chinese stardom as a web-based cultural phenomenon and examines how fans reshape and contend with the ethnic-yet-global image of Chinese stars. What does it mean to call these stars 'Chinese' in the global cyber setting? How is the fame of performers retained, extended, or altered in such space? How do web users' activities valorise the processes? In order to respond to these questions in a comprehensive and extensive manner, this book, unlike Yu's and Feng's volumes that focus solely on one single figure, encompasses five transnational Chinese stars. The five stars include Donnie Yen, Jackie Chan, Jet Li, Zhang Ziyi, and Takeshi Kaneshiro, who are the most celebrated transnational Chinese personalities and whose images are the most vibrant and opulent in the current cinematic scene. The justification of the choice of the stars is mainly twofold: first, prominence in cyberspace and, second, the potential capacity of provoking the concern of Chineseness, the theme of enquiry of this book. In this perspective, action stars Jackie Chan, Jet Li, and Donnie Yen are selected while Chow Yun-fat is not on the list. Chow's image mediates across various entertainment industries and cultural markets (Feng 2017: 1). Although Chow successfully captures Hollywood's notice with his performance in Hong Kong action films, his presence in the global and cyber arenas is relatively restricted, as compared to three other big names in transnational cinema. I choose Zhang Ziyi instead of Michelle Yeoh as the only female star in this study. It is true that Michelle Yeoh engineers a substantial transnational profile in her acting career. However, she is less visible in the Web 2.0 than Zhang, whose relatively youthful image and lucrative private life become part of the keen interests of web users. Takeshi Kaneshiro is preferred to Tony Chiu-wai Leung in this study. Both actors engineer screen personality as reticent and cosmopolitan. Kaneshiro's image, nonetheless, more readily provokes the exploration of the topic of Chineseness because of his bi-ethnic appeal that dominates the fan discourse.

It is also worth noting that the megastar Bruce Lee will not be a subject of discussion of any individual chapters of this book. Instead, the critical address of Lee will be disseminated in the analysis in Chapter 1 on Donnie Yen's Wing Chun persona. To elaborate, Lee will be discussed in a way that his cinematic presence serves as an axle for which Yen's image is associated to, extended, and altered from. I am well aware of Lee's global appeal and broad cult following. In the 1970s, a noticeable con- stellation of fanzines have been produced and they are mainly circulated locally in the viewers' circuit. In the cyber age that has seen a change of fan culture, his biography and martial arts philosophy together with his movie clips and interviews are available on certain fan sites, reaching a wider audience over the globe. The participatory web further facilitates the creative and dynamic endeavours of reworking Lee's materials, perpetuating the megastar's fame long after his death. It is undoubted that Lee's cyber appeals should be recognised. However, this book intends to study not only the fan-generated discourse in cyberspace but also the stars' potential attempt, no matter by personnel representatives or allegedly by the stars themselves, to respond to fans either on the web (as the chapters of Donnie Yen, Jackie Chan, and Jet Li vindicate) or in other media conduits (as the chapters of Donnie Yen, Zhang Ziyi, and Takeshi Kaneshiro reveal). This type of response, as part of star–fan interplay, is the missing part of the web-based phenomenon of Lee as a fallen star who suffers premature departure. It explains why Lee is not studied in an individual chapter of this book.

Chineseness as cine-cyber imaginary

By exploring the Chinese star image in cyberspace, this book situates the discussion of Chinese stars within the debates of Chineseness and intervenes in the critical analysis of Chineseness that is once largely situated in the cinematic culture. How can one approach and understand 'Chineseness' in the cyber context? How is the conception shaped, altered, and refashioned by web users? Here I propose a new hybrid form of Chineseness, or what I call cine-cyber imaginary, as a conceptual aperture to enter my formal discussion. Such imaginary refers to a quality of Chinese stars that is discovered in cyber discourse, as extended or evolved from the cinematic realm. As I will argue, it is highly plastic and dynamic, not confined in a fixed meaning-making context but subjected to relentless remaking. It is, hence, de-substantialised – present with or without any historical, cultural, or signifying coordinates. It becomes an open signifier in which various interests with regard to persona management, discursive power, and cinephilia may converge and interact. To elaborate, such a form of Chineseness may still evoke ethnicity, but it is not necessarily informed by the symbolic referents of which the meanings are steadily shaped by the diegetic conditions like those found in the martial arts genre in the previous cinematic period. Chinese star image becomes the digital model that is not read as a classical text but is explored interactively, exemplifying a certain autonomy of actions and reactions of web users.

This book also posits that the Chineseness serves as a kind of imaginary that straddles the cinematic and cyber worlds, of which their presence in these worlds does not rival or override each other. Such a specific quality coincides with the phenomenon of post-cinema. In the post-cinematic era, the star image appears elusive and capricious, of which the meaning is not fixed in a certain hermeneutic context. In his seminal book, *Post Cinematic Affect* (2010), Steven Shaviro innovatively and elaborately discusses the notion of the post-cinematic:

> Pop culture figures are *icons*, which means that they exhibit, or at least aspire to, an idealised stillness, solidity, and perfection of form. Yet at the same time, they are fluid and mobile, always displacing themselves. And this contrast between stillness and motion is a generative principle not just for celebrities themselves, but also for the media flows, financial flows, and modulations of control through which they are displayed, and that permeate the entire social field. (Shaviro 2010: 10; emphasis in the original)

The post-cinematic is a feature that emerges at the moment not utterly in sync with the one dominated by the cinematic culture. The edited volume *Post Cinema: Theorizing 21st-Century Film* (2016) continues to elaborate the notion by positioning stardom in the spectrum of history, arguing that post-cinema refers to a 'broad *historical* transformation' (Denson and Leyda 2016: 2; emphasis in the original) emblematised by the shift from one phase to another. With the consciousness of keeping the word 'cinema' as the concerned term, it prompts us to consider the *relation* (rather than mere distinction) between older and newer media regimes, rather than positing a clean break with the past (ibid.). Similarly, in his analysis of anime aesthetics, Alistair Swale (2015) denies that post-cinematic refers to the medium that is completely eclipsed through the emergence of new modes of image construction while acknowledging that cinema is subtly transformed by the digital means of image-making (4). Likewise, these 'post-cinematic conditions', as what Jeffrey Shaw and Peter Weibel (2003) theorise as 'future cinema', paradoxically bear long roots in artistic practices and influences of the existing communication channels. To further, it does not imply that cyberspace replaces cinema or that movie stardom is isolated from its presence in cinema.[3] In a similar vein, this analysis is situated at a point in time when cyberculture is on the rise while the cinematic culture remains robust and prolific, or 'is not made obsolete, but "recontextualised" and "repurposed"' (Shaviro 1993: 33–38). In short, this book considers Chinese stardom on the web not as an entirely new entity borne out from nowhere but as a continuation, extension, and modification of cinematic phenomenon. By so saying, it is, hence, helpful to critically assess the Chineseness in cinema.

Many ideas pertinent to Chineseness in cinema stem from the martial arts genre. The 'Chinese' world in martial arts films is an imaginary construct shared in the viewing of films, rather than something concrete and taken for granted. *Wuxia* films are typically set in the conceptual world of '*jianghu*', a filmic imaginary literally meaning 'rivers and lakes' and connoting the world 'out there' (Chan 2001: 490). It signifies a martial arts world that captures the portraits of the individual lone fighter who embodies 'the fluid condition of human existence caught in the sheer immensity of th[e] chaotic world at large' (491). While Chineseness in the martial arts genre is inherently indefinite and abstract, the martial arts body, played by Chinese actors and set in a 'Chinese world', can signify components to be appropriated by a collective consciousness such as nationalism. The 'imagined China' is also exemplified by the martial arts body that is celebrated by some Chinese filmmakers in the late twentieth century. Drawing on the director's exilic experience and cultural rootlessness, King Hu's films stemmed from a nostalgic 'craving for China', with components such as traditional ethical values and Chinese performing and visual arts (Rodriquez 1997). Tsui Hark made the *Once Upon a Time in China* series to represent China in a global political context, and to borrow Fredric Jameson's concept (1986: 69), these films can be taken as a 'national allegory' (Figure I.3). Tsui uses the legendary Chinese folk hero Wong Fei-hung as a nationalist icon who defends against imperialist invasion. While Bruce Lee only directs a couple of his own films, *The Way of the Dragon* and *Game of Death* (some portions completed before his death), the films that he starred in are also examples of allegorical nationalism. Lee plays a furious nationalist martial artist who fights back the invaders of China. His Chinese national hero image became popular in the political milieu of multi-ethnic anti-imperialism in the 1970s. Lee's films present the martial arts body as an imaginary frontier to explore the mystification of the nationalistic fiction, and this body emphasis carries no substantial national history or culture.

Considering this view of the martial arts body, one may reject the notion of Chineseness as a monolithic given bound to mainland China. Rey Chow (2000) acutely problematises the concept of Chineseness, associating it with a sort of cultural essentialism that produces an imaginary demarcation between China and the rest of the world (5). Chow's hypotheses intersect with those of Allen Chun (1996). By contending with the idea of 'decolonising Chineseness' in the context of diaspora, Chun, in his essay 'Fuck Chineseness: On the ambiguity of ethnicity as culture as identity' (1996) critiques certain reactions to the homogenous identity imposed by nation-states, as expressed in the voices of the marginalised.

Figure I.3 Jet Li's Wong Fei-hung in *Once Upon a Time in China* is exemplary to the national allegory of China

> While the diversity of 'voices' from the periphery can contribute to the decentering of the essentialism and hegemony of culture … one can hope to effectively decolonise the fiction of ethnicities authorised and institutionalised by the center only by questioning, at the same time, the legitimacy of existing identities to bind people to prevailing institutions and groups. (Chun 1996: 125)

In contrast, Ien Ang in her seminal book *On Not Speaking Chinese: Living between Asia and the West* (2001) adopts a space between Asia and the West to re-evaluate the notion of Chineseness. Echoing the hypotheses of Nestor Garcia Canclini (1995) and Ulf Hannerz (1996), she argues that Chineseness needs to be 'undone' in response to the politics of cultural globalisation today (2001: 87). For these writers, then, the elements composing what was conventionally called 'traditional Chinese culture', 'Chinese national culture', or 'Chineseness', and that was said to have been produced in the framework of 'national cinema', no longer stand as such. Instead, they point to what has now become fluid, volatile, and pluralistic.

Having said so, the heterogeneity and fragmented-ness of Chinese identities appear inadequate in understanding Chineseness in the age of global capitalism. Within the postmodern milieu of multiple and diverse identities, the Chinese martial arts body and movement can be the appearance that Chineseness is not grounded by substantiality, or it could even conceal the absence of substantiality, pretending that there is something inside (Lo 2005: 194–6). Films like *Crouching Tiger, Hidden Dragon* display an ethnically diverse China that mixes accents and origins, as is the case in the diaspora. As a diaspora director, Ang Lee employs Orientalist stylistics to manifest the imaginary China as a sort of cultural translation. Borrowing Tu Wei-ming's notion of 'Cultural China' (1994: 34) where the periphery – the Chinese diaspora – forms 'a new cultural center of Chineseness', this film could be read as an expression of the unique Chinese diaspora culture in light of the reciprocity between the centre and the periphery:

> [T]he center no longer has the ability, insight, or legitimate authority to dictate the agenda for cultural China. On the contrary, the transformative potential of the periphery is so great that it seems inevitable that it will significantly shape the intellectual discourse on cultural China for years to come. (Tu Wei-ming 1994: 27–8)

Tu articulates a 'cultural nationalism' marked by the Chinese diaspora's desire, expressed by both filmmakers and audiences, to 'identify with China and things Chinese, even though they may not have been born there or speak its national language or dialects' (Tu 1994: 111). Nevertheless, this yearning to identify with the nation China and Chinese culture does not mean full Chineseness. Ang Lee's film reveals a loss of an authentic cultural or national self that is disempowered in the nationalistic discourse (Lo 2005). The film presents an 'authentic' ethnic appearance, and projects a mythic cultural version of Chineseness under that appearance. The mystery under the appearance is, in Kwai-cheung Lo's phrase, 'a phantasmic deceit' (21), a tactic pretending that there is something inside while the film is actually devoid of historical and cultural substance. Lo (2005) argues for fluid identities conforming to the flexible logic of global capitalism:

> Because global capitalism is only an inconsistent amalgam of diverse elements, national and cultural direction will continue to be sought as part of an attempt to secure identities and political

> positions on what has become slippery ground. The Chineseness
> is a veil to cover up the loss of substantial national particularity in
> a world operating with the logic of global capitalism. (Lo 2005: 16)

Lo's emphasis on the absence of historical and cultural essence implies that Chineseness becomes 'fluid'. In interactive cyberspace, the 'fluidity' is pushed further, to the point that the martial arts body becomes an elusive and ambiguous entity that has inconsistency or even emptiness at its kernel.

This review of the extant literature on Chineseness in cinema provides a basis for my analysis of Chineseness in cyberculture. These works contend that the 'China' represented in martial arts films is imaginary and abstract, allowing for an allegorical and nostalgic articulation of the Chinese culture. As I postulate, on the one hand, Chinese film stars share similar contestation and attempts of assimilation with stars of other ethnic groups in face with the hegemonic white culture. Chinese stardom, on the other, draws upon the specific tradition of martial arts cinema. When fans transfer images from films to cyberspace, the conception of Chineseness becomes complicated with the plurality and openness it takes on in the cyber setting. Mindful of the prolific and continuing intellectual effort of Chineseness in cinema, this monograph situates the scrutiny in cyberculture and attempts to interrogate the meaning of conception within the context. In this way, this book will proffer a critical intervention of Chineseness and redress some inadequacies of the current literature on the subject by advancing the exploration of the dynamics borne out of technological apparatuses, cultural discourses, and network culture.

The goal of this book is, by and large, threefold: first, to orientate and ground the theory and practice of Chinese stardom in a participatory cyber context; second, to analyse the composition of the Chinese stardom that traverses the cinematic and cyber realms; and, third, to provide a new vision to the study of transnational Chinese stardom. In order to achieve these goals, I construct a new framework for the study of Chinese stardom, refashioning the concept of Chineseness as it transits from cinema to cyberspace.

The user/fan participation as methodological frame

The participatory nature of cyberspace predominantly shapes the methodological orientation of this book. Star construction becomes a popular endeavour that allows everybody to participate in the process. Using 'participation' as a critical, unique perspective to look at star-making, I will draw on Henry Jenkins's theory of the participatory culture and media fandom. His book, *Textual Poachers: Television Fans and Participatory Culture* (1992), is one of the pioneering works on the topic that begins in the pre-Internet era. For long, fandom has been analysed as rather more problematic: the stereotype of 'the fan' has been one of peculiar, excessive, and unhealthy obsession with (supposedly) culturally trivial objects such as TV shows (Sandvoss 2005). Turning fan experiences into academic texts is evidenced as an innovative effort of certain writers such as Stanley Cavell (1981), Randall Collins (1998), and Matthew Hills (2002) who have productively demonstrated the possible amalgam of academics and fandom in their works. Opposite to the consumer culture, participatory culture rejects the passivity of consumers, emphasising the critical and interpretive practices of fan community. As Jenkins avers, fans should be viewed more positively as establishing their own culture out of media texts, and as selectively 'poaching' meanings and interpretations from privileged media products. The advent of the World Wide Web collides with the evolution from zines, fan clubs, radio shows, and gossips to blogs, wikis, social networks, and podcasts, aggravating the participatory culture in vigorous manners. Henry Jenkins (2006b) elaborates the participatory culture in terms of four characteristics that correspond to Web 2.0 sites: first, affiliations: membership in online communities on Facebook, MySpace, and message boards; second, expressions: producing new creative content such as fan vids and mashups; third, collaborative problem-solving: accomplishing tasks and generating new knowledge by working together, for example, Wikipedia; and, fourth, circulations: shaping the media flow, such as with blogging. Jenkins describes the culture inhabited by fans as self-contained, evident to the potential and robustness of audiences for civic engagement and creative expression. This book will encompass three out of these four characteristics postulated by Jenkins's model – affiliations (Chapters 2 and 3), expressions (Chapter 4), and circulations (Chapter 1) – in its analysis of the role of fans in star construction, yet without using exactly Jenkins's terms.

This book concentrates on web users who are considered as the primary force of star construction in cyberculture. I delineate 'user' as part of spectatorship or fandom, as opposed to institution-based parties such as stars, studios, media, marketers, and personnel who have power in the traditional star-making scene. Star studies enter the arena of serious discussion in the 1970s, as mentioned, whereas fan studies remain a marginal discipline in a greater area of academia until the 1980s (Gray et al. 2007: 1). In considering key approaches to star studies, there has been critical reluctance to treat film audience seriously (Yu 2012: 22). Western theories of stardom are usually said to begin with Richard Dyer's *Stars* (1979), a groundbreaking text presenting the results of his study of Hollywood stars. Unlike earlier writings that emphasised the psychological, economic, and legal aspects of stardom (Walker 1970; Allen and Gomery 1985; Gledhill 1991), Dyer's work connects it to the mainstream film theory of recent decades, by developing a 'sociosemiotic' approach to illustrate that the star image is an 'intertextual construct' (Gledhill 1991: xiv) produced across an array of cultural and media practices. However, Dyer's hypothesis assertively departs from 'star hagiography' in popular biographies and autobiographies as well as from 'anecdotal and impressionistic star adoration' in fan magazines and trade publications (Hollinger 2006: 35). Bias of the populist debate of treating film spectators as a 'manipulated mass', furthermore, perpetuates with the rise of the mass entertainment. A critical tradition of evaluating the hypothetical worth of audiences' opinions is evident in Karen Hollinger's (2006) questioning of the use of audiences in her star analysis. Hollinger states, 'Box office statistics, fan magazine polls and letters, fan club news, fan mail, Internet fan sites, and reviewers' opinions have all been used to provide insight into the popularity of certain stars, but they do not always reliably reveal exactly why viewers feel a connection to certain stars' (43). Her argument reveals an omission of the potential importance of audience in the realm of stardom (Stringer 2003: 277).

While the audience is marginalised in film studies, certain academic effort has responded to the condition by putting it back at the centre of star studies since the late 1970s. As Christine Geraghty (2000) explicates, 'it is the audience's access to and celebration of intimate information from a variety of texts and sources which are important' (189) and this audience is best typified by the fan (Yu 2012: 168). The visibility of fans in the account of stars dates back to the early twentieth century. Throughout the decades from the 1910s to the 1940s, film critics began to approach stardom from a 'fan' perspective (Fischer and Landy 2004: 3). They composed praises about their adored actors in the forms of newspaper articles, movie magazine essays, and journalistic reviews. This trend was taken up in the scholarly essays and books of the early 1960s that have spanned an array of specific topics characterising the critical exploration of stardom until the present.

The hypothetical account of film spectatorship gives way to the critical studies of fan audiences in relation to star construction. In her original essay, 'Feminine fascinations: Forms of identification in star–audience relations' (1991), Jackie Stacey argues that the exploration of stars has stayed predominantly textual. Following Stacey's attempt of working against the textual determinism, Janet Staiger (1992) suggests a historical approach for examining spectators' responses to film. She argues that the presence of contextual discourses may illuminate the comprehension of published materials like reviews and articles. Her analysis indicates a methodological shift, as Stacey (1994: 16) describes, from the 'textually produced spectator' of film studies to the 'spectator as text' within cultural studies. Such a shift has given way to the burgeoning of publications that are often associated with gender and sexuality. Titles like *This Made Masquerade: Stardom and Masculinity in the Jazz Age* (1996), *Masked Men: Masculinity and the Movies in the Fifties* (1997), and *Gay Fandom and Crossover Stardom: James Dean, Mel Gibson, and Keanu Reeves* (2001) explore specific male stars in relation to an array of historical texts, such as fan magazines, publicity materials, and critical annotation. Jackie Stacey's *Star Gazing: Hollywood Cinema and Female Spectatorship* (1994), adopting the empirical approach, investigates the interplay between female stars and female spectatorship. In her volume *Growing up with Audrey Hepburn: Text, Audience, Resonance* (2003), Rachel Morley offers an account of the British female experience of adoring Hepburn in the 1950s, the 1960s, and the 1990s so as to unfold how enduring the star appeal is. Morley's volume has extended the star–audience interplay to the personal life and the everyday practices of the actress's followers. These erudite efforts work to open up an alternative threshold that is based outside not only the film text but even the mainstream culture, tapping into the realm of subculture that always runs to overturn and burlesque the dominant ideologies. In a similar vein, this book rejects the idea of passive, homogenous spectators. Rather, I intend to view the spectator as a culturally constructed, active, agentive subject who participates in the process of star-making.

Recent intellectual works unveil the burgeoning of fans' participation in the realm of movie stardom. Barry King's 'Embodying an elastic self: The parametrics of contemporary stardom' (2003) probes fan writing about stars. King uses the Hollywood star Sharon Stone to illustrate the concept of an 'elastic persona', showing how websites become a venue for constant rewriting of star personae and applying the notion of textual dissemination to human identity. Fans, in addition to the stars themselves, function as active players in the economic and interpretive machinery in generating commercial and cultural value. The star persona is, hence, under constant mutation enforced by fans. In a broad sense, King investigates online star systems as multimedia and intertextual phenomena, emphasising the growing power of fans and how it emulates and promulgates, rather than criticising or restricting commercial entertainment and popular culture. What is illuminated here is that the rise of the Internet and the increasing fan involvement make possible an evolving stardom from an industry-based phenomenon to a fan-driven phenomenon. Stars are no longer a presence in cinema but also in cyberspace, such that the star-making process is open for a multitude of fannish forces to work upon.

To adopt the audience-/fan-based approach, this book needs to address a question: Who are the audience/users/fans? This question is also extended to the concerns of anonymity and pseudonymity that are not uncommon in the cyber world. The stars attended to in this study gain their transnational fan following mainly in Hong Kong, mainland China, the East Asian region, and North America. Also, the World Wide Web is a global circuit that users around the world, presumably, can have access to. It can, thus, be inferred that the fans are of diverse identities and backgrounds. I roughly identify three categories of fans to be analysed: first, the Western fans who originated in countries in the West like Europe and North America; second, Chinese/Asian fans who are culturally closer to the stars' originating culture; and, third, Chinese/Asian fans who have migrated to the West and who have or have not assimilated to the new culture. By saying so, this book will consider a user or fan as a discursive position rather than a real person. Empirical audience studies assume the notion of a 'real' audience and intend to seek 'an accurate barometer of public opinion' (Butler 1991: 241). Even for empirical audience research, however, the picture of 'real' audience response is questionable because respondents' personal investment and the researchers' mediations and interpretations are inevitable (Yu 2012: 24). This book will demonstrate how the discursive positions of the web users are established textually and ideologically while examining the fans' participation in the star-making. The current analysis, furthermore, prefers regarding the users as a culturally constructed entity that possesses a hypothetical quality, similar to that of the spectator imagined by film theory (Mayne 1993: 8). This stance facilitates recognition of the flexibility of various modes of address. In this light, the authentic identity is not a determinant parameter in this study.

The book will analyse five Chinese movie stars on five groups of participatory sites in Web 2.0 (blogs, Flickr, Facebook, YouTube, and forums) respective to five types of fan practices (blogging, photo-sharing or 'flickering' photographs, socially connecting or 'friending', sharing online videos or YouTubing, and discussing). The intention of this approach is to create a set of five matrixes, each involving a specific type of fan practice in a participatory site and a matching star, which will form a corpus as the basis for critical discourse such as close readings and textual analysis and/as fan discourse analysis. The five matrixes shall include:

(1) blogging Donnie Yen
(2) 'flickering' Jackie Chan's photographs on Flickr
(3) 'friending' Jet Li on Facebook
(4) YouTubing Zhang Ziyi and
(5) discussing Takeshi Kaneshiro on fan forums.

In each of the matrixes, this study will identify the defining features of the participatory sites and the corresponding principal fan practice as the major force of shaping the star phenomenon of specific actors and actresses.

The twofold justification for matching the sites with the stars, frequency, and relevance is directed to the question of how recurrently and prominently the images of the particular stars are posted and circulated by cyber fans. First, the study ascribes a specific participatory site to a specific star because he or she shows more frequent presence than other actors or actresses (Chapters 2, 5). Second, the analysis assigns a specific actor or actress to a specific Web 2.0 site because such a site illustrates the relevant aspects of the star phenomenon of him or her (Chapters 1, 3, 4). Backed up with statistic count, a general survey, conducted in the period from 2013 to 2017, of each of the Web 2.0 platforms can provide evidence for the selection criteria, which are tied to the salient aspects of the star image, for each of the cases. It is followed by the identification of a small corpus of texts for close analysis.

While the cross-matching model pinpoints the most prominent and salient features of the respective stars in cyberspace, distinct from their cinematic personae, it implies that the analysis is not all embracing. Whereas all selected stars gain their presence in the selected participatory sites, such a cross-matching model will exclude the analysis of the stars in the sites other than the matched one. Also, this analysis will only focus on the main fan practices rather than covering all types of practices found on particular sites. The resulted analyses may be limiting but they will be focused on the star analysis with respect to the primary feature of the sites.

A couple of methodological notes are needed here. Awareness is given to the possible limitations of missing the messages and posts that are not tagged with the selected keyword. To consider the web as an open-source archive,[4] this book will use the English names of the Chinese stars for the keyword-searches to identify the corpus of texts for analysis. This means a selective access to the Anglophone sphere rather than to the Sinophone sphere and the spheres dominated by other languages. It is undeniable that Chinese-language materials are important in examining Chineseness. Given the English-language emphasis and the Anglophone sphere in this research, however, to include the large quantity of the untranslated Chinese materials and the wide range of issues raised would be impossible and beyond the scope of this study. Furthermore, English remains to be a lingua franca on the web (Vettorel 2014). As Vettorel (2014) avers:

> In a constantly interconnected world … in many cases via electronic media, English is most often employed as a commonly shared lingua franca. In these globalised transnational spaces of interaction English can serve both more pragmatic, utilitarian communicative purposes, and/or be appropriated and localised to express identities and meanings that are peculiar to the participants and to the inter-actional contexts. (Vettorel 2014: 1)

The presence of such lingua franca is necessary for Internet users to establish and retain contact in the context of 'wider networking' (Seidlhofer 2011: 86) that 'operate beyond territorial (and linguistic) boundaries by definition, be it at a local, national, international, intra-cultural or intercultural level' (Vettorel 2014: 1). This justifies the book's large, although not sole, use of English-language materials for analysis.

To establish analytical categories as the means for delineating the texts for analysis implies the choice of not limiting the selection of texts based on duration of accessibility. In principle, any cyber text is available for search and access until the uploader removes it (with the exception of censorship of certain offensive materials in some countries like the PRC). Furthermore, time for research in this book spans from 2010 to 2017. Due to the ephemeral nature of the Internet, certain materials that have been once accessible may disappear afterward. Since the critical factors in my selection were fan responses to and expository potential for the texts, the length of period of accessibility was not a highly relevant factor.

Chapter summary

This book aims to investigate Chinese movie stardom in cyberspace by establishing a new theoretical framework for considering Chineseness as the outcome of the participatory effort of fans. Chapter 1 examines Donnie Yen's martial arts body in the blogosphere. It argues that Yen's kinetic body, often the focus of bloggers' interest, is not only the corporeal entity that appears in individual films he starred in and became famous for, such as *SPL: Sha Po Lang* (2005), *Ip Man* (2008), and *Legend of the Fist: The Return of Chen Zhen* (2010), but it is also an outcome of sundry participatory forces, bridging the martial arts body to the elements in extra-diegetic settings such as the Hollywood science-fiction genre, martial arts culture, and hip hop culture. It, hence, appears as an intertextual phenomenon that bloggers keep reworking and renegotiating Chinese nationalism in tandem with the cyber legends of Ip Man, Bruce Lee, and Chen Zhen. The Chinese body of Yen is further questioned and complicated when users mix symbolic components drawn from Chinese or non-Chinese systems. Also, the offscreen existence of Yen shows both resonance and incongruity to his screen personae complicating his martial arts image. These new forms ultimately allow bloggers to revisit, represent, and contend the ethnic representation of Yen.

Chapter 2 focuses on Jackie Chan, arguing for his cyber presence oscillating in the interstices of the ethnically Chinese image and a cosmopolitan goodwill appeal. The discussion shows that Flickr hosts official photo albums featuring Jackie Chan's movies and goodwill events whereas these visual images present Chan as a still-thriving martial artist and a patriotic ambassador. Arguably, such a goodwill image is a token to retain the star value and to 'apologise' after a public mistake. Furthermore, considering that his star personae was once anchored in martial prowess and kinetic agility, giving him a strong ethnic branding, such an ethnically branded image has become increasingly universal. The image functions as crucial to his bridging role between his nation and the world.

Chapter 3 utilises a similar approach, examining Jet Li's celebrity-philanthropist personality in online social networks. The discussion focuses on a Facebook fan page named under Jet Li, and that presumably is run by the actor to promote not only his movie but, more noticeably, his charity The One Foundation. His charity has a slogan, 'One Foundation, One Family', evoking a world community in which human compassion and decency should extend to everyone, undermining the 'Chinese' element and bespeaking a kind of 'world' awareness. As a venue for the possible philanthropic mobilisation, the star presence in the cyber-network displays ambivalence of the notion of Chineseness.

Chapter 4 investigates the celebrity image of Zhang Ziyi on YouTube, of which users negotiate her debatable appeal, as situated in the politics of cultural nationalism, by sharing and commenting on Zhang's notoriety on the web. Zhang's international fame began with her performance in the martial arts epic *Crouching Tiger, Hidden Dragon* (2000). As she grew increasingly famous under the limelight of international media, her English-speaking flair and her amorous encounters become a point of fan attention. In press interviews, Zhang spoke broken English, which questions whether she is qualified as a star in the Anglophone global film culture. Moreover, her public personality is dogged by a series of quasi-sex scandals that chiefly draw negative domestic responses. The viewers' sentiments garner a force in cyberspace, expressing a kind of collective resentment of the star's nationalistic presence. Nonetheless, Zhang's hard work in improving her English and realising her ambition proves her upward mobility in global stardom. Taken together, the YouTube videos entail complexity of the star presence in ethnic, national, and linguistic terms in the global visual circuit.

While the subjects of previous chapters are all ethnically Chinese, Chapter 5 focuses on the half-Taiwanese (Chinese), half-Japanese Takeshi Kaneshiro and his star image on fan forums, where his mixed ethnic identity becomes a central feature of his transnational stardom. Such an identity renders the Chineseness he embodies onscreen ambivalent and unstable. Fans, moreover, compare Kaneshiro to the Hollywood star Johnny Depp, with respect to his famous good looks, and Keanu Reeves, with regard to his multiethnic identity. The impact of fan manipulation on Kaneshiro's fluid persona is shown by the exploitation of his half-Japanese identity for charity by some Japan-based fan sites. Responding to the 2011 Fukushima nuclear disaster, one such site exhibits a series of paintings by an affiliated artist employing Kaneshiro's image as the focus of representation. The malleability that fans find in Kaneshiro's star persona stems from this potential to embody either Chineseness or Japaneseness.

This book concludes with a theoretical formulation of Chineseness in participatory cyberculture. Subsequent to the brief revisit of the analyses from the previous chapters, a concluding remark will engage with Pierre Lévy's theory of cyberculture and David Rodowick's (2007) theory of the so-called new media image to argue that the open cyber setting enables dynamic fans' reworking of star texts and multiple ways of approaching Chineseness. The star presence becomes highly abstract, carrying no historical essence or stable meanings of the 'Chinese'. A new, hybrid mode of Chineseness as cine-cyber imaginary that is capricious and unstable emerges, redefining star personae in the web-based environment. By cogently uncovering the dynamics and debates of a vital relationship between Chinese stardom, web technologies, and fan discourse, this book provides insight for further explorations of stardom and the pertinent phenomena in the global digital culture.

Notes

1. Some examples are the videos entitled 'Martial Arts Meets Star Wars', 'Crouching Tiger, Hidden Dragon Mixed with Star Wars and Mortal Kombat', 'Crouching Tiger, Hidden Dragon Light Saber Fight', and '中國史上最強的劍' ('*Zhongguo shishang zuiqiang de jian*', literally, 'The Strongest Sword in Chinese History').
2. According to Vivian Lee (2011), films labelled 'pan-Asian' are effectively 'pan-Chinese' in terms of language, cast, and content (5).
3. As Denson and Leyda (2016: 2; emphasis in the original) continue to note, 'Post-cinema is not just *after* cinema, and it is not in every respect "new," at least not in the sense that new media is sometimes equated with digital media; instead, it is the collection of media, and the mediation of life forms, that "follows" the broadly cinematic regime of the twentieth century – where "following" can mean either to succeed something as an alternative or to "follow suit" as a development or a response in kind.'
4. Such an idea makes the World Wide Web the largest and most accessible vault for moving-image material. Archival users rather than archivists are the central figures in archival practice, realising a bottom-up mode of dissemination (Prelinger 2009: 268). Nonetheless, there are concerns about copyright and ownership, about losing control of records, and about the qualification of using and consuming the archival materials (ibid.).

Chapter 1

Blogging Donnie Yen: remaking the martial arts body as a cyber-intertext

Introduction: traversing between Hollywood and martial arts cinema

The latest *Star Wars* instalment *Rogue One: A Star Wars Story* (2016) has become a new sensation in cinematic and popular arenas. *Star Wars* is plausibly the most compelling title in the history of the science-fiction genre, successfully attracting a broad cult following all over the globe. The movies become fascinating cultural texts of which are anchored myriad user-generated practices of cultural production. *Star Wars* devotees eagerly poach, edit, and rework the imagery from the cinematic texts and share them in the fan-based circuits. As the seventh 'saga' film, *Rouge One* is the first standalone feature from the *Star Wars* series that is set prior to the events of the 1977 episode (Lee 2016). The blockbuster features an international cast, including the Mexican Diego Luna as Cassian Andor, the British-Pakistani Riz Ahmed as Bodhi Rook, and the Chinese Wen Jiang as Imwe's loyal friend Baze Malbus, vindicating the ongoing ambition of the *Star Wars* franchise to access the global audience. Part of the spotlight of both English- and Chinese-language media rests on the exceptional appearance of Donnie Yen, a top Chinese martial arts star, as one of the Jedi knights. Ranked as the sixth most influential Chinese celebrity in the Forbes' 2011 list (Xu 2011), Yen is one of the most prolific and bankable actors in Hong Kong cinema, gaining currency in the border-crossing market. *Rouge One* casts Yen as Chirrut Imwe, a blind benevolent monk, a character that Yen describes to American press, *USA Today*, as 'definitely an important guy' (Truitt 2016) who purportedly possesses the paramount fighting dexterity in the galaxy, or as what Yen simply puts, 'the best fighter' (Lee 2016). The description readily makes audiences expect to see Yen's superb acrobatic skill. Attention also points to the martial arts actor who beats out the peer candidates who have been prominent in the US, for example, Jet Li, Tony Leung, Stephen Chow, Chang Chen, Daniel Wu, and Leehom Wang, to win the role, becoming the first Hong Kong action star to perform in a *Star Wars* narrative (Baxter 2015). Yen once expresses in a press interview, 'Of course I'm feeling a sense of achievement . . . For a Hong Kong actor, and a Chinese actor, to be able to play such a significant role that is consistent with the spirit of the series – with the Force – it's a very precious opportunity' (Lee 2016). In another interview, which was originally released by Geek Culture and then reposted on YouTube, Yen elicits, in a similar sense, 'Asians have proven themselves can be as good as anybody else' (Lee 2016), as in a way that ethnicity emerges as the framework of approaching and discussing his personification in a *Star Wars* story in the public discourse. In other words, the appearance of Yen, as an ethnic Chinese, in a celebrated science-fiction hit, is no longer simply a matter of the personal pride of a star but is associated with a wider issue of ethnicity. Whereas these media materials have riveted audiences, certain web users have re-posted the interview clips on their blogs, not only for imparting the news but also for acknowledging and celebrating the actor's 'success'. In this fashion, the discourse of ethnicity of transnational Chinese personalities is relayed between various participatory websites, earning a relentless presence in cyberspace.

The concern of ethnicity is complicated when one closely scrutinises Donnie Yen's martial arts persona in *Rouge One*. While some cinephiles have probably much anticipated Yen's performance (STORMTROOP-ERLARRY 2016), some others wonder how the highly acclaimed Hong Kong action star, who is notable for his authentic kung fu, will fight in the pioneering Hollywood science-fiction title. Nicknamed 'The Strongest in the Cosmos' ('*yuxiu zuiqiang*' in Chinese) by the Chinese-language media, Yen is generally recognised as a star who possesses superb martial arts dexterity. From the inception of his acting career, Yen has daunted audiences and critics with the rapid-fire pacing and dense action in his fight scenes. Discovered by the choreographer-turned-director Yuen Woo-ping, Yen made his debut in *Miracle Fighter 2* (1982). Impressed by Yen's flexibility, speed, and sharpness, Yuen helps to formulate Yen's identity by casting him in a cop film, *Tiger Cage 2* (1990), in which Yen was the lead as well as the action director. As indicated on Donnie Yen's official website, many audiences regarded the fight scenes as standing out in the history of action cinema (sub-page about *Tiger Cage 2*). In the

2000s, Yen moved from Hong Kong to Hollywood, where the *Highlander* series was his first overseas project. He worked as the choreographer and played minor roles in *Highlander: Endgame* (2000) and *Blade II* (2002) two years later. His subsequent Hollywood appearance in *Shanghai Knight* (2003), in collaboration with Jackie Chan, won little acclaim that made his Hollywood prospect seemingly poor by mid-decade. Yen then returned to Hong Kong and attained newfound success with the titles *Empress and the Warriors* (2008), *Painted Skin* (2008), *Bodyguards and Assassins* (2009), and, most notably, *Ip Man* and *Ip Man II: Legend of the Grand Master* (2008 and 2010) and *14 Blades* (2010). Yet Yen's 'Chinese' screen image, which relies on his bodily rigour and martial authenticity, is crystallised especially with his breakthrough role in *Ip Man*. Hence, it is not surprising to note that the casting of Yen in Rouge One, the 'brand' that is almost equivalent to digital visual effects, calls forth questions of the star agency. Such ambiguity in the star identity is aggravated with respect to his experience of shooting *Rouge One* in Pinewood Studio in Britain, as Yen reveals to *The Hollywood Reporter*, which is similar to the one in a theme park, rendering as hyperreal and fanciful (Chu 2015). Arguably, Yen exhibits a star body not grounded on physical prowess as much as his earlier screen personae but more on a digitally altered surface. Therefore, Yen's performance in *Rouge One* proves Yen's transnational superstardom that capitalises on his genuine kung fu while challenging the substantiality of his kung fu presence.

Donnie Yen's ambiguous martial arts persona gains its presence in the blogosphere. It is not difficult to find a number of blogs that are established under the name of Donnie Yen. Blog, a truncated expression of 'weblog', refers to a discussion or informational website published on the World Wide Web. It primarily functions as personal diaries or, as Rebecca Blood defines, 'a frequently updated webpage with dated entries, new ones placed on top' (Blood 2002b: vi, 12). Blogging becomes a vital tool that revolutionises web publishing for an immense majority of users. It decentralises the right of writing, reporting, commentary, and publishing that were once in the hands of traditional media. Although blogs emphasise single authorship as one of the prime characteristics (Myers 2010: 16), they allow their readers to give annotation, which is a form of users' interaction. Two other characteristics of blogs include: first, interval of updates: it is distinct to a personal homepage that it is regularly updated; and, second, a web of links: it is unlike a traditional kind of diary in that it is built around links (ibid.). Discourse analysts and literary critics have sought for decades to dismantle the idea of the single unified text in blogs (Myers 2010: 8). As transitioned into the Web 2.0 era, blogs evolve to be increasingly interactive and intertextual. Blogs pertaining to Yen contain a mix of texts like biography, screen images, and martial arts philosophy of the performer. By virtue of the intertextual potentiality of blogs, users are endorsed to work on a multiplicity of star 'texts' to formulate new, versatile star–fan dynamics in the blogosphere.

This chapter analyses the blogged persona of Donnie Yen and the ways that bloggers approach, negotiate, and reinvent the martial arts body of Yen. How do bloggers write and publish about Yen? To what extent do bloggers draw on Yen's cinematic persona to construct the blogged discourse of the actor? What is the interplay between the onscreen appeal and the offscreen life of Yen, as interpreted by bloggers? To respond to these questions, I Google-searched with keywords 'Blog, Donnie Yen' on 25 June 2017, the day I conducted the survey. The quantity of search results counts as 3,850,000, out-numbering those of other transnational Chinese stars, including Jet Li, Zhang Ziyi, and Takeshi Kaneshiro, while just following that of megastar Jackie Chan, which counts 4,000,000. Such an outcome justifies the matching of Donnie Yen and the platform of blogs as a noteworthy object of enquiry. In total, I located five blogs that topped the list as major sites of investigation. They are: (1) Fightland Blog, (2) Burrello Submarine's Movie Blog, (3) The Blog of Alfred Hsing, (4) AWMA Blog, and (5) Azn Badger's Blog. While some bloggers poach and share photographs and interviews of Yen, some others create relatively personalised entries, chronicling their encounters as part of the star discourse. In both cases, as I hypothesise, bloggers reveal a tendency to recycle the martial arts persona that denotes Chineseness and, nevertheless, their texts often give way to a (re)reading of Yen's body. Along such a logical line, Yen's martial arts image in blogs is not isolated from its presence in cinema but is referenced, juxtaposed, and hybridised with components of other symbolic spaces than Chinese nationalism in film. To elaborate, bloggers keep renegotiating Chineseness through occasioning it with codes and the personae of different fighting models, genres, and cultures. They also blend diegetic and extra-diegetic materials where the blended images unnecessarily conform to the previous modes of star presence and finally complicates, if not de-emphasises, the Chineseness. Suffice it to say, Yen's martial arts image is no longer constrained by a specific nationalised setting but becomes a composite, ever-changing, and multi-directional 'intertext', which allows diverse meanings to emerge and develop.

The 'Wing Chun' phenomenon: bridging the film world and the martial arts world

It is undoubted that Donnie Yen's Wing Chun persona is a key theme of the actor's blog-oriented presence. As one of the few action stars who depicts Wing Chun on cinematic screens, Yen had, in fact, enacted his connection with the martial arts technique long before *Ip Man* (2008). As early as 1994, Yen played a supporting role in Yuen Woo-ping's kung-fu hit, *Wing Chun*. Starring Michelle Yeoh as the female protagonist Yim Wing Chun, an early pioneer of Wing Chun, the film demonstrates hardcore kung fu in combination with flamboyant wirework, consolidating Yuen's choreographic style. Yen plays the character of Leung Bok-chau, Yim's future husband, who later becomes Yim's student and names this type of martial arts after her. Yen's role thus foreshadows his part in composing the Wing Chun story on Hong Kong screens fourteen years later principally through the biographical role of Ip Man.

Ip Man does not only revive Donnie Yen's Wing Chun persona on cinematic screens, the hype it engenders also casts extradiegetic influence in the arenas of marital arts culture. The release of *Ip Man* has occasioned the Wing Chun fever, which has grown throughout the international film industry. For example, Hollywood actors reveal their passion for and praxis of Wing Chun. Robert Downey Jr discussed his Wing Chun experience in interviews with Oprah Winfrey and David Letterman. Similarly, Nicolas Cage exhibits his Wing Chun skills in *Bangkok Dangerous* (2008) ('Hollywood Star Learns Wing Chun' 2010). Across the Pacific, a Wing Chun craze has taken Asia by storm. An influx of martial arts aficionado has travelled southwards to Foshan, Guangzhou, and Hong Kong to visit the birthplace of Ip Man and to learn Wing Chun. In Hong Kong, hundreds of new Wing Chun schools have been opened ('Ip Chun (葉準), 84-year-old Wing Chun legend' 2009). Xie Xiaoyang, a writer for *Yazhou Zhoukan*, a Chinese-language news-weekly magazine, has provided an account of the popularity of *Ip Man* in relation to the rise and fall of Chinese martial arts in contemporary China (Xie 2009: 26). He uses the term 'disappearing *wulin* (literally, martial forest)' to describe the once collapsed yet now reinvigorated martial arts culture. With the cultural impact it summons, furthermore, *Ip Man* signifies come-back of an old subgenre of the 1970s kung fu films such as Bruce Lee's films and Shaolin-themed films advocating temple-based martial arts and southern kung fu that denote an intense pedagogic impulse. Concomitantly, it opens up a new subgenre of Wing Chun films composed of and led by an array of Ip Man-themed movies such as *The Legend is Born: Ip Man* (2010), *The Grandmaster* (2013), and *Ip Man: The Final Fight* (2013), starring emergent and established actors like Dennis To, Tony Chiu-wai Leung, and Anthony Wong respectively as Ip Man. Albeit that Donnie Yen has only practised Wing Chun mainly for the shooting of *Ip Man*, he is more widely recognised by fans as an icon of Wing Chun than other 'Ip Man' actors, or cleanly calling him, 'the best Ip Man' (Yip 2013).[1] Suffice it to say, the entire Ip Man phenomenon subsumes Yen's newfound star power, the resurgence of the Wing Chun culture, and the popularity of the screen persona.

In the movie *Ip Man*, Wing Chun is an important signifier of Chineseness. As a popular form of martial arts with a century-old history, Wing Chun is a highly codified entity conjuring a specific identification of Chinese culture. Ip Man is depicted as a respectable and dignified man in the community, incarnating an essential Chineseness by embodying Confucian virtues like propriety, modesty, family, and dignity. Similar to a Wong Fei-hung figure, the Wing Chun master appears as a good-natured family man who, as Yen puts it, is 'essentially a nerd who fights well' (Seto 2010). Unmatched in martial arts, he always holds back in the face of combatants' challenges and defeats them without hurting them. One illustrative scene is when Master Liu demands a duel from Ip Man. Liu comes to Ip Man during dinner time and Ip Man refuses to fight until the family dinner is finished. The fight is also held behind closed doors, as Ip Man does not wish to embarrass his opponent or harm the latter's public reputation. The other parts of the plot, in addition, depict that during the Japanese occupation of China, he is courageous enough to stand against the oppressors. He teaches Wing Chun to the locals, encouraging them to unite and offer a helping hand to one another. He is a man of honour who protects his family, friends, and fellow Chinese through his Wing Chun presence. Yen's Ip Man personality signifies an 'ideal Chineseness' with which most Chinese people are eager to associate.

By so arguing, Donnie Yen's Wing Chun body in *Ip Man* serves as a site of confrontation and resistance. Noting that Wing Chun may enable a woman to conquer a man, the cinematic persona of Ip Man incarnates the masculine ethos that is fuelled by patriotic vigour. Nationalism and masculinity articulate well with each other. Nation, as Joane Nagel (1998) posits, is an institution historically dominated by men (248). The prevailing norms, practices, and ideologies are adopted to define hegemonic masculinity like honour, bravery, duty, and cowardice.

Through the construction of patriotic manhood, thus, nationalism is sexualised and miliatarised. The intimate link between nationhood and manhood in *Ip Man* is epitomised by the colonised setting of the narrative. Living in China during wartime in threat of a Japanese invasion and the respective mayhem, Ip Man embodies the courage to confront and triumph over the invaders. It reverberates to Frances Gateward's (2009) argument that the body is the primary resource and means for self-articulation for the colonised, the working, and those subjected to oppressive regimes (65). The physical training further marks the martial arts body as a tool of defiance by disciplining it. It also corroborates Frantz Fanon's (1963) observation that the powerlessness of a colonised people leads to fantasies of greater physical power: 'The first thing which the native learns is to stay in his place, and not to go beyond certain limits. This is why the dreams of the native are always of muscular prowess; his dreams are of action and of aggression' (52).

The Chinese-fight-against-invaders theme continues in *Ip Man*'s 2010 sequel that connotes heightened collective nationalistic undercurrent. Scenes like Ip Man's defeat of the Western boxer can be read as victory of the 'East', or particularly China, over the 'West' (Funnell 2013: 128). Such East–West confrontation can be viewed in a broader context of the box-office performance of *Ip Man 2*, which was released concurrently with Jon Favreau's *Iron Man 2* (2010). While Hollywood blockbusters historically dominated the Chinese cinema market, *Ip Man 2* gained higher box-office revenues than its Hollywood rival, implying Chinese films' potential in the competing global film arena. The 'Ip Man' sensation has proven Yen as a viable player in relation to his Hollywood counterparts, cementing his status as a martial artist in the local and in-ternational audience.

Some blogs underline Yen's 'Ip Man' role but it is not necessarily meant to recognise the Chineseness signified by the Wing Chun personality. One of the instances is a blog named The Fightland Blog. Not a few entries address the personality in *Ip Man* while the blogger appears to be keen on discussing *Rouge One*, linking Yen's personalities in the films from two disparate industries and cultures. Dated 8 July 2015, the blogger named Sascha Matuszak posts an entry after Twitch Films broke the news of the latest *Star Wars* feature's casting of Yen. The title of the entry 'Kung Fu Film Legend Donnie Yen Lands Role in Star Wars' (http:fightland. vice.com/blog/kung-fu-film-legend-donnie-yen-lands-role-in-star-wars) readily provides the impression that the post centres on *Rouge One*.

Nonetheless, the majority of the content including the photograph, the video, and the text stress on *Ip Man*, unfolding how impressive the Wing Chun personality is to the blogger. What tops this entry is a movie still of *Ip Man*, which displays the hero in Chow Ching-chuen's (Simon Yam's) ruined cotton mill (Figure 1.1). Looking sombre with drawn eyebrows, Yen is captured in a medium-shot frame, put in the foreground on the right side. His tightly clenched fists, taut muscles, and ready-to-fight posture denote force and wrath, making his martial arts body a vehicle of Chinese masculinity. As the blogger appropriates the photograph from the film and posts it on his or her blog, he or she reduces the martial arts persona to solely a flattened image that is decontextualised from the diegetic signifying context of nationalism. Put another way, he or she diminishes Yen's presence to mere physicality and draws no connections to Chinese identity and subjectivity associated with a Wing Chun body.

Arguably, the post hints at Cornel Sandvoss's concept of 'neutrosemy' (2005: 832), which exists in textual openness that 'actual significa-tion value' is neutralised and surpassed by 'fans' existing schemes of perception and horizons of expectations' (835). It deals more with the

WORDS

KUNG FU FILM LEGEND DONNIE YEN LANDS ROLE IN STAR WARS

FIGHTLAND BLOG

By Sascha Matuszak

Figure 1.1 A movie still of *Ip Man* included in a blog entry of 'The Fightland Blog'

blogger's identity and desire than the perspectives and the mechanics of production of the Wing Chun combat scenes. Interest in the Wing Chun technique dominates the cyber presence of the martial arts body. The Chinese body becomes more a cinematic construct than a natural given. While it seems that there remains an obsession with re-staging the political allegory of how a Chinese Wing Chun patriot defeats the Japanese imperialists, the attention to human acrobatic ability does not survive that obsessive tendency. In such a context marked by the loss of cyber fans' aptitude to effectively govern significance (Scodari 2007), the Chinese body becomes a fetish deprived of substantial Chinese culture and intact Chinese subjectivity.

What follows, in the same post, is a YouTube video featuring the most-recalled scene in *Ip Man* of the Chinese hero fighting with ten karatekas, yet conveying a more problematised nationalistic spirit than in the celluloid version. The plot portrays that Ip Man seeks revenge for the death of a fellow Foshan master by engaging the karatekas in a bout. Underscoring the dynamism of the hero's body, the director adopts quick editing and moving frames to suggest the ferocity of the Wing Chun acrobatics and maximise the action's vividness. Although the film entails how Yen's presence defines the male-chauvinistic nationalism, the clip is transferred to the blog and re-situated in the context of Yen's international fame that earns him the *Star Wars* contract, having little to do with Chinese nationalism. This video is nothing more than a form of virtual reiteration, devoid of any nationalistic basis for its representation and articulation.

The Chineseness embodied by Ip Man becomes further vague as the blogger juxtaposes it to other action and generic categories. Bloggers reimagine Yen's star appeal subsuming a synthesis of Wing Chun and Mixed Martial Arts (MMA), extending the cultural undertone of the Chinese martial arts. Blogger Sascha Matuszak (2015) writes in response to the cast of Yen in *Rouge One*:

> It will be interesting to see what type of Jedi Yen will be. He is supposedly an ally of Han Solo, which present some interesting maverick possibilities. Maybe he pulls some particularly un-Jedi stunts that get him a little too close to the Sith side of life? Maybe he just dominates, plowing through Stormtroopers and Sith-Lords with MMA-infused kung fu (a style Yen has been developing over the last few films), keeping Solo's aging soul safe from harm.

While the blogger is electrified by Yen's Wing Chun personality, he or she is also aware of the fact that his kinetic agency is not bounded to a single paradigm. He has endeavoured to explore and design unique cinematic action styles, exciting audiences with novelty while retaining a sense of conventional realism. He develops his signature approach of the MMA style in cinematic action, which lends itself well to diversity and mutability, similar to Bruce Lee who invents Jeet Kune Do, a mix of techniques that is described as a liberation from form. MMA, a term coined by Rick Blume, the president of Battlecade, is a full-contact combat sports permitting a broad range of 'completely different' fighting styles such as judo, Brazilian Jiu-Jitsu, karate, kickboxing, and wrestling. Donnie Yen is among the rare action stars to have successfully transposed MMA from arena to theatre. A core manifestation of the MMA style in Yen's movies, in particular *SPL: Sha Po Lang* (2005) and *Flash Point* (2007), is hand-to-hand combat culminating in a display of the explosive power of the male body (Barretto 2016). Fighters' heads, limbs, and torsos evoke a kind of machismo through the crude, powerful manner of the fighting. As a self-professed MMA fan, Yen once expressed in an interview:

> As I was doing research the martial artist inside of me found something that I think throughout the years of my martial arts training that all of sudden just clicked. I have studied so many traditional martial art styles; traditional Kung Fu, Wushu, Taekwondo, Boxing, Karate because I was a martial artist before I was a film maker. Then I realised this whole MMA thing actually brought an answer to all martial arts; does it work? (Nic 2016)

According to Stephen Berwick's article published in *Kung Fu Qigong Magazine* (June 2000), moreover, MMA as Yen's approach to martial arts is not only the secret to his success as one of Hong Kong's most prominent directors, but also the reason to regard him as a contemporary martial arts master. By bridging the kinetic codes signified by Yen's myriad roles, the user reimagines the intertextuality of the actor's public persona.

The user Sascha Matuszak is not the sole blogger-martial arts lover who notices the intricate relationship between the two techniques. Another post on Fightland Blog called 'Wing Chun and MMA: Controlling the center', written by Jack Slack, reconciles the gap between the Chinese martial arts and the Westernised, modern technique, the two fighting paradigms that can be most distant, as many observe. As indicated in the title, the post focuses chiefly on the fighting principle 'controlling the centre', proving that the writer is savvy in martial arts. Slack points out some perceived prejudice of Wing Chun for the purpose of rejuvenating the value of traditional acrobatics in a modern setting. As the blog opens:

> Wing Chun remains the punchline of many jokes in the mixed martial arts community. In fact, I often receive tweets and emails asking me to come down on one side or the other in an argument between friends – one will say that Wing Chun is useless in a modern combat sports context, the other will argue that it is simply because no true Wing Chun masters feel moved to compete. (Slack 2015)

After explaining the principles of the Wing Chun, the blogger circulates the materials emphasising MMA. He or she has cut a number of videos of MMA fights, noticeably kickboxing and Muay Thai, which underscores the 'occupying-the-centre' principle and how it collides with that of Wing Chun. The clips operate on the auto-repeating format that exhibits the movements of the professional athletes as well as their physical verve and skill. Since this post is hyperlinked to other entries under the 'Donnie Yen' tag, the extra-diegetic components widen the public appeal of Yen in the blogged space.

Ip Man, Bruce Lee, nationalist consciousness

The intertextual potential of Yen's blogged presence is not only shown through various fighting paradigms but also through the anti-imperialist themes shared by various ethnic and cultural communities. Straddling Chinese nationalism and hip-hop culture, Yen's Wing Chun body becomes a vehicle to triumph over imperialism, applauded by Chinese-Americans and African-Americans alike. A blog named 'Burrello Submarine's Movie Blog' is one of the instances. The subtitle of the blog – 'Cinema Esoterica Obscura' – hints that the blogger is a huge cinephile. The blog archives an inventory of movies that the web user describes as 'weirdest', cataloging in alphabetical order. Searching with the tagging keywords 'Donnie Yen', the blog generates a list of entries that uncover the perceived proximity between Yen and the *Star Wars* series. One of the entries emphasises the possible associations between Donnie Yen's 'Ip Man' image and Bruce Lee. In fact, the two personalities from the different periods, Donnie Yen and Bruce Lee, have certain overlaps. With a short filmography of five titles, Lee's meteoric rise to international fame has made him 'the most popular kung fu star in the West' (Lo 2005: 86). He is celebrated for his physical rigour, martial dexterity, and profound philosophy in martial arts. The untimely death of Lee left the kung fu fans hungry for a type of screen action that can be achieved by Lee only. Hong Kong filmmakers tried seeking the next martial arts dragon to fill the market gap. Yet the attempt seemed failed until the rise of Yen as the first Chinese star-choreographer in Hong Kong cinema whose image, fighting skill, and philosophy appear comparable to those of Bruce Lee (ibid.) – not to mention that Yen, as a long-time fan of Lee, persistently acknowledges Lee's inspiration in his works (Fury 2011: 20).

The 6 December 2011 post entitled 'Everybody was Kung Fu Fighting: The Story of Ip Man', was originally published *for The Alternative Chronicle on 12 January 2011* and quotes the opening line of the lyrics of Carl Douglas's song 'Kung Fu Fighting' released in 1974 on the edge of a 'chopsocky' film craze in the United States. *It also concurs Ip Man with hip hop,* two subjects that presumably have little to do with each other. Hip hop refers to a form of musical expression originating in African-American communities in New York in the second half of the last century whereas Ip Man is a Wing Chun martial artist who lived in China in the turn-of-the-century period. The concurrence stems from America's fascination with Hong Kong martial arts in the 1970s. According to David Desser's analysis (2000), an unprecedented, phenomenal domination of foreign films on American cinematic screens happened during the week of 16 May 1973 (20–21). *Fists of Fury* (1971), *Deep Thrust: The Hand of Death* (1972), and *Five Fingers of Death* (1973) were ranked the top three on *Variety*'s box-office list. This was the only time that such a number of foreign films casting non-white actors were so well-received. The popularity of these features in turn notably influenced Blaxploitation, an American subgenre targeted to the urban black audience that, although short-lived, attained box-office success and an enduring influence on American cinema through such low-budget cult films as *Scream, Blacula, Scream* (1973) and *The Mack* (1973) (Ongiri 2005: 252). Having said so, the esteem of Hong Kong kung fu films among African-American audiences of the time has often been overlooked (Gateward 2009: 55). Publicity for films like *Deadly Duo* (1971) and *The Water Margin* (1972), both directed by Chang Cheh, appeared in the *New Amsterdam*, the most widely circulated black newspaper in New York City. Martial arts films had theatrical distribution not only in Chinatowns, but also in black communities in such cities as New York and Washington, DC, one of the most segregated cities in the US (ibid.) As late as the 1980s, black theatres were still showing kung fu films, reflecting the power of the genre in African-American populations in the US.

In addition to the historical ties, the competitive and confronta-tional allusion shared by both hip hop and martial arts films becomes an imperative aspect of the cross-text account. These dual genres, one musical and the other filmic, designate forms of resistance to an oppressive hegemony, which is well observed by Frances Gateward (2009):

> Hip hop attempts to negotiate the experiences of marginalisation, brutally truncated opportunity, and oppression within the cultural imperatives of African American and Caribbean history, identity, and community, while in kung-fu films, the Chinese attempt to negotiate the same in relation to Japanese, European, and sometimes – as in the case of Bruce Lee and *Enter the Dragon* – White American powers. (Gateward 2009: 64)

Hip hop originates as a ghetto youth subculture developed by African-American, Caribbean-American, and Latino-American young people in the 1970s in the area of New York City and shaped by the hardships of urban African-American life in a racism-laden sociocultural milieu (Gateward 2009: 53). It demonstrates a transformation through painting, film, fashion, video, dance, and, most remarkably, rap. Hip hop aesthetics constitutes an intervention against the mainstream culture: the music is cacophonous, yet in perfect pitch in articulating defiance to domineering authority. Moreover, hip hop entails an aesthetic sublimation of violence, as illustrated by pioneers like Afrika Bambaata who 'asserted his concept of youth solidarity by rechanneling violent competition into artistic contests' (Keyes 2002: 47). According to M. T. Kato, Bruce Lee's art is 'a progressive foundational concept of the hip hop aesthetics' (2007: 176). Lee is probably the martial arts actor who enjoys the greatest fame among African Americans. 'Images of Bruce Lee were at least as popular in many black homes as were images of Martin Luther King, possibly even more so' (Ongiri 2005: 252). In this sense, martial arts films can readily speak to the African-American viewers, whose history lends appeal to stylised action and aggression, such that the films become a locus for cross-identification.

Bruce Lee becomes an icon of resistance and triumph for the Third World minorities against racism in a diaspora setting, as what Chris Berry has dubbed the 'third world underdog' (2006: 218). Lee's 'underdog' image in defiance of racism is most largely shaped by his Chen Zhen personality in *Fist of Fury* (1972). It would not be an exaggeration to describe Chen Zhen as one of the most iconic figures in Chinese cinema. Originally created by Hong Kong writer Ni Kuang, this fictional character is based on Liu Zhensheng, a disciple of Huo Yuanjia, an acclaimed martial artist who became the title character of *Fearless* (2006) starring Jet Li. As Chris Berry (2006) posits, *Fist of Fury*, among Lee's films, is his 'most evidently nationalistic work' (220). In the setting of semi-colonised

Shanghai, Chen Zhen is a student of the founder of the Jinwu martial arts school who seeks to avenge his master's death from rival Japanese. The Japanese sneer at him with a sign bearing the 'sick men of Asia' (*'dongya bingfu'*) slogan. The scene unmistakably inspires the aforementioned Ip Man-verses-ten-karatekas fight in the 2008 Wing Chun epic, such that the vengeance-seeking plotline turns the pacifist martial artist to be a furious avenger, further uncovering an affinity between the personae of Donnie Yen and Bruce Lee. The climax of *Fist of Fury* is a contest with a Russian (white) champion introduced by the Japanese. As the police come to arrest Chen Zhen, he charges them with audacity. The film closes with a freeze frame of Lee in mid-leap, accompanied by his signature scream *in tandem* with the sound of gunfire. Chen Zhen presents as a patriotic hero that all Chinese threatened by imperialism would be keen to associate themselves with. His anti-imperialist presence not only conveys the hero's physical dynamism but also defines the nationalism of the cinematic space.

Instead of *Fist of Fury*, however, the blogger posts a movie still of Bruce Lee's fourth movie *Enter the Dragon*. Led by the box-office success of Lee's previous production, *The Way of the Dragon*, *Enter the Dragon* (1973), is the James Bond-style movie Lee made for Warner Brothers. Continuing his image as a furious fighter, this time, Lee plays the familiar role of an international police agent who combats against a well-off criminal named Han. Lee is a Shaolin martial artist whereas Han is a strayed Shaolin disciple. Lee goes to Han's fortress, where he joins forces with a white American and an African American. While the latter dies, Lee and his white colleague manage to destroy Han's fortress and arrest the evildoer. The movie still of *Enter the Dragon* that the blogger chooses exhibits Lee's stripped-off body, covered with spilt blood, underscoring the 'body as a weapon', as he or she explains. The caption of the picture reads: 'Still one of the best', indicating the blogger's fondness of the screen personality as the exemplary heroic image of Lee. This proves that the martial arts body is a contested venue to explore Chineseness, rightly exemplified through the star body of Bruce Lee. Tony Rayns and Stephen Teo debated over Lee's body in terms of narcissism and nationalism. In his essay, 'Bruce Lee: Narcissism and nationalism' Tony Rayns (1980) emphasises the martial expertise and self-sufficiency in Lee's characters that are manifested and culminated in a series of fight scenes. He cites a scene in *The Way of Dragon* (1972) as an instance in which Lee's character exercised in a room and took pleasure from the self-image in the mirror. As Rayns argues, the sequence is narcissistic to the extent of being

EVERYONE WAS KUNG FU FIGHTING: THE STORY OF
IP MAN

For all the serious, highfalutin movies I watch, I do confess I have a weakness for the kung-fu flick. Action is fun to watch and as a guy it's sometimes hard not to be fascinated by violence and destruction in movies. Watching a building collapse or a high speed car chase or dinosaurs fighting each other or Bruce Willis jumping off a roof with a fire-hose bungee cord is fun and exciting. Naturally the martial arts epic must enter one's peripheries at some point. Ever since I saw a Jackie Chan marathon on TV as a kid I was hooked. The kung-fu movie gets a lot of flack sometimes for being fairly thin when it comes to plot, but the incredible athletes and personalities that have emerged from it are what draws us. Every move Bruce Lee does is astonishing to watch and there's something eternally fascinating about using only your body as a weapon.

12.06.11
by Burnello
Submarine

Figure 1.2 The cinematic personality of Bruce Lee in *Enter the Dragon* in the entry entitled 'Everyone was kung fu fighting: the story of Ip Man'

onanistic (111). Lee's kinetic body functions as to bespeak a satisfaction of ego. However, Stephen Teo is suspicious about such an approach to Lee's body. In his essay, 'The true way of the dragon: The films of Bruce Lee' (1992), Teo challenges such a view by arguing, 'To perceive of Lee as only a kung fu martial artist without understanding his nationalistic philosophy is to perceive of Lee only as an illusion, an image in a mirror, Lee as Narcissus' (79). As Teo elaborates, these critics, rejecting sharing Lee's nationalistic ethos, partake in a paradox of their own invention by stressing Lee's obsession with ego and physical perfection. While Rayns and Teo adopt very different approaches to examine Lee's body, a point that both essays have concurrently insinuated is that the martial arts body is something more than a physical entity; rather, it is a venue for suggestive debates surrounding the issue of cinematic Chineseness in the genre.

The historical presentation of historical personae, yet appearing as fragmented and abstract, orchestrates part of the intertexual discourse of Donnie Yen/Ip Man. In the latter part of the blog entry, the Wing Chun theme re-emerges that the blogger includes an archival black-and-white picture of Ip Man and Bruce Lee, simulating certain documentary legitimacy (Figure 1.3). From its inception, the media hype of *Ip Man* revolves around the teacher–disciple relationship in reality. Photographs and anecdotes of the two martial artists circulated in the public discourse, providing a good deal of exposure for the film. These extra-diegetic materials include the personal story of Ip Man, the encounter of Bruce Lee and Ip Man, and the Wing Chun training they undertake. In the

The sequel, *Ip Man 2* (2010), brings the cast back and features Sammo Hung as a cantankerous martial arts master in Hong Kong and sees Ip Man fighting a cocky, belligerent (and rather obnoxious) British boxer (reminded of Mr. T in *Rocky III*). Although the stakes are never quite as high, more fights seem bloated or forced, there's an influx of what appears to be some wire-fu, and the western boxing is never as interesting to watch as the kung-fu business, it is a fun sequel about restoring national pride through the unifying power of martial arts. For fans of the martial arts epic, *Ip Man* might be exactly what you've been waiting for.

The real guy alongside his student, Bruce Lee.

Originally published for "The Alternative Chronicle" Jan 12, 2011

Figure 1.3 The blogger poaches and posts an archival picture of Bruce Lee and the Wing Chun master Ip Man

blogosphere, Yen fans copy and share documented texts of real-life figures, formulating a new archival and discursive space that permits users to revisit and recirculate the history at any time. In this way, historical narrative intertwines with fictional personalities. This kind of composite presentation insinuates that the persona construction oscillates between documentary and fictive modes, occupying the middle ground of the real and the fabricated.

Furthermore, the photograph exposes a temporal and spatial displacement. The story and the character of the history about the Wing Chun culture in the 1960s have been framed in the 2010s. Interestingly, while the blogger posts a historical picture, he or she does not provide any account or footnote on this piece of history. The blogger does not even imitate a narrative voice, guiding the audience to interpret the past. Such cyber-documentation of Ip Man and Bruce Lee does not necessarily mean an enhanced and stable sense of historicity regarding martial arts, in view of the elusive and inconsistent qualities of cyberspace. It is true that film per se lacks an essential historicity in that Ip Man is positioned in a fictitious nationalist diegesis and is equipped with a hyperbolic Wing Chun physicality. Such an instance unfolds more superficiality than substantiality. In cyberspace, the history of the master–student relationship of Ip Man and Bruce Lee is represented in neither a coherent nor linear fashion. Instead, materials, divulged of historical essence, are searched, presented, and accessed in a fragmented, isolated manner. As this blog entry indicates, although fans are interpellated to historical witnesses of the Wing Chun culture and the icons, the fragmented image can only suggest that history and memory have faded. It entails a documentary effect but not documentary authenticity. The blogger employs the documented history more to reimagine the possible relations of the Wing Chun personae of Ip Man, Bruce Lee, and Donnie Yen than to show how authentic the history is. Hence, the modality of archival access and cyber citation is not necessarily grounded by historicity but is shaped by representability and changeability.

Yen's martial arts lineage and the 'family man' image

If it is Yen's characters that largely denote the Chineseness in his star appeal roles, then some blogs have complicated and perhaps obscured such 'Chinese' codes by emphasising the private life of the actor. The offscreen existence carries significance in image building. Scholarship has vindicated that it is the duality of the image consisting of onscreen persona and offscreen presence, publicised and circulated via fan magazines, press interviews, gossip columns, and fan clubs, that makes a star (Dyer 1979; Allen and Gomery 1985; Geraghty 2000). Furthermore, Christine Geraghty (2000) posits that the distribution of the stories about stars' 'real' life should not occupy a secondary position to the film itself (189). The questions of how the life stories are articulated and consumed is equally significant to those of how actors' films are produced and promoted. Considering the blog-oriented presence of Donnie Yen, one can certainly observe fans' access to and celebration of the intimate information of the icon. Whereas audiences hail his martial prowess on screens, they also show curiosity in the extra-filmic appeal pointing to his family life, martial arts upbringing, and the back-screen physical training. Yen's private life may or may not denote a kind of Chineseness as what his characters usually do, muddling his status as a well-known martial arts star.

By arguing so, it is note-worthy that Yen's offscreen publicity both overlaps with and contrasts to the onscreen image. As Sabrina Yu (2012) elucidates, the film industry often employs two strategies of star-making: one is to stress conflict and the other coherence between the screen personality and private life (168). Richard Dyer, in his seminal book, *Stars* (1979), suggests that tensions and contradictions between cinematic roles and personal life always appear. Judith Mayne further argues that the precise personae of stars emerge with 'constant reinvention, the dissolution of contraries, the embrace of wildly opposing terms' (1993: 138). In a different light, certain scholars discern the correspondence, consistency, and integration between the personalities in and out of films. Richard DeCordova (1991), in his account of the early film star system in America, purports that a public icon's private existence was chiefly represented as a reflected image of his or her characters. It is observed that the contours of dual strategies of star construction, crisscrossing, diverging, and overlapping with one another at times, is evident in the blogged persona of Yen. To elaborate, Yen's offscreen presence can be considered along two axes: first, his ample martial arts background and, second, his 'family man' image. I attempt to argue that while the first image conflates Yen's screen image as a marital arts fighter, the second shows incongruity, if not denial, to his profession. Such a twofold approach informs the star phenomenon of Yen, curtailing the complicated dynamics between the personae within and outside the diegetic worlds.

Certain blogs concentrate on Donnie Yen's family background without totally abandoning his association with kung fu. A blog called 'The Blog of Alfred Hsing' presumably run by Hsing, a US-based martial artist, actor, and stuntman, provides an illustration of this idea. With a Californian background, Hsing has won at the World Wushu Championships in 2009, which accredits him to move within the transnational martial arts filmmaking network. Capitalising on his academic training in a computer profession, he unfolds his Internet knowledge by establishing his blog persona, of which he simultaneously – and consciously – forges a connection with celebrated icons including Jackie Chan, Jet Li, Zhang Ziyi, and Donnie Yen. To further prove his martial dexterity, the blogger addresses and publicises his encounter and experience in an array of martial arts movie productions. In an entry dated 30 December 2012, Hsing writes about his screen debut in China playing a monk character in *The Sorcerer and the White Snake* (2011), a martial arts epic starring Jet Li and Zhang Wen. A 9 March 2013 post chronicles Hsing's participation as actor and choreographer in *My Lucky Star* (2013), a Chinese-language adventure romantic movie featuring Zhang Ziyi who endeavours to be the producer. A 5 June 2015 entry records that he has worked with the JC Stunt Team in the Jackie Chan vehicle *Dragon Blade* (2015), which has been awarded at the 16th Huading Film Awards with Best Action Design. In addition, as indicated in a post dated 22 March 2017, he becomes the subject of *Hero in All of Us – Alfred Hsing*, a short film about his own career of and commitment in *wushu* produced by JetLi.com, a website established by Jet Li allegedly for promoting martial arts. Hsing writes in an entry released on 19 March 2016 about his experience of working as a stunt coordinator with the American-based Hong Kong choreographer Yuen Woo-ping in *Ip Man 3*, which contains the co-appearances of, as Hsing esteems, the 'greatest martial arts legends' Donnie Yen and Mike Tyson. Hsing's blog signposts his growing profile and his ambition of establishing status in the martial arts and cinematic worlds by relating himself with martial arts pop icons.

One point it is worthwhile to consider is that Yen's presence in Hsing's blog is not solely constructed around his movies and screen roles but also through the megastar's lineage and upbringing. Cinephiles are probably aware of the fact that Yen's superb martial arts skill is drawn from his lifelong martial arts background, bridging the onscreen image and offscreen existence of Yen. As a child, he was taught martial arts by his mother Bow Sim Mak, a world-acclaimed Tai Chi master who is the founder of the Chinese Wushu Research Institute. After living in Boston for some years in his teens, Yen was sent by his parents to Beijing for two years of formal martial arts training, learning from the same master as Jet Li. Yen has often stressed that his onscreen kung fu is 'real' in that he has learnt martial arts and does his own action rather than using doubles or stuntmen. To keyword-search 'The Blog of Alfred Hsing' with the phrase 'Donnie Yen', one can obtain the results focusing on both Yen's screen persona and martial arts pedigree, of which the latter is more intriguing to me. Dated 23 April 2010, an entry from Hsing's blog entitled 'Sister to Donnie Yen, Daughter to Bow Sim Mark: Lunch with Martial Arts Star Chris Yen' obliquely recognises Yen's martial arts appeal. Hsing introduces Chris Yen in a way that capitalises on her martial arts lineage and the fame of Donnie Yen. Perhaps better known as Donnie Yen's sibling than her own name to the general public, Chris Yen follows the similar trajectory of receiving martial arts training and developing a career as an entertainer. Generally considered as an emergent face in the entertainment world, nevertheless, Chris Yen exists as 'an awesome martial artist and entrepreneur', as Hsing describes, underlining her multi-vocational status and the capitalistic potential of her name.

This blog piece is a showcase of the multimedia persona of Chris Yen, recycled and reframed in a repertoire of attractive and marketable imagery of the starlet by Alfred Hsing. The blogger republishes the magazine cover of *Inside Kung Fu*, using Chris Yen as the subject that is framed as 'Leading Kung-Fu's New Breed'. The cover image shows Chris Yen, with a sobre and confident face, wearing an Oriental-styled costume exhibiting a 'wushu pose' (Rosenbaum 2009) characterised by virility and femininity. Self-referenced, the blogger also re-posts an online article written by S. I. Rosenbaum from a wushu news blog that he posted in 2009, which delineates in detail the heroine's background and vocation, corroborating with the intertextual capacity of his blog. Hsing, moreover, embeds in this post a video entitled 'Chris Yen Action Reel', which was originally broadcasted on YouTube on 9 November 2008. The video encompasses an array of the actress's media appearances, for instance, the hyper-stylish promotion footage for Fox's Fuel Television network created by Los Angeles-based artist Jason Irwin, movie clips from the 2009 Hollywood action thriller *Give 'Em Hell, Malone* and a 2004 Hong Kong action comedy, *Protégé de la Rose Noire* (directed by Donnie Yen). This assembly of personae not only displays the physical prowess of the female body but also vindicates the escalating visibility of Chris Yen in global media. What closes the entry, moreover, is the advertising image for Martial Arts Complete, an emergent merchandise of martial arts equipment and supply. The caption of the photograph reads, 'International Martial Arts Star Chris Yen', identifying Chris Yen as an established name in the public arena.

Whereas the blogger unveils the predisposition of recognising Chris Yen as someone of notable fame, such fame is not fabricated without relying on the status of Donnie Yen. Hsing shows no intention to relinquish the association to Donnie Yen in constructing the star discourse of Chris Yen. The entry includes a brief account of Donnie Yen, 'the brother', as the paragraph reads:

> Her brother Donnie Yen has appeared in more than 40 films and TV shows, including: **"Ip Man"**(2008)**, "Flash Point"** (2007), **"Saat Po Long aka SPL"**(2005), **"Shanghai Knights"** (2003), **"Hero"** (2002), **"Blade II"** (2002), **"Highlander: Endgame"** (2000), and **"Iron Monkey"** (1993). (Hsing 2009; emboldening in the original)

Arguably, the martial arts status of the two 'Yens' can be strengthened by underlining the brother–sister relationship. Hence, this shows how Donnie Yen's appeal interlocks with the other personae that are not only from the industrial network but also from kinship.

A unique trademark of a 'family man' becomes the core of Yen's extra-filmic existence, which is loosely resonant to his onscreen persona. In his early career, Yen's private life does not seem to come to much media limelight. He was once divorced in 1993 but the news was scarcely reported. All the public is conscious about is Yen's second marriage with his present wife Cecilia Wang, a former beauty queen from Toronto, Canada in 2000. The public exposure of affection to his wife grants him the accolade as 'the best husband', as certain media coin ('Your husband is great, but Donnie Yen is even better' 2017). The celebrity couple also become the subjects of various advertising campaigns. Resorts World Sentosa's 2016 endorsement to the Yens as brand ambassadors is an example. Furthermore, unlike some celebrities who intend to hide their children from paparazzi, Yen from time to time posts family photographs on Weibo, forging by himself an identity as a responsible father. As an actor who earns fame through his martial arts persona that highlights masculinity, gallantry, and power, Donnie Yen publicises his private existence that is feminised, emotion-driven, and sentiment-saturated.

Donnie Yen's family-based livelihood is not hidden from the awareness of bloggers. The blog 'AWMA: Asian World of Martial Arts, Inc.' has linked Yen's private life to his casting in *Rouge One*. An entry entitled 'Donnie Yen created a new martial art for Rouge One: A Star Wars Story' (http:blog.awma.com/donnie-yen-created-a-new-martial-art-for-rogue-one-a-star-wars-story/) appears on 15 December 2016, one day prior to the theatrical release of *Rouge One* in the US, which is probably generated by the hype of the science-fiction extravaganza. The blogger consolidates a series of Yen's interviews from English-language press such as the BBC, *Variety*, *People* magazine, *Empire* magazine, Yahoo, and Geek Culture, cueing the hyperlinked potentiality of blog texts. One of the interviews was originally produced and publicised by Geek Culture, an online network of devotees of popular media and culture such as video games, science-fiction, toys, and gadgets on titles as famous as *Transformers* (2007–2017), *Star Wars* (1977–2016), and *Star Trek* (2009). The clip was then posted on YouTube and now is copied-and-pasted by the blogger. The conversation informs Yen's original plan to refuse the invitation of shooting *Rouge One* and the reason, which sounds unusual for a professional actor, is his reluctance to be away from home. Yen also expresses similar will on some other occasions, for example, 'Here [China], I can go home to have dinner after a day of filming. No films [shot outside China] could give me that. Actually, it'd be perfect if the shoot of a film could take place in my backyard' (Lee 2016). In the 'Geek Culture' interview, Yen continues to elicit his story about the family celebration of Halloween in 2016, following his wife's idea, by preparing his kids the *Star Wars*-themed outfit. Countless *Star Wars* fans all over the globe herd to sundry web-based platforms to upload and share images of their costumes with like-minded others. Yen, likewise, posts on Instagram the photographs of his son dressed as Chirrut Îmwe and his daughter dressed as a Stormtrooper (Figure 1.4). The narrative articulated by Yen and relayed by the blogger not only advertises Yen's personification in *Rouge One* (or the move itself) but also foster Yen's offscreen existence as a responsive and accountable husband-father.

In fact, news and photographs of Yen's son adopting the image of a miniature Chirrut is already in circulation in the globalised media space. For instance, comicbook.com appropriates an Instagram picture of Yen's family on a *Rouge One* marketing event and publicises it on 22 December 2016 on Blast Points Podcast, an online platform to garner *Star Wars* aficionados and to share news on a weekly basis. Hashtagged with 'RougeOne', the caption of the picture reads, 'Shoutout to Donnie Yen's son for being the coolest kid possibly ever' (Seigel 2016). The 'costumed' son, reportedly a *Star Wars* fan, becomes 'a poster child of sorts for representation in genre films' (ibid.). In this regard, the public discourse juxtaposes and annexes Yen's offscreen existence as an accountable father with his cinematic appeal. Such approach of image-making seems closer to that of Hollywood actors like Brat Pitt, Johnny Depp, and Tom Cruise than Yen's Chinese counterparts, unveiling the alternative aspects to Yen's martial arts persona.

Figure 1.4 An online image of Donnie Yen's son dressed as Chirrut Îmwe and his daughter dressed as a Stormtrooper as part of the family's Halloween celebration

Continuing the argument, Donnie Yen's heterosexual relationship stands him out from other Chinese celebrities, becoming an important venue for bolstering his fame. As mentioned, Yen does not mind exposing his affection to his wife. He often posts on Weibo photographs of birthday dinners, vacations, and Valentine's celebrations. Entertainment reporters are also keen on inviting Yen to provide tips of a happy marriage, as if the hero epitomises the key to a successful family. Yen's high-profile romantic life is distinct from his predecessor, Jet Li. As a famous screen fighter, Li engineers his stardom dominated by his screen persona, and Leon Hunt (2003) once argued that Li does not exist outside his screen roles (141). Li's private life appears to be inaccessible, or, in Sabrina Yu's (2012) phrase, 'even a little mysterious' (174) for his viewers. There has been news about Li's marriage with the former beauty pageant champion, Nina Li. Even Li himself has exposed some anecdotes on his website by depicting himself as a traditional, reliable 'family man' (175). The media exposure of his private life is, however, limited. Moreover, Hong Kong media observe that Li, on purpose, avoids discussing his private life in public. For example, a headline in a local newspaper *Ming Pao* dated 3 October 1994 reads, 'Jet Li's Three Secrets: Family, Money and Romance'. Whereas audiences may express curiosity with respect to his private life and romantic encounter, Li candidly admits that he is not good at expressing passionate feeling and tactfully attributes this to his shy, reticent personality (Yu 2012: 175). Furthermore, the lack of romantic scenes in Li's films is mainly due to the actor's 'discomfort' in filming intimacy, moderately resulting from his 'conservative, puritanical upbringing' (ibid.), different from Yen's instance that he avoids bed scenes in order not to upset his wife (Pulumbarit 2015). In this light, Yen strategises his persona management otherwise, by providing explicit expressions of adoration. Such expressiveness increasingly generates intimate discussion about his marriage from the public (ibid.), cementing his image as a reliable, affectionate sexual partner.

Donnie Yen's commitment to family also distinguishes him from Jackie Chan. While Yen has hardly found himself entangled in any controversy about sexuality throughout his career, Chan is notorious with respect to his romance affairs. Gossip columns have exposed that Chan got married to a Taiwanese popular actress Joan Feng-jiao Lin who gave birth to Jaycee Chan, a Taiwan-based, American-born Chinese pop singer-actor. Simultaneously, Chan is usually linked with the names of women as well-known as Mando-/Canto-/J-pop queen Teresa Teng and screen diva Brigitte Lin. Audiences may be more aware of Chan's affair with Elaine Ng, a Hong Kong beauty queen, who publicly accounted her pregnancy in 1999 and that made some tabloid headlines. At the time, Chan admitted his imprudence by saying that he had 'only committed a fault that every single man in the world commits' – a response that annoyed many audiences and netisens (Fam 2017). Compared to Chan's image as an 'irresponsible' man, Yen holds an appeal that is more positive, mature, and stable.

By saying so, one may notice that dedication to the household is a trait not utterly absent in Yen's cinematic realm. *Ip Man* perhaps is one of the few narratives that personifies a Chinese hero who is good at fighting and simultaneously fond of his wife and children. As previously discussed, such a narrative emblematises Confucian values of serving in honour of community and family that are, nevertheless, not much extended in blog texts. Most of the footage from *Ip Man* that is poached and posted onto blogs exhibits and evinces the martial prowess of Yen/Ip rather than showing a dedication to family. From this perspective, the discourse of Yen's private life indicates miniscule overlaps to his cinematic personality.

To sum up, the twofold offscreen life of Donnie Yen shows both resonance to and discrepancy of his onscreen appeal. Some blog entries address the persona of Yen's sister, which is resonant to his fame as a martial artist. Some others include the texts of Yen's marriage and fatherhood that diverge from the fighter persona on celluloid screens. If Yen's martial arts personality solidifies a kind of Chineseness in his stardom, then his private life destabilises the 'Chinese' ethos by making an image wavering between consistency and incongruity in the star construction.

Problematising Yen's martial arts appeal in the post-*Ip Man* period

Donnie Yen's recent screen persona further vexes the Chineseness by generating computer-generated image (CGI) spectacles of the martial arts body. The blog 'AZN BADGER'S BLOG' (https:aznbadger.wordpress. com/tag/donnie-yen/) displays a predilection to Yen's appeal marked by clues of flexibility and diversity. The host of the website is an American-based blogger called 'Trevor' who has eclectic interests in media and sports, including retro video games, boxing, old-school pro-wrestling, comic books, kung fu, and Godzilla movies, as the web-page of the blog indicates. Tagged under the keywords 'Donnie Yen', a number of entries exhibit Yen's personalities in films like Peter Chan's *Wu Xia* (2001). This 2001 epic is said to pay homage to the Shaw Brothers' martial arts movies of the 1960s and 1970s in general, and Chang Cheh's *The One Armed Swordsman* (1973) in particular (WU XIA – SentieriSelvaggi meets Peter Ho-sun Chan 2011). It portrays Liu Jinxi (Donnie Yen), who is the former member of the 72 Demons clan, seeking refuge in a remote small town in the Yunnan province in southwestern China. His seemingly accidental murder of two ignominious bandits who disturb the town has provoked the suspension of the investigator Xu Baijiu (Takeshi Kaneshiro), who epitomises a synthesis of Western science like forensics, physics, and psychology with Chinese medicine such as meridians (*jingluo*) and herbal medicine. The movie is well known for its innovative use of digital effects, allowing viewers to 'look through' the body, engaging with an alternative vision to the *wuxia* physicality. It takes a perspective in accordance with pathological anatomy, borrowing the visual rhetoric of the television crime series *CSI: Crime Scene Investigation*. The digital effects emulate the representation of blood cells, blood nerves, bodily fluids, and internal body parts and the degree of hurtfulness that a well-aimed blow casts on to the organ of the heart as part of the diegetic visuals. While traditional *wuxia* films generally emphasise the overt choreographic performance, *Wu Xia* modernises the genre by exposing the interior of the human body enabled by simulationist effects. It demystifies the heroic physique while offering to cinephiles and fans the fascination aligned with the principles of technologically based ocularcentrism.

Hiring martial artist Donnie Yen as *Wu Xia*'s choreographer supposedly aimed at reinforcing the impression of its kung fu's authenticity but the outcome sounds rather self-defeating. Director Peter Chan once said of Yen's action style, 'Donnie's work has always been realistic because his action has always been very grounded, you know, very powerful but yet very realistic. It's humanly possible. We never see Donnie's film where ... everything defies physics and human possibility' (WU XIA – SentieriSelvaggi meets Peter Ho-sun Chan 2011). However, what *Wu Xia* demonstrates is the opposite; it focuses not on what Donnie Yen's body can perform, but on what it cannot. The wide circulation of *Wu Xia* affirmed its marketability to both local and global distributors and audiences. According to the *Hollywood Reporter*, the film scored seven-digit presales in Asian countries like Singapore, Malaysia, and Indonesia. Outside the Greater China region, there was keen bidding interest from buyers in the

US, the UK, France, Germany, Australia, and New Zealand (Lee 2011). The film's success is partly on account of the longstanding appeal of the martial arts genre, the fame of director Peter Chan, and the star power of the major actors like Donnie Yen and Takeshi Kaneshiro. But the digital imagery and the new visual aesthetic it heralds have also played a role in its distribution success. Consider how the incorporation of simulation technology in *Wu Xia* is made a focal point of publicity of the movie, appealing even to fans of Hong Kong kung fu films. In this sense, the movie is laudable not only for its use of new technology but also for its capacity in complicating and obscuring the martial arts representation.

Donnie Yen's persona of a martial artist is further vexed by *The Monkey King* (2014), a Chinese-speaking CG-cluttered fantasy epic based on the Chinese classic novel *Journey to the West*. This action-driven spectacle capitalises on the martial arts cinematic legacy while incorporating considerable special effects in orchestrating screen choreography. On top of the animation crowding the background, the film renders CGI to display actions like frequent flying and floating above heaven. Co-starring the huge Hong Kong stars Chow Yun-fat and Aaron Kwok, Yen plays the titular character of Monkey King, subsequent to Jet Li's playful 'Monkey King' role in *The Forbidden Kingdom* (2008). As film critic Maggie Lee comments, 'It [the movie] provides Yen with little room to flex his acting muscles or otherwise emote effectively; in fact, the thesp looks unrecognizable in his hairy suit and heavy makeup' (Lee 2014). Put another way, the 3D blockbuster is a Donnie Yen vehicle where the limited martial flair and substance challenges the 'authentic' bodily presence of the performer-choreographer. Nevertheless, it is speculative that the launch of the movie on multiple IMAX screens will break the box-office records during the Chinese New Year (Lee 2014). It is similar to the instance of *The Stormraiders* (1998), a watershed film for rendering CGI in Hong Kong martial arts cinema, of which the digital spectacle displaces the martial arts body while it appeals to a broader market. According to Kwai-Cheung Lo (2005), the history of the Chinese body manufactured by Hong Kong popular culture is the history of its gradual virtualisation (100). The movie embodies the new void of Chineseness where the choreographic presence is intertwined with the imagined or the reproduced, questioning the star body in the martial arts cinema.

The ambiguous bodily presence of Donnie Yen endures in his subsequent cinematic appearance in the big-budget marital arts epic *Crouching Tiger, Hidden Dragon: Sword of Destiny (2016)*. Directed by

Yuen Woo-ping this time, *the movie* is another visual piece of digital arts of which CGI-propelled action carries more weight than real fight. It is a project chiefly driven by the American film mogul Harvey Weinstein who has restored Yuen Woo-ping's *Iron Monkey* (1993) and has remade King Hu's *Come Drink with Me* (1966) and Sun Chung's *The Avenging Eagle (1978)* (Mottram 2016). Exploiting the success of *Crouching Tiger, Hidden Dragon, the sequel* cast Donnie Yen, in replacement of Chow Yun-fat, alongside Michelle Yeoh, making viewers speculate about elaborate sword fights between the two martial arts megastars who have reunited for screen choreography for the first time after *Wing Chun* in 1994. Similar to *The Monkey King,* the choreography is, nonetheless, 'frequently marred by unnecessary CGI embellishment' (Sims 2016). As *Netflix's first original film (Child 2014), Crouching Tiger, Hidden Dragon: Sword of Destiny* signposts a new era of viewership of wuxia movies and the consumption of the aesthetics as well as altering the emphasis on the physical flair of martial arts personalities.

In the interactive blogosphere, moreover, fans' responses to Donnie Yen's personae in *Wu Xia, Monkey King,* and *Crouching Tiger, Hidden Dragon: Sword of Destiny* are not as numerous or prominent as his previous roles. In blogs, one finds only limited entries concerning these recent titles, not compatible to those of *Ip Man* and *Legend of the Fist: The Return of Chen Zhen.* It is not utterly clear if the scarcity of posts is because of the fact that these features are relatively new films, or other reasons. Further research is needed at this point to qualify a conclusion. Yet one may remain open to considering that blending the simulated and the corporeal has problematised Yen's star presence, which pivots on fans' recognition of the kinetic authenticity. Put another way, the star text of Yen becomes ambiguous in a way that his fans do not easily attach and respond to, as what the blog discourse manifests. Therefore, Yen's wooly martial arts image not only shapes bloggers' responses as limiting but also alters the star presence that has been already extended in the cyber realm.

Where Donnie Yen's martial arts persona has grown vague, there is no less ambiguity in the image of action megastars like Jackie Chan and Jet Li whose professional statuses are well-accepted and longstanding. As the most prominent transnational Chinese stars, Jackie Chan and Jet Li are celebrated for their spectacular stunts and martial prowess. As they are now entering middle age, their declining suitability for high-action roles begins to compromise their masculine images that were established in the early part of their filmographies. Chan possesses a battered body that is obviously not as agile as it was in his youth, exemplified in *Rush Hour 2* (2001), *Accidental Spy* (2001), and *Shanghai Knights* (2003). Likewise, Jet Li's recent screen roles diminish his status as a martial artist on which his vocational success relies. For his Hollywood film *Romeo Must Die* (2000), he was asked to perform high-wire stunts instead of hardcore blows and kicks. His ineffective father figure in *Ocean Heaven* (2010) and 3D-augmented swordplay in *Flying Swords of Dragon Gate* (2011) are other examples. With the problematic image of Chan and Li, we notice a transition in their star appeal that changes from fighting to goodwill. Through the work of their publicity personnel, they have both pursued a global persona through charitable effort in China, Asia, and America that helped unschooled children, promoted mental health, and supported disaster relief. Chan's ambassadorial engagement probably redeems his relations with the mainland and Taiwan audiences and thus preserves his popularity. Also, Li has launched his own charity, One Foundation, to maximise his international visibility. How do fans from all over the world approach and negotiate the appeal of Chan and Li in cyberspace? The subsequent two chapters will explore this question in detail.

Note

1. The subtitle of Yip's article includes, 'Four actors may have played the gonngfu master but Donnie Yen is the best of them all, say fans.'

Chapter 2

'Flickering' Jackie Chan: the actor-ambassadorial persona on photo-sharing sites

Introduction: between an ethnic actor and a global ambassador

Chinese movie star Jackie Chan appeared at the White House on the evening of 19 January 2011. He joined President Barack Obama for the State Dinner honouring the President of the People's Republic of China, Hu Jintao. It was a highly prestigious occasion with a guest list including politicians, celebrities, media elites, and musicians, plus two former American Presidents, Jimmy Carter and Bill Clinton. As is his habit when attending overseas events, Jackie Chan wore a mandarin collar shirt and a black jacket with no tie, and he was praised by *Politics Daily* as 'the best dressed man' at the dinner ('Jackie attends state dinner for Hu Jintao' 2011). In a journal entry posted on his official website, Jackie Chan recalled an anecdote from the dinner: 'While I was talking to him (Hu Jintao), President Obama came over to the table and said, "You know, Jackie Chan is very famous here in the States." President Hu Jintao replied, "He's more famous in China!" Laughter followed' ('My visit to the White House' 2011). This presidential dialogue exchange, brief and causal, that revolves around the celebrity's fame paid homage not only to Jackie Chan as a Chinese actor, but also to his transnational star power as a bridging agent between the two countries.

Jackie Chan epitomises the transnational capacity of Chinese stars yet without abandoning his ethnic identity. Following Bruce Lee, Chan succeeded in establishing his status as one of the best known and longstanding martial arts actors in Hong Kong cinema. Journeying throughout China, Asia, and the West for four decades, Chan gained countless fans, Chinese and international, through his distinctive personality that blends martial arts with slapstick comedy. He also impressed Hong Kong and international audiences with his death-defying stunts that are mostly performed by himself. His 1980s movies introduced him to audiences beyond Hong Kong as the result of the films' distribution in Southeast Asia and overseas Chinese communities. In 1995, he established his foothold in North America with a wide release of *Rumble in the Bronx* (1994) in America. The *Rush Hour* series (1998, 2001, 2007) and *Shanghai Noon* (2000) and its sequel *Shanghai Knights* (2003) are familiar titles that generated a cult following for Chan, which is unusual for Chinese martial arts movie stars. His extra-diegetic personality also signifies his fame's international reach. He holds honorary citizenship of Paris, Chicago, Tongyong, and Seoul, moving across Asia, North America, and Europe. In 2008, he received a star on the Hollywood Walk of Fame. He appeared alongside Arnold Schwarzenegger in a government advertisement combating copyright infringement. In 2005, he, in joining Mickey Mouse and Donald Duck, appeared as a guest in the opening ceremony of Hong Kong Disneyland, an emblem of global consumer and fantasyland culture. His reception of an Honorary Award at the 2016 Oscars further solidifies his star power in Hollywood. As a successful border-crosser, Chan engages in the experiences of displacement and accommodation in national and transnational intensities. He becomes the agent who navigates various geopolitical, spatial, and cultural positions within the global capitalist system, confronting and contesting the contradictions within mainstream institutions and ideologies. To be precise, Chan's perspectives emerge from his experiences departing from his native homeland, Hong Kong, and continual development in an increasingly transnational setting of media production, distribution, and consumption.

Although his global persona stems primarily from his martial art stunts and physical prowess, Jackie Chan's recent films demonstrate a decline in action-heavy sequences, attenuating his personality as a martial arts fighter. Now in his mid-fifties, Chan possesses a battered body that is obviously not as agile as in his youth. In recent films such as *The Spy Next Door* (2010), *Chinese Zodiac* (2013), and *Police Story 2013* (2013), Chan shifts roles, playing a resigned and passive man who is symbolically castrated, lacking his previous heroism and virility. The problematic masculinity Chan now embodies on film coincides with Chan's high-profile and extensive goodwill engagements. As early as 1995, the Hong Kong Tourist Association appointed Chan the Hong Kong Tourism Ambassador, making him an icon of the city. In recent years, his ambassadorial assignments have multiplied, fostering Chan's status as a representative of China and utilising his international popularity. He was appointed to bear the torch at the 2008 Beijing Olympics and Deaflympics as well as serve as the Promotion Ambassador for the 2010 Shanghai World Expo and the sixteenth Asian Games of that same year. By grasping every opportunity to show the world his goodwill commitment, Chan presents himself as, in Laikwan Pang's phrase, the 'Ambassador of the World' (2007: 214). In consideration of Chan's paradoxical star presence, both in the real world and in the cyber world, how does the web realise a new method of star construction that helps redress undesirable images and ensure good standing in the global entertainment arena? How do cyber occurrences illuminate or shape Chan's star appeal – a construct marked by both Chinese ethos and global consciousness?

To attempt to answer these questions, this chapter examines Jackie Chan's contentious stardom in cyberspace. I hypothesise that both fans and star personnel participate as fans in the same network for star-making as a strategy to reinvigorate the fluctuating fame of Chan. While enchanted fans celebrate Chan's onscreen martial arts star appeal, Chan's publicity teams circulate an offscreen ambassadorial persona to rectify the star's negative image. I identify Flickr, a photo-hosting and sharing site, as the primary venue of investigation. While social media is typically represented by Facebook, My Space, and Twitter, some scholars, critics, journalists, and active Web 2.0 users consider Flickr as an example in this group (Mislove et al. 2008). 'Social' becomes a key word at Flickr as it was one of the first sites to make sharing user content its central activity (Leonard 2010). The capability to add annotations and notes, as Caterina Fake, one of the founders of Flickr, explicates, grants the users a sense that they are 'part of something social' (Terdiman 2004). Rendering the act of photo-sharing a 'social medium' ('Quote of the day: Photo sharing a "social medium"' 2005), Flickr users are socially connected, forming communities similar to the fan clusters prior to the web era. Flickr allows its users to write comments and descriptive tags to others' pictures, creating a topic-oriented group, which can be public or private. Giving a similar comment, Andy Baio elucidates the distinctive significance of Flickr, 'There may have been other sites that allow photo sharing, but Flickr takes it all to the next level. It's social software, but the interface never gets in the way of what you're trying to do' (ibid.). In this analysis, I use the master web page to search the name 'Jackie Chan' in English – the medium most widely used by international audiences. In the following, I will focus on three albums of which

Figure 2.1 'Jackie Chan's Star' – the title of a tourist's photograph posted on Flickr

the photographs are either the fan-based activities or goodwill activities that are most relevant to the discussion of Chan's shifting status and value that attends his ethically Chinese-yet-transnational star phenomenon. They include an album posted by tourists who visited Hollywood's Walk of Fame, one posted by an Australian fan of Chan 'Adelaide Flashmob: Quest for Jackie Chan', and the other two posted by the event official photographers – 'Jackie Chan & Friends Free Concert' and 'Jackie Chan in Myanmar, July 2012'. This chapter will show that Chan's stardom on Flickr renders itself into an entity that negotiates the boundaries between star and celebrity, onscreen martial arts image and offscreen goodwill image, and Chineseness and globalness.

Tourists' reenactment of the martial arts persona

The market appeal of Jackie Chan's star persona has attracted much interest from the tourism industry. In 1995, the Hong Kong Government appointed him as Hong Kong's official Tourism Ambassador, a role for which he has shown immense enthusiasm, promoting the image of Hong Kong to the world. One may readily remember that Chan touted the Hong Kong International Airport as a tourist hub (*Takungpao*, 8 August 2003, quoted in Pang 2007) after the SARS outbreak in 2003 (*Hong Kong Daily News*, 8 July 2003, quoted in Pang 2007) in order to revitalise the once-stagnant tourism in the territory. As a Hong Kong icon himself, Chan is readily associated with the city by many people all over the world. In 2002, the Discovery channel invited Chan, described as 'the city's favorite son' on its DVD cover, to host a one-hour programme on Hong Kong. Chan also participated in the opening ceremony of Hong Kong Disneyland in 2005, appearing with Mickey Mouse and Donald Duck. All these activities are symbolically subsumed in the Honorary Professorship conferred on him in 2004 by Hong Kong Polytechnic University's School of Hotel and Tourism Management.

Among the more prominent signs of Jackie Chan's international success is his star sign on the Hollywood Walk of Fame in Los Angeles (Sandell 2010). In 2002, he cemented his legendary status with the star, the 2,205th star on the Walk, following Bruce Lee as the second Chinese movie actor to earn this distinction. His star lies in front of the Dolby Theatre (formerly the Kodak Theatre), the venue of the Academy Award ceremony, reinforcing the centrality of Hollywood to Chan's international appeal.

Visitors to Jackie Chan's star seem to enjoy emulating a kung fu stance, validating to the importance of his kung fu publicity. There is no shortage of such extra-diegetic reenactments of Chan's cinematic persona on Flickr. A number of photograph entries depict either the star itself or tourists posing 'kung fu style'. The latter category is of most interest for my purpose of exploring Chan's kung fu body and fans' reconstruction of the body. In August 2006, a user self-dubbed 'just an average Asian', a name explicitly referencing his ethnic identity, uploaded a picture entitled 'Jackie Chan's star', taken at the Hollywood Walk of Fame (Figure 2.1). The frame of the photograph includes the 'Jackie Chan' star and an Asian man in T-shirt, shorts, and sandals, presumably the user, squatted on the ground next to it, with both arms extended in front of his body and both palms open, unmistakably alluding to Chan's status as a kung fu star. Judging by the photo-stream of this user, this is the only photograph taken at the Walk of Fame while there are no other pictures even pertaining to celebrities. The exclusion of other 'stars' on the avenue perhaps reflects the implications of his chosen user name, highlighting his ethnic affiliations in a way that reinforces Chan's status as an ethnic Chinese, which is particularly suggestive in this context, that is, Hollywood in the United States. Arguably, what a user calls himself or herself on Flickr can impart an ethnic tinge to the global stardom.

Western fans of Jackie Chan are also well-represented among the Flickr 're-enactors', reflecting Chan's broad fan-base across cultures and genders. User 'Lacy Renee' posted a picture entitled 'Jackie Chan', straightforward and direct to her fandom, taken on 27 April 2011 in a nearly identical setting. Well lit by the abundant sunlight, the focus of the picture lies on the woman who occupies the central part of the frame, captured in a horizontal long shot; the name of the star on the ground is under-sized and seems translucent. With her bending leg and stretching arms, she poses in a playful, or perhaps womanly, fashion that recalls the martial arts acrobatics of Chan.

When Jackie Chan's onscreen persona is removed from a cinematic setting and found instead in a tourist setting, it alters the nature and significance of the martial arts body and stardom. While tourists 'perform' his kung fu moves, I argue that the performative acts actually deplete his star power. The photographs neither convey the dynamism and martial prowess that Chan is famous for nor articulate any cultural meaning signified by his image. It may be true that tourists' performative re-enactment, made possible through their bodies and marked by a kind of self-reflexivity, is a form of identification with Chan's martial arts persona. According to Judith Butler (1993), the body has 'no ontological status apart from the various acts which constitute its reality' (136). Fans generate a sort of identification in relation to Chan's martial-arts status though iteration and performances. Considering Chan's body as a 'site of performative enunciation' (Szeto 2001: 123), a double-fold iteration – fans performing Chan's performative persona – emerges. Tourists' re-enactment of the martial arts postures appears to rejuvenate the Chineseness once incarnated by Chan on cinematic screens. Nevertheless, here Chan's martial arts body and kineticism are reduced to a coral-pink terrazzo sign, corroborating with an absence of cultural substance exhibited by the body of Jackie Chan. While the performative acts of the tourists make token reference to Chan's status as an ethnic Chinese actor, what they try to do is to revivify substantial existence of Chineseness from emptiness.

An ambassadorial persona is always performed. As the nineteenth-century English essayist and businessman Walter Bagehot (1867) observed, 'An ambassador is not simply an agent; he is also a spectacle', suggesting that an ambassador is sent abroad both for substance and for show. In the society of spectacles, critiqued by Guy Debord (1995), all historical particularities are subsumed into the universal logic of capital; whereas in participatory web culture, these particularities are reinvented by cyber fans by uploading and sharing images of the spectacle online that still subsume themselves to the star's capital. On Flickr, where visual culture and participatory culture overlap, Jackie Chan's ambassadorial activities are channelled into the global construction of the spectacle collaboratively by his fans. According to Debord, the spectacle is more than a mere collection of images: it is a social relationship between members of the society that is utterly mediated by commodification and images. The cyber fans who reinvent the spectacle of Chan's persona have thus reinvented the social relationship between themselves and the star. This amounts to a re-interpretation of the star's performing agency and enables further interplay among the viewers. Through these activities, the ambassadorial image is not merely appearance; rather, it epitomises a paradigm of social life that is now conducted through interaction with spectacles circulating on the web.

'Jackie, Jackie, Jackie, Jackie . . . Chaaaaaan!': Adelaide Flashmob and Jackie Chan's Australian connection

Jackie Chan's transnational stardom has long extended to Australia, yet in contrast to the extensive literature on his Hollywood movies and ethnic presence in America, few have explored his Australian connection. Chan's parents are long-time residents of Canberra, having lived there since the early 1970s, and through them he gained Australian citizenship. His Australian connection further entails nationwide fame through his Hong Kong-based action movies and his martial arts prowess. He even chose Australia as the major shooting location for *Mr. Nice Guy* (1997). Moreover, he appears as a publicity icon alongside five other internationally famous figures, including Yao Ming, Zhang Ziyi, Lang Lang, Jet Li, and Zhang Yimou on the web page of China National Tourist Office Sydney. Jackie Chan's star presence in Australia proves his border-crossing persona beyond Asia and earns him a far-reaching fan following in cyberspace.

A Flickr album entitled 'Adelaide Flashmob: Quest for Jackie Chan' highlights Jackie Chan's transnational stardom, which is appropriated in a grassroots activity chiefly mobilised on cyber platforms. This album consists of 104 photo entries, uploaded by the user 'Hello Ben Teoh'.

The pictures document a flashmob event of the same name, which took place on 11 September 2010 in Adelaide. The album is hyperlinked to the website of Adelaide Flashmob (www.adelaideflashmob.com) of which a 5 September 2010 blog explains 'the quest'. The entry comprises a list of instructions, including the dress code and equipment, for readers who intend to take part in the event. The participants met at a square called Hindmarsh Square and rehearsed several planned 'mob' activities, including rushing into a coffee shop in masks chanting, 'Jackie, Jackie, Jackie, Jackie . . . Chaaaaaan!'; shopping at a mall; approaching the front counter of the mall to ask a preset question, 'Do you have any night vision goggles?'; and heading to a food court. Like other flashmob groups around the world, The Adelaide Flashmob organises and promotes their activities through the social networking environment in cyberspace.

Although this album has drawn only thirteen views, perhaps seemingly making it unworthy of attention, the event it documents has broader connections to Chan's Australian stardom. Actually this flashmob activity is part of *Quest for Jackie Chan*, an independent multimedia reality film project initiated and directed by Maria Tran, a twenty-five-year-old Australian-based filmmaker, actress, and social-media personality. The film aims to showcase and celebrate Australian fans of Chan. A major part of Tran's work is travelling across Australia to meet and interact with Chan's fans, recording personal messages and collecting fan mail for the star. The project also utilises a range of digital media technologies like Facebook, Twitter, Flickr, YouTube, and Vlogging to connect and engage with the people and organisations pertinent to Chan.[1] A hyperlink to the website for this project appears on the cover page of the Flickr album, inviting the users to learn more about it. Fair enough to claim, it is this film and the Jackie Chan fandom it captures that make the Flickr album significant.

It is interesting to contrast Jackie Chan's star presence in Australia with that in America. If America is a frontier for Jackie Chan to explore and contend as an ethnic actor who goes global, then Australia is a second home for him, a place to recuperate and reconnect with family. After the young Chan graduated from Master Jim-yuen Yu's opera school, the kung-fu film industry underwent a decline and Chan considered relocating to Canberra, the adoptive home of his parents. He spent a couple of years living in the city. During his stay, he learned English and worked in construction, where he was given the nickname 'Jackie', later to be his internationally known name, by fellow workers. Eventually,

Chan received a call from Hong Kong director-producer Lo Wei, bidding him to return to the territory for films. Although he afterwards quit his citizenship, he still valued his Australian connection. In the Inaugural Australia–China Film Industry Forum held in December 2010 in Beijing, Chan expressed gratitude to Australia for taking care of his father for forty-seven years, saying he regards Australia as a place that provides the motherly nurturance that feeds his family ('Jackie Chan at the Australia–China Film Industry Forum (translated)' 2012).

If Australia has been a place of nurturance for Jackie Chan's acting career, America has, by contrast, tested and challenged it. Hollywood is a frontier of America's 'Wild West' that is never easy to conquer, especially for foreign film talent. Consider Jackie Chan's failed attempt at Hollywood stardom in the early 1980s with his first two forays into Hollywood, *The Big Brawl* (1980) and *The Cannonball Run* (1981) through Golden Harvest. Following these box-office failures, Chan returned to Hong Kong to continue his career. Not until 1995 did he earn American audiences' enthusiasm with *Rumble in the Bronx* (1995), after which he regularly appeared in Hollywood movies. Even then, while Chan managed to secure Hollywood contracts, his roles were merely ethnic stereotypes lacking agency within the plot of the film. For example, Chan plays Inspector Lee in *Rush Hour* (1998) as 'perpetual foreigners' (Szeto 2011: 130) embodied through first the self-imposed silence and then by the joke of Carter's assumptions about Asians. Such image draws upon, as Kin-yan Szeto frames, 'the stereotypical misrecognition of Asian' (ibid.), erasing the subjectivity of the ethnic Asians, or the ethnic Chinese. In *The Tuxedo* (2002), Chan's character of Jimmy Tong, a cab driver, similarly, embodies the Chinese stereotypes with the appropriation of the comic spectacle. His character is turned into a high-tech equivalent and, consequently, his action is not as stunning and fast-paced as that in his earlier films, altering his onscreen persona. His kinetic agency is undermined by having the mechanical gadgetry in his body. The presence of special effects denaturalises the established perception of Chinese choreography and defamiliarises the martial arts star quality.

It is commonly known that Asian film workers in Hollywood have long held ambivalent and secondary roles. Hollywood has a long history of émigrés and foreigners: from the 1920s through the 1950s, Russians and East Europeans who were Jews fleeing pogroms formed part of the effort that created Hollywood. Nonetheless, as they slowly assimilated into white Americanness, they acquired that group's prejudices against blacks, Asians, and Hispanics. In the 1970s and 1980s, a flood of talents from Australia also entered Hollywood studios. But, arguably, these 'foreign' filmmakers have had an easier time assimilating into Hollywood due to their shared whiteness with the racial majority in the US. In the 1990s, with the influx of Asian and Chinese film talents to Hollywood, the identities and cinematic representation of ethnic Chinese become a point of attention. Their conspicuous arrival did not equal to a definitive position in the filmmaking system: 'Asian' characters were generally either represented as insignificant, or slotted into stereotypes reinforcing the hegemonic racial discourse of Hollywood. Ironically, rather than selling out his ethnicity to succeed, Chan capitalised on his ethnic image and transnationalises his Chineseness as means of forging his perpetual appearance in Hollywood movies.

By contrast, Jackie Chan has never tried to establish himself in Australian cinema. Part of the reason may be its limited size and art-house nature. But it also reflects Chan's relationship to Australia, in the sense that he does not allow himself to be ethnicised by Australia as he has been by Hollywood. Instead of acting in Australian movies, Chan uses the country as a venue for filming his Hong Kong projects. He shot most parts of the Thunderball-style action film *Police Story 4: First Strike* (1996) in Queensland. Soon after, he opted for Melbourne to shoot *Mr. Nice Guy* (1997). By taking major roles in these two films, he exhibited his agency in narrative and choreography by fashioning his action star status. In Australia, Chan appears less alien than he does in Hollywood. Whereas Chan's nationwide fame in both America and Australia is largely based on his Hong Kong movies, the difference in the fan discourse is distinctive: Chan's Hong Kong martial arts image is challenged and altered by his ethnic appearance in Hollywood movies, leading American audiences to see him as ambiguous. But his martial prowess in Hong Kong films remains the centre of the fan discourse in Australia.

Jackie Chan's ties to Australia also highlight the Australian connection to Hong Kong action cinema, which is acknowledged by film producer cum kung fu enthusiast, Bey Logan (Tran 2010). *Police Story 4: First Strike* (1996) was also the Hong Kong debut of the Australian wrestler Nathan Jones, who later starred in *The Protector* (2005) and *Fearless* (2006), fighting with Jet Li and Tony Jaa. In *Mr. Nice Guy* (1997), an Australian actor, Richard Norton, plays the antagonist role of an eccentric, edgy gangster. As a karate black belt, he earned acclaim for his stellar performances in a series of Hong Kong films directed by Sammo

Hung in the mid-1980s, co-starring Jackie Chan. Norton's Hong Kong stardom made him a frequent cover subject of global martial arts and film magazines. When filming *Mr. Nice Guy*, Chan also encountered two Australians, who have joined his stunt team as key members. Brad Allan plays a supporting role in *Gorgeous* (1999), supplying Jackie Chan a remarkable foil. He also appears in the documentary *Jackie Chan: My Stunts* (1999) to showcase a Jackie-style fight and has become a stunt coordinator in his own right on films including *Rush Hour 3* (2000). Paul Andreovski, too, joined Chan's stunt team and is his personal boxing coach. It is noteworthy that when these white actors appear in Hong Kong films, they typically play the minor roles that are stereotyped or demonised, much as Asian actors do in Hollywood – the reciprocity suggesting that racial politics are ubiquitous.

More recently, Jackie Chan's Australian ties have extended to his goodwill ventures, donating money rather than shooting films. In 2008, he funded a new science education centre at the first-class cancer research institution at Australian National University. Upon the opening of the science centre, the Australian Prime Minister Kevin Rudd hosted a dinner at his official residence to which Chan and his family, along with some diplomats from China and America, were invited (Furbel 2008). Considering China as the biggest trading partner of Australia, Rudd discussed with Chan the ways to help Australia strengthen its ties to China. Moreover, as an ambassador for the Beijing Olympics, Chan invited Rudd to attend the Games, indicating how his ambassadorial role draws on his ethnic Chinese identity as well as his transnational appeal. I will elaborate on this 'China's representative' image of Jackie Chan in a later section.

Refer back to the album 'Adelaide Flashmob: Quest for Jackie Chan'. It is based on Jackie Chan's fandom and it reflects his popularity in Australia on account of his Australian connections. However, the entire album is marked by the absence of Jackie Chan; no images of him appear, nor does the album exhibit the acrobatics and martial arts that characterise his stardom. The pictures do not, in visual terms, relate to the star persona for which Chan is acclaimed among Australian audiences. What dominate are images of the flashmob crowds performing actions on the street, in the park, and in the mall; they look indistinguishable from any other flashmob activities that can be imagined. The only sign of Chan in these pictures is the 'Jackie Chan' masks that the participants wear, as instructed by the host of the event. The fabricated 'appearance' of Chan reveals nothing to the viewers about Chan as a martial arts star.

The new 'drunken master': the 'official photos' of *The Forbidden Kingdom*

The sets of Flickr pictures convey the fame of Jackie Chan over his Chinese cinematic persona while they have limited capacity to augment Chan's star power as a martial arts actor. Only a few Flickr entries present actual movie stills of Chan's choreography and charisma on film screens. Flickr is a contemporary site with its emergence subsequent to the heyday of Chan's fame. This may explain the scarcity of stills from Chan's most well-known projects, such as the *Police Story* series (1985–96), the *Project A* Part I and Part II (1984, 1987), *Rumble in the Bronx* (1995), and the *Rush Hour* series (1998, 2001, 2007). For an ethnic star who achieved an international status only after many years in the industry, this is not too encouraging. Even though Flickr, like other photo-sharing sites on the web, enables users to post images from any era as long as they can obtain the images digitally, Flickr users seem disinclined to share images of Chan as a martial arts star. Consider Chan's declining martial prowess and acting appeal in his recent films like *The Karate Kid* (2010), *Little Big Soldier* (2010), and *Shaolin* (2011) in which he has shifted roles, playing a resigned and passive man who is symbolically castrated and no longer heroic and virile. His screen performance begins to depend more on character acting than on action choreography, signalling Chan's biggest challenge, which is to 'manage the unavoidable effects of aging' (Reid 1994: 23). It is thus potentially a pressing concern for his publicity team to seek ways to reinvigorate his established kinetic persona with this audience. Adopting the user-oriented cyber platforms to access the audience is one of the most effective ways to boost Chan's martial arts stardom. Practising top–down dissemination, the star's publicity personnel pose as ordinary users, uploading and sharing images of the star in order to manipulate the star construction in grassroots settings.

On Flickr, some albums marked with an 'official' label serve the executive record or visual presentation of Jackie Chan's star presence. For example, the album entitled 'Official Photos' comprises 114 photograph entries, all movie stills from *The Forbidden Kingdom* (2008), posted in the period from 6 July 2007 to 30 April 2008. As compared to another album named 'Behind the Scene' created by the same photographer that only consists of twenty-seven entries, the relatively large size of this album suggests the potentially greater attention paid by fans to the stars' screen roles that underline martial prowess and acrobatic physique than to the offscreen presence. As indicated on the webpage, this collection of pictures is provided by Lionsgate and The Weinstein Company, which co-distributed and released the movie. Here a collision of corporate and grassroots interests appear. While Flickr is a site allowing ordinary users to post photographs, studios and distributors have employed the platform to release 'official' pictures for publicity through individual user accounts. In other words, Flickr postings can be both industry-driven and user-driven.

One of the selling points of *The Forbidden Kingdom* (2008) was its first-ever onscreen pairing of Jackie Chan and Jet Li. Publicity for the film sought to stir anticipation and excitement among martial arts cinephiles and fans over the co-appearance of these two megastars (Rahner 2008). Since the inception of their acting careers, both had worked on their own projects without ever crossing trajectories for nearly four decades. Jackie Chan's *Project A* Part I and Part II (1984, 1987) and the *Police Story* series (1985–96) spanned a decade from the mid-1980s to the mid-1990s, solidifying his foothold in Hong Kong action cinema and simultaneously bridging his name to international audiences. Jet Li's *Shaolin Temple series (1982–6)* introduced the novice actor to the Hong Kong audience, and his fame grew with the *Once Upon a Time in China* series (1991–3). One may trace the cause of Jackie Chan's reluctance to be coupled with Jet Li to the clamour of fans following the insinuation against Chan in Wong Jing's 1995 action comedy film, *High Risk*. The film casts Jet Li as the police officer who displays physical virility and macho spirit and Jackie Cheung, a Hong Kong Canto-pop singer, as the other protagonist who is an indolent and action movie star. As the general audience perceives, the latter's personality is apparently a spoof of Jackie Chan as a womaniser, a boozer, and a fraud who does not do all his own stunts (LaSalle 1995). With the suspicion going on, Jackie Chan was said to be offended by the satire; thus, it is not surprising to see the two stars not collaborate on movies aside from their competition as martial arts stars.

Even after migrating to Hollywood, the two actors seldom have their screen performances crisscrossed in any ways. Chan performed in the well-received *Rush Hour* series (1999–2007) while Li worked on several separate projects. Chan had occasional collaborations with other Chinese actors and actresses, like Zhang Ziyi in *Rush Hour 2* (2001) and Donnie Yen in *Shanghai Knights* (2003) but not with Jet Li. It is speculative that since Chan and Li engineer similar star personae, their publicity teams had sought to avoid co-appearance in movies, since proximity in star agency leads to keen competitiveness.

The Forbidden Kingdom (2008) was far from a success in terms of popular reception, notwithstanding the opportunities for both actors to showcase martial arts agility and skills.[2] In the Flickr album called 'The Forbidden Kingdom', in which a majority of the images stress martial arts and choreographed action, the acrobatic rigour of the actors appears as rich and fascinating as in the movie. For example, a series of stills from the combat scenes between Lu Yan, Silent Monk, and Jason depicts in detail the sequence of bodily movement. The shots reveal how Jackie Chan's character, Lu Yan, thrusts out his hand, defends himself from the staff hurled through the air, and delivers a hard blow to an adversary in the fight. Many of these images are picturesquely widescreen framings, their depth enabling visual exploitation of the action detail. The choice of these photographs as publicity images is attributed to the spectacular visual quality of these scenes, albeit, as with all still images, the action is presented as isolated bits, rather than an integral whole. While the photographs help augment the grace and strength of Chan's martial arts star persona, that alone cannot guarantee the popularity of the film among fans.

Moreover, some pictures in the album highlight Jackie Chan's character, retroactively calling to mind his early, youthful cinematic persona. In *The Forbidden Kingdom*, Chan plays the dual roles, Lu Yan and Old Hop: the former character was from the ancient era whereas the latter is situated in a modern time. A photograph, entitled 'The singular Jackie Chan', shows Lu Yan, an inebriated travelling scholar who is knowledgeable about kung-fu (Figure 2.2). This medium-long shot underscores the star's acrobatic performativity through a diversity of performance elements like stretching legs, guarding arms, and upright waist, signalling ready-to-fight posture, accentuating the locking eyebrows, and tightly closed mouth. All of these signs connote belligerent aggression and kung fu adroitness in a visually exhilarating manner. The tilted shooting angle further signals the explosion of physical energy, alluding to the dynamism of Chan's body. As this part of the plot is set in ancient China, the ornamental portrait of the Buddha on the wall in the background and the stone statue in the middle ground likewise visually convey Chineseness, in a manner readily perceptible to global audiences.

Those familiar with Hong Kong martial arts cinema and Jackie Chan's early movies will not miss the fact that this photograph recalls Chan's

Figure 2.2 Lu Yan in *The Forbidden Kingdom*: showing Jackie Chan's acrobatic performativity

role and performance in *Drunken Master* (1978), the first movie to truly establish his name with Hong Kong audiences. Directed by Yuen Woo-ping, *Drunken Master* is a martial-arts action comedy featuring Chan as a young kung fu neophyte in a relatively contemporary setting. Nicknamed the 'Drunken Immortal', Lu Yan is also a 'drunken master', remaining agile and alert even when drunk. Moreover, in this photograph, Chan's fighting pose brings to mind the style of 'drunken fist' (the Chinese title of *Drunken Master*). Some critics unfavorably compared *The Forbidden Kingdom* to *Drunken Master*, claiming the latter allowed audiences to appreciate the physical vigour and martial arts virtuosity of Jackie Chan while the former capitalises on computer-generated imagery, downplaying the acrobatic dexterity of the actor. The deployment of the digital technology seems to portend a response to the aging of Chan. In fact, an earlier Hollywood film of Chan's, *The Tuxedo* (2002), has incorporated computer-generated effect in its action. This Jackie Chan vehicle shows the hero performing traditional stunts with the technological-and-corporal interface in the tuxedo. As the tuxedo proffers mechanical power to Chan, Szeto (2011) argues that the incorporation of special effects denaturalises the conventional perception of martial arts, 'valoris[ing] defamiliarisation precisely by making the accustomed interpolation of identity and subjectivity visible' (138). If *The Tuxedo*, an action movie in a modern setting, has made the interpolation visible through computer-generated effects, *The Forbidden Kingdom*, a costume drama based on the ancient-China fable, would have intervened such interpolation, as embodied by Chan, in the masquerade of something authentically Chinese.

The photographic allusions to the earlier cinematic roles played by Jackie Chan rejuvenate the star's onscreen image. They disregard Chan's declining physical prowess in the recent films, and instead retain memories of the actor's previous persona, thereby serving to acknowledge Chan's status as a perpetual martial arts star. Presumably, one can conceive of a star's image as distinct from the specific characters he or she plays in film. It is true that stars are given a character constructed in the narrative world (for example, through script and mise-en-scene) for them to signify (Dyer 1979: 99). In the case of Jackie Chan on Flickr, users post the movie stills to demonstrate not only how his muscular body signifies, but also how the actor's already-signifying image is re-enacted. This demonstration speaks to the relationship between a star and his or her screen roles, offering a point of departure to comprehend the persona in the extra-diegetic setting. However, the reiteration of the kinetic pose of the martial arts hero is of memory value and the gesture does not renew the actor's capacity to signify virility and masculinity, resulting in lack of identification from cyber users. This may be one of the reasons why on Flickr only the 'official' pictures are available for promotional purposes whereas none are uploaded by users to express their appreciation for this film.

The Flickr album exemplifies a hyperlinked structure and the manner in which fans relate themselves to the personalities. The 'singular Jackie Chan' photograph was appropriated and copied from a Chinese movie website called 1905 *Dianying Wang* (literally, 'Movie Net') (www.m1905.com). Below the photograph, the user self-named 'silent_monkey' has attached a hyperlink to the source of the image, the embedded webpage entitled 'movie stills' (in Chinese) that is devoted to *The Forbidden Kingdom*. This collection of images consists of more than a dozen movie posters and nearly a hundred movie stills, many of which are downloaded as 'wallpaper' for personal computers. This page also contains links to other text-based information about the movie, such as synopses, behind-the-scenes news, and commentary. Moreover, the name 'silent_monkey' is a blend of the dual characters Jet Li plays in the movie – Silent Monk and Monkey King.

As a clone of the Monkey King, of which the idea proposed by Li himself (NIX 2007), the Silent Monk possesses prodigious acrobatic dexterity, allowing Li to showcase the martial arts prowess for which he is known to Hollywood producers and international audiences. Naming suggests identification. The label 'silent_monkey' evidently expresses acknowledgement of not only Jet Li but also the martial arts cinematic tradition and the 'Monkey King' folk legacy, or perhaps the paying of a tribute to these narratives. Albeit that the photographs are placed under the category of Chan, the user's fondness is not exclusively restricted to him.

'My beloved country': Jackie Chan's ambivalent patriotic image

While Jackie Chan has an increasingly international status, his relation to his mother country has at times been ambiguous or even hostile. It is not unusual for Chan to make politically controversial remarks at publicity occasions, provoking concerns or even outrage from the Chinese public. In April 2009, during a panel discussion at the annual Boao Forum for Asia, the international Chinese movie star, Jackie Chan, made some politically controversial remarks about the PRC, Hong Kong, and Taiwan.[3] In a paternalistic tone he said, '[I]n the decade after Hong Kong's return to the Chinese sovereignty, as I gradually see, I am not sure if it is good to have freedom or not . . . If you are too free, you are like Hong Kong now. It is very much in chaos. Taiwan is chaotic, too' (Jacobs 2009). One could interpret a comment as such as intended flattery to China. Nevertheless, Chan's words enraged politicians, journalists, academics, and citizens in Taiwan, Hong Kong, and the PRC alike, with social media the locus of the lion's share of vitriolic responses. Scholar Hu Xingdou led a group of Chinese locals in a boycott of Chan's 'Believe in China' charity concert held that year at the iconic Bird's Nest stadium in celebration of Labor Day (ibid.). In an email message to hundreds of Chinese dated 24 April 2009, Hu advised the Chinese people to guard the freedom of the PRC, Hong Kong, and Taiwan by shunning the concert. On 19 April, Hong Kong newspaper *Apple Daily* gave the front-page headline 'Jackie Chan Is a Knave', followed by the publication's demand for an apology from the superstar on the next day. Indignant enough, some bloggers lambasted Chan as 'fascist', 'evil', and 'racist' (Ray 2009) and some others urged a boycott of Chan's films, with the impending theatrical release of *Shinjuku*

Incident in Asia. Moreover, pervasive censure appeared in discussion groups on the social media site, Facebook. A group called 'send Jackie Chan to North Korea', citing the North Korean government's disinclination towards freedom, summoned a signature petition that rapidly earned more than 6,600 members in four days ('Row over Jackie Chan deepens' 2009). On 21 April, the Hong Kong Tourism Board of which Jackie Chan has worked as an ambassador since 1995, received 120 e-mails and calls from the public in one single day, most of them expressing displeasure at Chan's remarks – such intensity of complaints being 'unprecedented', as the agency's spokesperson described ('Chan faces film boycott over comments' 2009). The public dissatisfaction extended to the web. Chan's 'too much freedom' comment, which was later segued into a critique that 'a television made in China might explode' (Moore 2009), invoked an array of e'gao videos, a 'new art form' (Wu 2007) where web users parody some popular music to variously sourced imagery as a creative voice to intervene in the public appeal.

As a response to the intense complaints, a Chan spokesperson later explained that Chan's reference to freedom was being misinterpreted, noting that the freedom to which Chan referred pointed only to the entertainment industry, rather than Chinese society in general. The explanation, however, did not assuage public anger. In the light of the complicated modern history of China and tense cross-strait relations,[4] Chan's remark on the freedom-and-control issue can be considered an attempt to bolster China's authority, uncovering his nationalistic proclivities. Whether Chan's 'explosion theory' contradicts his support of his nation or is a different register of nationalism that offers a reflective take on the problem of the PRC's manufacturing standards is hard to say. However, Chan's comments attracted much attention throughout greater China and the West, inciting concerns about his legacy and public image. The cluster of responses unfolds the critique and contestation of Chan's public persona on a web-based, grassroots level. It illuminates that even for an international star of Chan's volume of fame, the question of nationalism cannot be easily dismissed and will be continually resurfaced through fan discourse in the cyber network.

In view of such controversies, Jackie Chan and his publicity personnel are aware of the need to redeem his star image and to redress the problematic relationship with China. In 2011, Chan made the movie *1911* (2011), tapping into a cinematic current of propaganda films to celebrate the centennial of that turning point in modern Chinese history.

Furthermore, as Olympic ambassador, Chan condemned the pro-Tibet protesters as attention-grabbing 'naughty boys' contending for television fame, partially a response to Tibet's uprising in March 2008 in which a peaceful protest for the release of imprisoned monks and nuns led to tear-gas-and-gunfire suppression by Chinese police ('China: Alarming new surveillance security in Tibet' 2013). Intriguingly, the turmoil came at a sensitive moment for China as it was at the height of preparing for the 2008 Beijing Olympics. The issue called for the international attention and scrutiny of China's human rights record, which then caused some foreign leaders to boycott the Beijing Olympic opening ceremony. Whereas Olympic torch-bearers in many countries are the human rights protestors, Jackie Chan showed disapproval of the pro-Tibet protesters in a national-istic tone that downplayed the international denunciation of China's cruel crackdown in Tibet just months ago. As part of the phenomenon of fame, these aforementioned acts can be regarded as strategies working to redeem the ill reputation that grew adjacent to the machinery of 'industrialised celebrity' (Rein, Kotler, and Stoller 1997: 1). Alternatively, Chan may also have profited from the positive 'value of visibility' (14) – for a celebrity, any press is good press.

Charitable ventures are one of a few highly favoured means of counteracting the decline of a star's talent, accomplishment, and merit (Redmond and Holmes 2007: 8). They bear a persistent association with fame as ubiquitous and devalue currency (Marshall 1997). For Jackie Chan, they also serve as an important means of highlighting his ties with China. While *Flickr* encourages users' participation on a grassroots level, Chan and his publicity personnel employ it to post photographs about his activities to promote China, which they want to expose to the public. For example, an album entitled 'Jackie Chan & Friends Free Concert in Chinatown', posted on *Flickr* by the user 'mamba909' in June 2009, reveals Chan's border-crossing capacity and articulates his nation-alistic tendencies. It concerns an evening concert held in Central Plaza in Los Angeles' Chinatown on 22 June 2009. Performers included a group of pop singers and martial arts performers from China, a Korean performer, and a Chinese-American performer. According to the official website of Chinatown Los Angeles ('Chinatown Los Angeles'), run by the Chinatown Business Improvement District, the concert was an encore of the one held in Beijing, which the Chinese public boycotted after Chan's Boao speech. As narrated on the 'Chinatown' website, Chan was introduced as the star of the action thriller *Rush Hour*, underscoring his status as an action celebrity among Americans and Chinese-Americans. Moreover, Chinatown Los Angeles was the location of the filming for *Rush Hour*, described by the website as Chan's first US feature film (disregarding his special appearance in 1997's *An Alan Smithee Film: Burn Hollywood Burn*). Such articulation undeniably buttresses the link between the star and the place. There are four tag terms, namely 'Chinatown', 'Los Angeles', 'Central Plaza', and, of course, 'Jackie Chan' attached to the *Flickr* album, which comprises altogether forty-four photographs, some in colour, others black-and-white, capturing both on-stage and off-stage scenes. This visual record of the event promotes Chan's seemingly paradoxical status as a cosmopolitan Chinese.

For the cover of this album, 'mamba909' has chosen a frontal medium shot capturing Jackie Chan smiling amicably, waving his hand to the attendees and, symbolically, to the world. Concentrating on the diasporic Chinese community, Chan forges a connection with those to whom he shares ethnic ties. Some photographs in this album capture ceremonial moments, such as when the California Legislative Assembly presented Chan with a plaque they had awarded him three years prior but had been unable to give him until then. Additionally, they pinned a medallion on his T-shirt and presented a piece of jade artwork as commemorative souvenirs, praising him for his 'great' undertaking of encouraging young people to practise martial arts, to stay away from drugs, and to resume school after dropping out (Liu 2009). By choosing the Chinatown in Los Angeles, the largest Chinese-American community in the USA, for the activity, Chan emphasises his commitment to what I call 'diaspora outreach', emblematically indicated by the show's bilingual presentation in Mandarin and English. His ambassadorial agency fashions bonds among an array of Chinese communities scattered across the globe.

Jackie Chan's transnational image functions as a strategic means to strengthen his association with the national culture, which actually underpins his global celebrity value. A focal point of the Chinatown concert was Chan's premiering of his new song entitled '*Guojia*', which literally means 'country' or 'nation'. '*Guojia*' won nationwide acclaim in China, according to the press release available on the Chinatown Los Angeles website. Described by some media as 'patriotic', it is a song composed in honour of the sixtieth anniversary of the establishment of the PRC, co-presented by Jackie Chan and acclaimed Chinese female singer Liu Yuanyuan. A photograph with a caption 'Jackie Chan feeling the love of his country' depicts Chan, eyes closed in intense concentration and singing with evident feeling, expressing his deepest affection towards his 'guojia', that is China (Figure 2.3). Chan, together with members of his kung-fu teams, also performed the 'standard' set of hand signs while singing. They made the 'L' shape with their right hand, signifying 'miracle', as the lyrics read. Moreover, Chan's red uniform with the Chinese characters, *guojia*, exhibits his association with China through colour and symbol. In political terms, the PRC has also been called 'Red China' since its establishment on 1 October 1949. Red is used as the major colour of her national flag. In cultural terms, the colour red is used by Chinese people on a broad range of occasions such as weddings, celebrations, and the New Year festival (MDeeDubroff n.d.). As a whole, the concert is a publicity event not only for Chan's song and album but also for a nationalist culture. According to Fanon (1967), a nationalist culture can serve as a venue of collective endeavour to construct one's own identity and thus to instigate a shared experience towards authority. In the global age, a nationalist discourse articulates per se neither an embrace of local community, family, and kinship (Brennan 1990: 45) nor an incessant turning to local resources, allowing past myths and heroes to return to the scene (Nairn 1977: 348). In addition, as Arif Dirlik (1997) elucidates, 'national essences are constructed to legitimise incorpora-tion into Global Capitalism' (156), rather than providing alternatives to the capitalistic structuring of the world. While nationalism 'seems to provide an attractive and viable option for the cultural imaginary of post-revolutionary China within the context of globalisation' (Chu 2008: 190), we have to be aware that it is an outcome of discursive production that emphasises appearance more than essence. In *Whither China? Intellectual Politics in Contemporary China*, Zhang (2001) discusses 'China' in the post-Tiananmen epoch:

> The China produce and packaged in the new cultural market of the 1990s – a China in which state propaganda, the advertising industry, the market-driven popular media, as well as semiau-tonomous intellectuals all act as competing agents – has created a dazzling collage of images and a cognitive vacuum to be detected by a new critical practice. (Zhang 2001: 69)

In the milieu of the late-capitalist popular media, Chan's persona is represented and consolidated in social networks; it is also produced and packaged as part of the global culture of images. A matrix of transna-tional flows of capitals, images, and peoples is evident in the age of global capitalism. Chinese narratives are refashioned for global consumption. Chinese star images are commodified, becoming the currency in the

Figure 2.3 'Jackie Chan feeling the love of his country'

global market. The nationalistic essence of the stars displays complicity to capitalism, legitimising an incorporation of Chinese stardom into globalising processes. In such a context of global economy, on the one hand, transnational Chinese stars capitalise on their ethnic personae in order to capture the world's market. On the other, the Chinese star images are configured by the capitalistic logic of which the marketised and commodifying tendency of Chinese stardom provides a viable and appealing option for the cultural imaginary of Chineseness. Therefore, in the Flickr album I examine, if Chan has embodied anything about Chinese nationalism, such embodiment is reified into a commodity (Chu 2008: 190), an image that can be marketed and sold in the celebrity machinery of the global order. Chan's ostensibly nationalistic Flickr images are used by the star's personnel to secure his global star status and marketability in the global cyber-cultural politics.

A Chinese star in Maynmar

Jackie Chan's global sensitivity is evident in his ambassadorial image that applies not only to Chinese diaspora communities but also to other non-Chinese communities in Asia. Capitalising on his celebrity status, Chan gains visibility in an array of causes, such as public health, human immunodeficiency virus (HIV) prevention, action against child trafficking and violence to children, and mine-clearing operations in Southeast Asian countries such as Maynmar, Cambodia, Vietnam, and Timor-Leste (Kritsadaj 2016). As early as 2004, Chan was appointed Goodwill Ambassador for the United Nations Children's Fund (UNICEF) and part of his ambassadorial task focus on the regional network in East Asia and Pacific. Yet not until 2012 did Chan make his first visit to Maynmar, a site where UNICEF's work commenced in the 1950s ('UNICEF in Maynmar' n.d.). The star's three-day trip in Maynmar is marked by the advocacy of protection of children from illegal and exploitative trade. As the International Labour Organization reports, human trafficking is the second most lucrative criminal industry in the world, gaining annual profits of thirty-two billion in 2005. It produces countless children victims who are coerced into prostitution and the cheap domestic labour market ('Trafficking in children' n.d.). UNICEF also launches projects for developing and strengthening systems of health, education, and nutrition in assistance to the well-being of children. As the Ambassador of UNICEF, Jackie Chan visited schools, vocational centres, community projects, and residential care facilities that provide services for trafficked children who manage to return home and who are orphaned in the streets (Kandel 2012). He has also met with press and government officials to communicate the anti-trafficking endeavour in the country. All these efforts creditably and efficiently valorise Chan's border-crossing personality in charity and humanism.

A Flickr album entitled 'Jackie Chan in Mynamar, July 2012' is an online record of Chan's goodwill endeavour. It contains, in total, twenty-eight entries, uploaded by the user called 'UNICEF East Asia and Pacific' on 6 July 2012, and visually chronicles the star's encounter in Myanmar. The photographic archive is presumably official, evidencing how the institution adopts the grassroots-based cyber platform for publicity. Not a lack of snapshots captures Chan spending moments with the children, highlighting his amicable image. For example, a photograph posted by 'UNICEF East Asia & Pacific' shows Chan agreeably and patiently listening to a girl from the Basic Education Middle School in Mandalay, Myanmar's second largest city. Another entry, posted three days later, reveals Chan sitting in the midst of the young crowd from the School for Deaf in Mandalay, emulating the sign language in order to show his name. The uploader tags these pictures, alongside other entries of a similar theme, as 'Jackie4kids'. The tagging is, practically, for easy searching but, strategically, it was for promoting Chan's image as the ambassador for children.

With the ambassadorial appeal, Jackie Chan is presented as a figure of bridging cultures that are supposed to neighbour peacefully, and advancing cultural heterogeneity. In a press conference held at the end of the trip, as validated by one of the photographs, he greets them with the *sampeah* gesture – pressing the palms together with a slight bow. Another photograph exhibits Chan joining the Maynmar Shan dance performed by the members of the Girls' Training School. While Chan was in his UNICEF uniform of a blue T-shirt and white pants, the girls wear the traditional costume for the performance, embodying the cultural contrast of the subjects. In this manner, Chan, with decorum, diplomatically navigates and is conversant with Southeast Asian culture, accentuating both foreignness and willingness for cultural accommodation.

Furthermore, the *Flickr* photographs corroborate with a powerful media appearance of Chan, pinpointing his authority as a male star. In a photograph, he stands in front of a swarm of journalists and photographers with his arms wide open and his fists firmly held (Figure 2.4). As the Flickr caption suggests, Chan solicits support from the media for the cause of 'saving' the children. His gesture dramatises strength and determination, providing a visual impression of the mastery of his agenda. As a piece of press release of UNICEF (2012) enunciates, a speech that Chan plans to deliver to the young audiences in the trip reads:

> It is very important that young people know how to protect themselves … Simple things, like knowing not to trust anyone who promises you a dream job in another country; never going to an unknown place alone; knowing your parents' and your own full name and age; and being able to explain where you live, help children guard against traffickers. ('UNICEF Goodwill Ambassador Jackie Chan in Myanmar: "Children are not for sale"' 2012)

Both the visual image and the verbal discourse of Chan can be interpreted as a manifestation of the star's paternal clout, reverberating to how the Chinese-language media coins Jackie Chan as '*da ge*', literally 'big brother'. Referring to Teresa Odendal's (1990) critique of the philanthropic elite, many wealthy people use their giving not only as a means to ensue status but also to 'paternalistically flaunt their own cultural capital and expertise' (16). Claiming a turn from capitalistic to humanitarian concerns, Chan invokes a cosmopolitan mentality, which is part of the star's 'cultural capital', yet to be realised in his paternal position. Without exposing his intention to serve a dominating purpose, Chan presents himself as endeavouring to work on something he thinks meaningful to the younger

Figure 2.4 As a UNICEF ambassador, Jackie Chan displays his paternal power in front of the press in Myanmar

generation in Myanmar. His rhetoric sounds profound yet fanatical and it articulates the star profile carrying 'the possible connotations of depth, intelligence, and commitment to his or her public persona' (Marshall 1997: 110).

What Jackie Chan, as a Chinese star, does is legitimise his culturally superior position while speaking for humanitarian concerns. However, in the world order nowadays, both China and Myanmar are categorised as the exotic 'Orient' and so what makes Chan, as an ethnic Chinese, superior to the Myanmarese, as imagined by the West as 'the Other'? One may recall an episode from *Rush Hour* as a source of hint: while Chris Tucker portrays himself as a black man oppressed by white people, he also brags of himself as 'tall, dark and handsome', calling Jackie Chan 'Third World ugly'. The movie, in fact, is enough to ethnicise Chan who is placed in the milieu of 'Chinese' as he appears in the Hong Kong chicken market, karaoke lounge, and massage parlour. By slamming Chan as the 'ugly' in the 'Third World' category, Tucker implicitly positions himself as the 'First World',[5] asserting his advanced status over Chan merely through emphasis of physical features. Chan assumes his position similar to that of Tucker, although in a milder degree, that he acknowledges his standing as an ethnic Chinese virtuoso and ascribes subordinate-ness to the Maynmarese subjects. He demonstrates his discursive power as if he is in the 'natural' and 'rightful' position in a cross-cultural context. It can be inferred that it is not Chan's Chineseness but his transnational power to grant him privilege to transcend his ethnic/national category. Conversely, if Chan is an ethnic Chinese star lacking such presumptuous ethos, he will, otherwise, appear less capable than what he does now of teaching a lesson to the Maynmarese 'inferior'.

To conclude, star publicity is a noticeable component of the star construction in cyberspace. The above analyses show that the star discourse surrounding Jackie Chan on Flickr can sometimes result from publicity and packaging initiated by the stars and their agents. As Flickr is an open territory where everybody can participate, stars post and distribute photographs, videos, and texts that they want exposed to the public, so as to manipulate their star presences on the sites. For Jackie Chan, the movie marketing team uploads an 'official' set of movie stills to embellish or enhance his martial arts persona and kinetic power. Photographs of the activities at overseas Chinatowns and in Myanmar reveal Chan's efforts to build bridges between China and other parts of the world, producing a patriotic and ambassadorial image. Chan has increasingly taken on a global appeal that stretches beyond a Chinese identity, engineering a compelling and legitimate new star image. To 'flicker' Jackie is not purely a grassroots practice but also a publicity strategy engendering a kind of lateral interaction between fans and stars.

Posting these selected materials online also impels fans to respond and interact, creating the stardom in a collaborative manner. While Jackie Chan is conscious in fashioning their global goodwill personae, fans do not always exhibit an ardour comparable to that elicited by his cinematic persona. Flickr fans post pictures of themselves at Chan's 'Walk of Fame' star, paying tribute to his martial arts kineticism, whereas they seldom upload photographs of Chan's goodwill events. Since his screen appeal has a more longstanding presence in the fan discourse than his ambassadorial personae, fans are more prone to identify with his martial arts prowess than his charity as the kernel of the stardom. In this way, fans negotiate with the actor in the star construction process, interrogating the martial arts body in an interactive, capricious fashion.

Jackie Chan's ethnicised, border-crossing imaginary in cyberspace is parallel and inspiring to that of another Chinese martial arts actor, Jet Li. Consider the roles of Jet Li in *Romeo Must Die* (2000), *The One* (2001), and *Danny the Dog* (2005) that reveal compromise to the ethnocentric sensibilities. Colliding and negotiating with the politics of ethnic representation, this sort of star texts unfolds the question of Chinese stars' engagement and survival in multiple systems and cultural forms in today's global Hollywood. In the following chapter, I will analyse Li's ethnic-yet-global image by focusing on his philanthropist mobilisation in online social networks.

Notes

1. In 2010, Maria Tran gave a guest lecture at The University of Hong Kong. Interestingly, as she wrote in her blog entry dated 11 April 2011, she discovered the negative connotations of the 'Jackie Chan brand' among young people (Tran 2011). Although she showed indifference toward those connotations and kept assuring the fame of Jackie Chan, what she elicited here exactly unfolds the 'oppositional' discourse about Chan given by anti-fans.
2. One concern of the fans was the director, Rob Minkoff, who is known for children's films rather than the action genre. Some had already raised such doubts immediately after the launch of the project, according to a fan self-dubbed 'Drunken Reviewer' (probably a reference to one of Jackie Chan's roles 'Drunken Immortal') (merrick 2008).
3. For decades, the Chinese central government has held complicated yet sometimes intimidating relationships with Hong Kong and Taiwan, which were once the colonies of the UK and Japan, respectively, in the nineteenth and twentieth centuries. Hong Kong returned to the motherland in 1997, finishing the ninety-nine-year lease of the territory to the British. The Japanese were ousted from Taiwan in 1945 when the Nationalist Chinese (the Kuomintang) took over the island. Now, although both places were handed over to China, its legitimacy and authority over the prior colonies are at stake (Tucker 2008).
4. The 'One country, two systems' policy made Hong Kong a Special Administrative Region of China. Allegedly autonomous, Hong Kong could retain all internal affairs under its control, leaving merely its foreign relations and defence policy to Chinese authorities. Besides, Taiwan shows unwillingness towards unification with China, renouncing independence. Backed by the power of the United States, who enabled Taiwan to defy Beijing in the Korean War and the Vietnam War, China regards Taiwan as a remnant regime supported by a key capitalist enemy.
5. That involves the racial politics of the black in the white America, which is a topic I do not yet go into details on.

Chapter 3

'Friending' Jet Li on Facebook: the celebrity-philanthropist persona in online social networks

Introduction: leading the way for Chinese philanthropy

Transnational Chinese movie star Jet Li reappeared on the cover of *Time* magazine's Asia edition in November 2008, six years after a previous cover spread publicised his starring role in Zhang Yimou's martial arts blockbuster *Hero* (2002). Titled 'The Liberation of Jet Li', the later issue features Li and his charity, One Foundation, which was founded in April 2007. The article explains how the movie star-cum-philanthropist leads the growing wave of China's charity culture. Widely known throughout Chinese popular culture for his volunteering and charity work, Li is an exemplar of crossing over from celebrity to philanthropy. He has served as the philanthropic ambassador for the Red Cross Society of China and its governing bodies, the International Federation of Red Cross and Red Crescent Societies ('Celebrity Jet Li becomes first goodwill ambassador' 2010). He has volunteered for relief work enthusiastically and spoken at forums for humanitarian issues, such as mental health awareness, suicide prevention, and disaster relief. His various collaborative work with world leaders such as former United States President Bill Clinton and former British Prime Minister Tony Blair, including American business moguls and philanthropists Bill Gates and Warren Buffett as well as the 2006 Nobel Prize winner Muhammad Yunus, in highly publicised charity events and fundraising initiatives has further bolstered his global visibility and philanthropic credibility (Saunders 2008; Bishop 2009; 'Tony Blair and Jet Li launch new climate change partnership for a low carbon future' 2009; Associated Press 2010). All these endeavours have helped establish and consolidate Li's reputation as the planet's most high-profile Chinese philanthropist.

In 2004, the PRC permitted private charitable foundations to be registered for the first time. The next five years saw the establishment of approximately 1,500 such foundations, which by 2008 were thought to be worth some 100 billion RMB; this represented a great leap from the meagre total of 2.2 billion RMB in 2002 ('The celebrity' 2009). In addition to Li's One Foundation, other Chinese celebrities were at the forefront of this flourishing development. In 2006 Canto-pop singer and actress Faye Wong, with her former husband Li Yapeng, launched the Smile Angel Children's Hospital Project; this marked the beginning of private, non-profit hospital services for children in mainland China. Other well-known Chinese celebrities extended their star image by becoming United Nations ambassadors for global humanitarian and environmental concerns. For example, actress Li Bingbing, the first national Goodwill Ambassador from China for the United Nations Environment Programme ('Li Bingbing UNEP Ambassador in China' 2010), was also a World Wildlife Foundation (WWF) Earth Hour Global Ambassador. Her LOVE Green movement advocated an environmentally friendly, low-carbon lifestyle (United Nations Environment Programme (UNEP) 2010). Actress Yao Chen, on the other hand, became the honorary patron of the United Nations High Commissioner for Refugees (UNHCR) and visited Ethiopian refugee camps in 2012 (Wu 2013).

Jet Li reportedly led the way in the escalating trend of Chinese celebrity activism (Dien 2008). The founding of the One Foundation, undertaken in conjunction with the Red Cross Society of China, represented the keystone of Jet Li's star-powered philanthropic image. This start-up charity advocates an innovative culture of broad-based participation in philanthropy that focuses on disaster relief, child welfare, and philanthropy development; it trains public welfare professionals and has received donations, totalling in the region of fifty million RMB, from the Lao Niu Foundation and the Tencent Foundation – among others ('One Foundation' n.d.). Although One Foundation is a PRC-based charity, it accedes to contemporary notions of 'new philanthropy' or 'venture philanthropy' (Anheier and Leat 2006: 21) that encourages transnational, business-like models of giving, while concomitantly inviting public scrutiny of its operations. Its work is therefore unrestricted by geographical, cultural, or national boundaries, evidenced by active involvement in disaster relief for Japan's 2011 earthquake and tsunami, and Typhoon Morakot in Taiwan in August 2009. By actively managing the One Foundation, Li becomes a global philanthropist.

Jet Li often cites his harrowing experience while vacationing in the Maldives in 2004 as inspiration for his philanthropic dedication. As he has recounted to globally well-known media such as *CNN*, *The Times*, and *Newsweek*, he and his family were on the beach when a tsunami swept in without warning. Li grabbed his four-year-old daughter. The giant wave nearly drowned them. Luckily, they were rescued. Surviving the horrendous disaster marked a radical turn in his life. Then forty-one years of age and already a globally established movie star, Li underwent a soul-searching process and ultimately resolved to commit himself to charity, which he now deemed as an infinitely worthier pursuit than accruing wealth and power ('The tsunami that changed my life' 2008). He thus opted to become 'a full-time relief worker', devoting himself to philan-thropic tasks 'intensely' (Fitzpatrick 2008).

If film stardom is the blueprint for global celebrity, then Jet Li's shift from film to philanthropy is crucial for scrutinising celebrity presence in Greater China today. Besides martial arts legends Bruce Lee and Jackie Chan, Jet Li is arguably the world's most famous martial arts superstar. Fans identify his kinetic body and martial arts prowess with male potency. Without having to cope with as many interrogations and criticisms as his contemporary Chan, Li lacks the attendant visibility of notoriety. Yet Li's authentic martial arts dexterity distinguishes him from Chan, who is more famous for his action-packed stunts and action comedy. Li's films may not top the box office, but he has established himself as, in Julian Stringer's phrase, 'more of a sure-fire commercial bet' (2003: 278) with his bona-fide martial arts credentials. Though not an A-list mega-star in Hollywood, Li offers a sufficient commercial package that promises habitual attention from the American media (Stringer 2003: 279). Although not the first of Hong Kong film talents to set foot in Hollywood, Li remains where his compatriots left long ago, proving himself as one of the most flexible and adaptable Chinese stars (Yu 2012: 5). Despite critical scrutiny of his acting skills, he retains a broad cult following around the globe.

The role of celebrity philanthropist is not a natural transition for martial arts stars like Jet Li, whose stardom rests on clearly established fight choreography. The history of Hollywood philanthropy, by contrast, dates back to the late-1910s and continued throughout the twentieth century (Trope 2012: 157). The modern-day philanthropic image is often associated with contemporary Hollywood stars such as Richard Gere, George Clooney, Brad Pitt, and Angelina Jolie, becoming standard for many entertainment personalities. Yet Li's career tells a different story.

With a lengthy acting filmography spanning more than three decades, Li's lasting star appeal crosses geographical and cultural boundaries. His star personality developed within a transnational framework, occupying a place in the local and global playing fields. His fame as a film star began with *Shaolin Temple*, which was planned in 1979, filmed in 1980 and 1981, and released in 1982. The film gained Li instant popularity and led to two sequels (1984, 1986). In the 1990s, his celebrity grew through titles such as the *Once Upon a Time in China* (1991) series. His films proved local successes, and overseas distribution of these films in South East Asian markets brought Li regional fame. His martial arts skills earned him his first Hollywood role in the 1998 cop-action film *Lethal Weapon 4*. Although he plays a minor antagonist, Li's performance and his martial arts skill earned him subsequent Hollywood contracts. From 2000 to 2005, Li starred in five Hollywood productions, a remarkably prolific record for an expatriate Hong Kong entertainer. Li also found time to return to Asia and star in transnational martial arts blockbusters, such as *Hero*, *Fearless* (2006), and *The Warlords* (2007). Although Li's reputation as a martial arts actor had never been more salable, his career came to a turning point mid-decade when he began publicly emphasising his philanthropy over his screen roles. Li's increasing focus upon humanitarian engagement opens up various cinematic, social, and ideological possibilities for decoding that persona, which contrasts sharply with his already-established cinematic presence, and provokes further investigation into that discursive shift.

The shifting focus from cinema to charity coincides with audience dissatisfaction with Jet Li's latest movie roles, which suppress his fight choreography and martial arts prowess. In his middle age, Li accepted roles that diminished his image as a martial arts fighter. In *Romeo Must Die* (2000), an action-packed movie, the director utilises computer-generated special effects in nearly every fight scene. Producer Joel Silver aimed to recreate the avant-garde visual effects from his previous big hit *The Matrix* (1999). Li's action scenes consist of high-wire stunts, which, according to Jet Li's official website, disappointed fans and made Li realise that he should rely less on wirework and more on his real martial arts skills. Similarly, *Hero* and the Hollywood remake of the Monkey-King narrative, *The Forbidden Kingdom* (2008), employed wirework, colour-coding, and digital editing to accentuate the fights as spectacle (Farquhar 2010: 122). The 3D-augmented swordplay in *Flying Swords of Dragon Gate* (2011) suggests Li's attenuated agility. The use of digitalised visual effects to substitute for combat problematises Li's status as a martial arts actor. Furthermore, some of Li's Hollywood roles tend towards ethnic narratives perpetuating the stereotype of Asian male effeminacy. For example, *Danny the Dog* (2005) casts Li as Danny, a lethal martial artist raised in captivity since childhood who explodes in violent fury whenever his collar is removed. Kept in a cage in the underground floor of a Glaswegian gangster's headquarters, only to be used as a formidable weapon, this controversially inhumane character offended some viewers who found the portrayal humiliating to ethnic Chinese. Suffice to say, ineffective martial arts performances and ethnicised portrayals contribute to Li's waning cinematic verve, and alter his star persona.

Promotional rhetoric for *Fearless* (2006) portends the fading of Jet Li's screen vigour and star image. The marketing personnel extensively publicised the film as 'Jet Li's last martial arts movie', as indicated on movie posters and DVD covers, attracting media and public attention (Swifty 2006). Premiering four years after his last appearance on Chinese screens in *Hero*, *Fearless* was eagerly anticipated by Hong Kong fans. Considering his declining number of film appearances, the 'last martial arts movie' discourse surrounding *Fearless* hinted at Li's declining enthusiasm for martial arts performance. Although Li ultimately did not retire from acting and featured in more films such as *The Warlords*, *The Forbidden Kingdom*, and *The Expendables* series (2010, 2012, 2014), those films noticeably downplay his martial prowess and patriotic heroism. Li himself identified *Fearless* as the picture concluding his onscreen life as a martial arts star (Rafferty 2006), marking the beginning of the development of his full-fledged goodwill image, chiefly mobilised by his serious pursuit of philanthropy.

Compelling and legitimate, Jet Li's new philanthropic persona emerges almost simultaneously with his perceptibly diminished screen image. In the epoch of user-generated media, it is not surprising that celebrities take active roles in promulgating news about themselves and fostering positive self-images, enhancing the cultural values they represent and, therefore, their 'star quality' (Dyer 1979). In the entertainment business, charitable work is inextricably linked to public relations efforts. Celebrities such as Jet Li are often subject to the symbolic and commercial value of their giving. Many contemporary celebrities hire philanthropic advisors and organisations to recommend philanthropic causes congruent with their image in order to further their credentials (Trope 2012: 158–9). Ties between celebrities and charities augment the social significance of the celebrity image by underlining the 'possible connotations of depth, intelligence, and commitment to his or her public persona' (Marshall 1997: 110). By making the public cognisant of their philanthropic efforts through various publicity conduits, celebrity-philanthropists reveal the cultural beliefs their image stands for, in the hope of gaining the audience's recognition of those beliefs as well as of the star image. Facebook, a social networking site, forges the celebrity–charity ties on a global level and enables Li to effectively establish and extend his values beyond film into philanthropy.

Philanthropy on Facebook as a means of accruing star values

Although Jet Li's philanthropic ventures in recent years coincided with his waning career as a martial arts actor, they nevertheless have added value to the image of the star (Marshall 1997: 110). Facebook presents an emergent locus in which Li's star persona is negotiated, potentially redressing his deteriorating cinematic profile and rejuvenating his public personality. Facebook possesses the capacity for accruing social significance through connecting and interacting with users. Some theories of media sociology contend that individuals accumulate social capital – through favours (human capital) or new information (intellectual capital) (Resnick 2001) – which functions as a resource embedded in social relationships and interactions within the network (Lin 2001; Putnam 2000). The social network's stated objective is to help people connect (or re-connect) with people they know through the act of searching for and adding 'friends'. Users make conscious investments in social interaction by bridging ties with friends, colleagues, or even strangers in the same circuit (Resnick 2001). Users create profile pages and forge links with friends and acquaintances, paralleling many other social networks. In view of its function in star construction, users can also build Pages and Groups dedicated to their favourite celebrities, serving as advanced forms of fan clusters like fanzines and fan clubs calling for and uniting supporters. By 'joining the Group' or 'liking the Page', users become part of a virtual community tightly organised around sharing information about their mutual object of interest. In this light, Li's philanthropic cyber-persona serves to strategically accrue social capital and manage fame, with respect to Li's declining martial arts prowess and cinematic appeal. It also demonstrates the 'association with both capitalism, where the celebrity is an effective means for the commodification of the self, and democratic sentiments' (Marshall 1997: 25, 26).

Facebook hosts myriad Pages devoted to Jet Li in which his celebrity power is established, maintained, and accentuated on a cosmopolitan level. Facebook Pages is an organised virtual space displaying content including user interactions and microblogging known as a timeline. Users can freely post news, photographs, and videos pertinent to Li, simultaneously inviting others to 'like', 'share', and 'comment' on the posts. The range of posted information includes biographical information, media interviews, photographs of publicity events, trailers of upcoming movies, and other similar material. Although Weibo is the leading social networking site in the PRC (Rapoza 2011), Facebook is an apt venue for scrutinising Li's online presence because he is a transnational Chinese celebrity whose philanthropic activism operates on a cosmopolitan level. Li's Facebook persona is, moreover, represented collaboratively by fans from cultures both inside and outside his country of birth. As international credibility is a key accessory to the Chinese celebrity (Hood 2010: 89), it is justifiable to choose a non-PRC-based online social network, notwithstanding its prohibition in territorial China (Gibson 2009).

By setting my discussion in the context of online social networks such as Facebook, this chapter investigates Jet Li's celebrity philanthropist image in cyberspace and its signification. Can the cosmopolitan goodwill image, which operates outside film, compensate for Li's declining visibility on cinematic screens? As Li's star image is transposed to the Internet, via Facebook, how do his fans respond to, rework, and re-negotiate this image? What does Li's cyber-image signify to his fans? What does this mean in the milieu of global cyber-cultural politics? In order to respond to these questions, this chapter will analyse Li's appeal as an actor-philanthopist, as a result of star–fan dynamics in online social networks. The subject of this analysis is a Facebook Page entitled '李连杰Jet Li', obtained through the keyword-search facility of the site with the search words 'Jet Li'. The page ranks first on the list of outcomes, suggesting its predominance among Facebook users. In a six-year period, the site has received 18,687,937 'likes' (a virtual vote of approval) since its launch on 16 June 2008, attesting to Li's large Facebook fan base. In the subsequent sections, I will also investigate the ways that Jet Li and his fans engage and interrogate the actor's martial arts persona and philanthropic image, as well as the dynamics involved. This chapter will argue that while his star persona was once anchored in martial prowess and kinetic agility, giving him a strong ethnic/national branding, this ethnically/nationally branded image has become increasingly cosmopolitan as he engages in philanthropy, dealing with global humanitarian concerns. In doing so, the discussion will try (re)positioning Facebook as a new and promising venue for understanding and contesting Li's celebrity status as a martial arts master and philanthropist, which has decidedly yet contradictory nationalist and cosmopolitan configurations.

'Hello, my FB friends': forging imaginary direct links with fans

Based on the public's familiarity with Jet Li as a film celebrity, or as an 'intimate stranger' (Schickel 2000), Li functions as an authoritative and credible voice in an array of humanitarian causes, exerting influence on the public – an influence that includes numerous forays into Facebook. The '李连杰Jet Li' page spotlights the star's philanthropy. Offering minimal personal information, Li's profile on the page states his birthplace as Beijing, China, while the sections on education, work, interests, and favourites are left blank. Although the host of the page makes limited use of Facebook's multimedia sharing capacities by posting only a few videos and photo albums, the timeline changes often as he or she updates the status on a weekly or even daily basis. The majority of the posts make reference to Li's charity projects, including the UNESCO Charity Gala 2011, Red Cross's relief effort in Japan's 2011 earthquake and tsunami, and Li's designation as the International Red Cross and Red Crescent's first Goodwill Ambassador, further substantiating his cosmopolitan cyber-celebrity activism.

The posts about Jet Li's charity allow fans to access and engage with Li's philanthropic public personality. The posts and commentary pertaining to the earthquake in Yushu, Qinghai of 14 April 2010 is available. Measured 7.1 on the Richter Scale, the earthquake caused 2,698 deaths, left 270 missing, and more than 12,135 injured, according to the Xinhua News Agency ('China to mourn quake dead, public entertainment to be suspended' 2010). The quake destroyed more than 85 per cent of buildings, leaving thousands of people homeless and without power ('The Yushu, Qinghai earthquake has caused over 400 deaths', 2010). Li and his team went to the epicentre of the quake-hit zone to provide medical assistance and distribute survival goods. Li's relief work nurtures social relationships and encourages interaction with users connected to the network. Such activity fosters feedback from users and builds trust between Li and his fans. On the '李连杰Jet Li' Page, an album consisting of thirty-four photographs of this trip details the celebrity's spontaneous charity work amid the devastated ruins of buildings and livelihoods. In the photographs, Li consoles victims, converses with the local government officials, and supplies food and water. One photograph, which is selected by the uploader as the cover image of this album, as allowed by the Facebook setup, shows Li hugging a heartbroken and desperate male victim, signifying a generous compassion and brotherly love that transcends class boundaries (Figure 3.1). This photo collected 10,653 likes, 2,435 comments, and 104 shares by 24 June 2014, while other photographs in the album attracted numerous 'likes', ranging from several dozen to several hundred. 'Likes' and comments are the visible markers of attention (Ellison, et al., 2014: 858), also signalling the strength of the fan–celebrity relationship. As Ellison and her colleagues argue, a Facebook status update without 'likes' or comments reveals a lack of interest from one's network, or the update goes largely ignored, and thus

Figure 3.1 A Facebook picture shows Jet Li lending a shoulder to a weeping victim during the relief work of the Yushu earthquake

is pushed downwards in newsfeeds by the site's content display algorithm. Plausibly, similar logic applies to the Timeline-posted photographs. Hence, the moderately impressive numbers of 'likes' and comments on the aforementioned posts show that users notice and generally identify with Li's goodwill, contributing to relationship maintenance between Li and his fans. This increases the public's perceived access to Li and demonstrates a structure for promoting celebrities in cyber-networks. As Resnick (2001) argues, one's ability to access useful information resources is pertinent to the composition of one's network and one's position in the network. The users create information pathways that close 'structural holes' (Burt 1992; Granovetter 1974), narrowing the gap between themselves and fans.

Although both Facebook Pages and Facebook Causes promote charity and raise public awareness of certain issues, a Page is the venue in which Li's philanthropic image is readily mobilised. Launched in March 2007 by Internet entrepreneur Sean Parker and political organiser Joe Green, Causes is an application that runs no websites of its own but is a subset of Facebook, allowing users to add it to their profile pages. Causes has raised awareness and rallied supporters around social issues, ranging from pro-life, to wildlife protection, and acquired immune deficiency syndrome (AIDS) prevention. Via Causes, organisers can build a community of supporters, establish volunteer capacities, mobilise fundraising campaigns, and launch petitions. While Facebook Causes allows a wider public reach and more enhanced exposure in the cyber-network than Pages and Groups (Gibson 2009), the preference of Pages over Causes works to propel Li's charity, informing the changing concept of philanthropy in celebrity culture in the cyber era. Functionally speaking, Causes holds a dual purpose of recruiting people for a cause and providing resources for joining existing causes (Pring 2014), allowing online users more politically active participation such as signing petitions or making donations. However, Li's Facebook Page neither acquires a list of contributors and their donations, nor demands personal information. While Causes is clearly and exclusively positioned around building communities of action and supporting specific issues, Pages is for sharing news and updates. Philanthropy is no longer considered a humanistic or social category that demands specific knowledge and expertise. It is, too, not necessarily a separate regulatory regime supported by sufficient rationale and thorough scrutiny. Rather, it can be something as widely and readily accessible like information with the Internet, the democratised communications avenue. In Li's case, the use of Pages over Causes illustrates that the celebrity-propelled philanthropy denotes the star's considerable proximity to the public, realising Facebook's full potential to develop networks and to invite collaboration.

Jet Li's Facebook Page is marked by an impression that the Page is established and operated by Li, or his assistant, and the resulting posts seem to be part of his 'authentic' image. The use of personal pronouns 'I', 'my', and 'me' characterise the fan page text, as many posts are written from Li's perspective. For example, the host writes a status update on 29 September 2010, 'Today I attended Madame Tussauds in Hong Kong to reveal my wax Jet Li figure. Now I have a twin!' In another post on 25 December 2010 Li festively greets his fans, 'Merry Christmas and Happy New Year everyone! I just spent my Christmas eve finishing up my last day of filming on my latest movie New Dragon Gate.' Li's assistant also writes some of the posts, usually making his identity clear. Examples include this post on 27 July 2010, 'This is Alfred Hsing Jet Li's Assistant – We are in Shanghai', and another on the following day, 'This is Alfred Hsing Jet Li's Assistant - We are back in Beijing and this morning we visited one of Jet's old training grounds where he used to practice *wushu*.' While Li's official website also acknowledges this Facebook Page as run by Jet Li himself, these posts presumably heighten the authenticity of the star discourse and testify to Li's willingness to engage with his fans through online platforms.

Moreover, the use of direct address proves a significant factor in framing Jet Li's philanthropic image. As his posts indicate, the host speaks directly to the users that have 'liked' this Page, forging links with them in the cyber-social circle. It is not uncommon to see 'statuses' (microblog entries akin to Twitter 'tweets') on a celebrity's Page, that begin with 'Hi everyone', 'Hello everyone', and 'My FB Friends', thereby personalising the updates as if addressing the fans directly. For instance, a post created on 3 June 2009 advertises a new partnership with Adidas Shanghai. Part of the message reads, 'Hi everyone, thanks again for being so supportive, it always means so much. Today I have some exciting news. Recently Adidas Shanghai launched a new project that has been in the works for several years.' Another status update posted on 6 July 2009 publicises an online game launched by the One Foundation in order to promote a sponsored walk to raise relief funds for the 2008 Sichuan earthquake in China (Figure 3.2). Measured 7.8 on the Richter Scale, the earthquake happened on 12 May 2008, causing nearly 70,000 deaths, approximately 18,000 displaced, and five million homeless ('China – Sichuan earthquake:

Figure 3.2 An online game launched by the One Foundation as part of the fundraising for the relief work of the Sichuan earthquake in China in 2008

Facts and figures' 2008). The message of the post states, 'My FB Friends! Join the Global One-walk game online with the One Foundation to support the ongoing work in Sichuan and keep the walking spirit alive! Just print, shoot and upload!' By no means neutral, the propagandistic penchant of the status update actively campaigns for Li's humanitarian causes. The direct address shapes Li's online persona by fabricating an ostensibly amicable and approachable image on Facebook and, thus, the imaginary close links with fans.

The technological apparatus of the online social networks makes the process of celebrity-making more democratic than through traditional media because of fan participation. The Web is open for all to participate, including celebrities and media companies that present themselves as part of the fan community through online social networks. They can launch 'fan' accounts at these sites to post 'desirable' news and photographs. In this sense, celebrities and fans become collaborative agents constructing the star persona. This phenomenon eases the constraints that large-scale commercial media place upon individual celebrities, allowing them to control and regulate their own reputation through a newfound alternative agency. In this manner, celebrities, often together with their personnel, wrest control of their personae away from traditional media, legitimising celebrity publicity within the capitalist entertainment milieu.

Actually, the joint effort of celebrities and fans in image construction is not something new to Jet Li's stardom. Well aware of the potential of new media technologies for connecting with fans, Li used the Internet to respond to fans' letters and gifts in the late 1990s. 'Although I don't know much about computers, I am grateful that Internet technology makes it possible finally for me to let all of my fans know how much I appreciate them', he states on his official website (Li 1999). Li further promises to provide recurrent website visitors with information about his life, films, and viewpoints, creating an interactive exchange with fans (Yu 2010: 227). Thus, his official website augments Li's down-to-earth appeal through a 'low-key public presence' (ibid.), while also forging stronger ties with his fans.

Jet Li's online persona signifies new star–fan dynamics and results in effective image making. Li becomes part of a fan's 'social graph', as Mark Zuckerberg, the founder of Facebook, calls this network (Kirkpatrick 2008) that allows celebrities to manage fame and maintain relationships with fans at lower cost (Ellison et al. 2014: 3). To manage their reputations, celebrities invest in 'social relations with expected returns in the marketplace' (Lin 2001: 19). Celebrities are highly constructed cultural commodities and their personae entail perceived capacity for reciprocity, a key factor in social capital that facilitates resource exchange with fans. Fans generate desires and fantasies about their idols while celebrities gain affection and identification from their supporters, securing their power. Charity, in Li's star phenomenon, becomes a nexus of this web of relationships that expand the significations of the star image and structure the elaborate system of celebrity-philanthropists.

Jet Li's onscreen presence and his offscreen image are never two disparate realms in his stardom. The signification of his image as a martial arts fighter becomes part of the publicity of his goodwill status, gesturing towards a multi-dimensional star personality. Rather than completely abandoning his screen personality, Li's goodwill image reveals hints of capitalising on his long-standing and profitable cinematic appeal, which functions as his 'brand'. As Dyer argues that stars are manufactured for profit (1986: 5), Li's established celebrity status appears as an auspicious cultural commodity allowing rich yet volatile exchange with his fans through the entertainment market, encapsulated by his wages and bankability. The celebrity magazine *People with Money* reports that Li topped the annual list of the highest-paid movie actors in the world for 2013 with an estimated USD75 million in combined earnings (Kearney 2013). More than a decade ago, Li earned 70 million yuan (USD 9.1 million) for his role in *Hero* (2002). For *The Warlords*

(2007), he was paid 100 million yuan (USD 40 million), a record salary for a movie actor in a Chinese-language film (Wenn.com Source 2007), making him the most expensive actor in Asia ('Jet Li breaks film salary record' 2007). Before his marked physical decline in the mid-2000s, Li was more than capable of being cast in Hollywood star vehicles, such as *Lethal Weapon 4* (1998), *Romeo Must Die* (2000), *The One* (2001), and *Kiss of the Dragon* (2001). Fans mainly admire Li for his acrobatic skills. In explicating Li's celebrity power, Julian Stringer (2003) argues that viewers watch Jet Li movies expecting vigorous kicks and punches that justify the cost of the movie ticket.

Despite the changing focus of Jet Li's fame from martial arts actor to philanthropist, Jet Li's contemporary image suggests no intent to isolate the actor's charity from his film career. *Ocean Heaven* (2010) and its publicity campaign represent one such example of this synthesis of film and philanthropy. Lacking fight choreography and special-effects spectacle, *Ocean Heaven* was produced on a small budget of seven million yuan and represents one of Li's few forays into melodrama. The film tells the story of a terminally ill father, played by Li, struggling to care for his autistic adult son. Written and directed by emerging female director Xue Xiaolu, a long-time volunteer for Beijing Stars and Rain, a non-governmental educational institute for children with autism, the film wears its charitable mission on its sleeve. More than just cinema, the film represents a goodwill vehicle that draws public attention to autism as well as to Li's charity ('Jet Li plays with heart in "Ocean Heaven"' 2010). An array of Li's Facebook Page posts during the film's publicity period demonstrates this view. For example, on 19 June 2010, Li uploaded a photograph of the red carpet at the Shanghai International Film Festival where the film premiered. In the caption, he congratulates actor Wen Zhang and director Xue Xiaolu for winning the awards for Best Actor and Best New Director respectively at the CCTV Movie Channel Media Awards. A week later, Li re-publicises the event by posting a different photograph of the cast and crew onstage. Arguably, Li advertises not only the film but also his philanthropic agenda. In addition, Li's role in the film as an ineffective patriarch departs from his well-known screen persona marked by physical virility and martial arts machismo, and yet, the role clearly connects with his charitable personality and corresponding star qualities. Projects such as *Ocean Heaven* alter or reinvent his cinematic persona in a way that unfolds and supports the symbolic function of Li's goodwill image.

Buddhism, *Youxia* virtues, the goodwill image

Predicated on his martial arts fame, Jet Li's philanthropic persona unhesitatingly reveals his changing view of martial arts. Early in his acting career, Li declared that he made films to 'preach' Chinese martial arts as a healthy mode of athletics (Yu, quoted in Yang 1991a: 231). However, the focus of the star discourse shifted in recent years from the physical to the spiritual aspects of martial arts. According to Li, the emphasis of martial arts should not be power but inner harmony; the greatest enemy is always the self. This view resonates with Bruce Lee's famous dictum stressing the importance of self-knowledge as part of his martial arts philosophy, largely derived from Taoism and Buddhism (Bowman 2010b: 193). Lee states: when you're faced with looking at your own life with awakened eyes, you will have increased a bit in the knowledge of yourself, and knowledge of anything outside of yourself is only superficial and very shallow. To put it another way, self-knowledge has a liberating quality ('The philosophy of Bruce Lee' n.d.). Jet Li's *Fearless* thematically showcases this liberating power of self-knowledge. The film is a fictional account of the Chinese martial artist Huo Yuanjia, the founder of Jing Wumen, a famed martial arts school in Shanghai. He was also the master of Chen Zhen, the protagonist of Bruce Lee's *Fist of Fury* (1972) and the 1994 remake, *Fist of Legend*, which starred Jet Li. *Fearless* represents a prequel of sorts. In both diegetic and extra-diegetic terms, we see interstices between the two martial arts stars. In *Fearless*, supreme martial artist Huo undergoes personal trauma and fights his way out of darkness, arriving at the true meaning of martial arts. Victory is found not through the defeat of the invaders but by breaking away from the fragile, wounded, and evil self, revealing a pacifist image that gradually replaces Li's violent screen personality. In some press interviews, Li explicates that the meaning of '*wu*' in *wushu* or martial arts is to stop fighting, which contrasts with its literal meaning of 'military' or 'bellicose' (Yu 2010: 232), even commenting that today's *wushu* championship stresses form more than the essence of being a martial artist. As Li (2000) explains on his official website, 'I never say to myself I'm the best fighter in the world . . . If someone learns martial arts solely to pick fights on the street, to lean on it as a keystone weapon in conflicts, to use it to bully and intimidate others – then that person, in my opinion, cannot be considered a true martial artist' (Li 2000). As an art form, *wushu* is the outward expression of one's tranquility and internal cultivation, Li argues. Acquiring internal harmony allows practitioners to become vessels that facilitate unity across cultures and nations. By publicly professing his martial arts philosophy, Li shows a proclivity for pacifism befitting his goodwill persona.

As a pious Buddhist, Jet Li's non-violent image is an outgrowth of that religious faith. His official website reveals that one reason that Li has not retired from acting is his mission to spread the Buddhist philosophy of 'loving-kindness' and unconditional love 'in non-traditional ways and through non-traditional media', inspired by his Buddhist mentor, Lho Kunsang Rinpoche, who is a respectable spiritual master of Tibetan Buddhism (Li n.d.b). Although here Li does not elaborate, 'non-traditional ways' and 'non-traditional media' might be construed as new media such as online social networks, which allow him to connect and communicate with his fans in a seamless and instantaneous fashion. Li's One Foundation is decidedly personal and intimately connected to his religious belief in 'loving-kindness' and 'unconditional love'.

A video posted on the '李连杰 Jet Li' Page epitomises this particular integration of Buddhism with philanthropy. Li's Facebook 'friend' Vincent Lee posted a video clip celebrating Li's forty-sixth birthday on 27 April 2009, titled 'Happy Birthday, Jet'. Such actions build trust and engender expectations of reciprocal communication (Donath 2007), serving as an observable marker of attention that initiates and maintains contact between friends (Ellison, et al., 2014: 858). Short and philanthropically conscious, the video features episodes of Li's religious activity such as spiritual contemplation and prayer recitation (with prayer beads in hand), as well as his hectic journeys to various charity functions (Figure 3.3). The Buddhist music on the soundtrack intensifies the religious dimension of the imagery. As a response to the video, the host, who is representing Li, writes on the timeline: 'Thank you everyone for your wishes. For the past 46 years, I have been searching for the meaning of life. But now, I know that I can do my best to help our global family, our ONE family. Thank you for being with me here, and let's join hands to build a better future' ('李连杰 Jet Li' Page). Drawn to the altruistic goals of meeting global humanitarian needs, remaining aloof to worldly fame and wealth, the host propitiously grasps every chance to promote Li's charitable image and the virtues of charity. Using the first-person point of view, the host's reply to the video denotes Li's devout pursuit, while concomitantly aggrandising the reputation of One Foundation.

Figure 3.3 A video post celebrates Jet Li's birthday yet promotes the actor-philanthropist's Buddhist-based image.

Jet Li's charity is publicly recognised on Facebook, validated by the copious responses given to the aforementioned video-post. The video has earned more than 3,366 'just-click' approvals, 394 'shares', and 1,450 comments in various languages, showcasing the polyglot characteristics of the platform. Many comments directly supporting Li's philanthropy reveal a cobweb of fans' identification with Li's heroism. For example, user 'Kiarie Dennis' writes on 8 December 2010, 'Thanks to you Jet, for the support you give to the people who are in much need. God bless you so much and add you happy days in you life.' The wording demonstrates that 'Kiarie Dennis' perceives Li as an 'actual friend' with whom she maintains a relationship through Facebook. Other comments idealise Li as a moral figurehead. For instance, on 4 March 2012, user 'Aracely Lopez' writes, 'You're an awesome human being. Keep helping the world; you can do it. GOD BLESS YOU.' Graciously labelling Li 'an awesome human being', fans see a contemporary hero exceeding the realms of entertainment and martial arts. For many fans, Li is not just a violent fighter like his cinematic roles, but also a moral role model (Yu 2010: 234). His public persona gives, sacrifices, and empathises with sheer dedication, gaining respect from the media and public. Regarding Li, journalist Liam Fitzpatrick remarks: it is difficult to name any other A-list celebrity, not even Bono, who has made such a total commitment. There are plenty who touch down in Africa between albums or movies, but none has actually walked off the job as Jet Li has done, at the top of his game (2008). Li's charitable image reflects the trope of the knight-errant (*youxia*), a heroic figure in *wuxia* narratives. The *youxia* often travel alone in *jianghu*, which is a conceptual world of the 'imagined cultural China', protecting ordinary folk from oppression by means of martial arts prowess. They hold moral codes above the law and prove their chivalric virtues through adventure. According to James Liu, the knights-errant were 'inspired by an altruistic spirit and a strong sense of justice and . . . acted on a universalistic principle' (1967: 11). The knight-errant persona appears in many of Li's onscreen roles such as the legendary Wong Fei-hung (*Once Upon a Time in China*), Chen Zhen (*Fist of Legend*), and Huo Yuanjia (*Fearless*), all renowned for their martial arts potency and altruistic virtues. Extending to the extra-diegetic milieu, Li personifies a modern version of the knight-errant by helping the vulnerable and upholding a distinctive moral code. His philanthropic persona places the interests of society and nation above his own, which is a noteworthy feature of the knight-errant and all other heroic figures (Hood 2010: 98). This image of a 'moral exemplar' circulates among his Facebook fans, shaping a socially ideal figure as a result of interaction among members of the social network.

While some commentary threads of the 'happy-birthday' video-post praise Jet Li's philanthropic acts, others still delight in his filmic persona and martial arts choreography. Some of Li's cyber fans respond more readily to his cinematic persona than to his charitable image. Emblematic of Chinese martial arts, Li's screen roles inevitably inform part of his cyber presence; some fans solely acknowledge that dimension of his celebrity persona. For example, user Ronald Regonios writes, 'My favorite actor is jet li'; [*sic*]' on 8 December 2010. User 'Hamed Ahamdi' likewise enthuses on 31 July 2011, 'Hi Jet Li, I like your all films very much and your fight. you are the best [*sic*]'. Lengthy gaps between the post (in 2009) and comments (in 2010 and 2011) are common. Like most participatory sites, Facebook allows users to respond to a given post at any time unless the uploader or administrator removes the post. Thus, discursive elements related to Li's celebrity persona readily reappear at any moment in the cyber-fan network. The seemingly incongruous response to the content of Li's posts demonstrates the continued appeal of his onscreen persona to fans, despite the philanthropy-centred content. Although potentially an outcome of Li's long-time appeal as a martial arts actor, these fan responses, nevertheless, demonstrate overlap between his cinematic and philanthropic personae.

Jet Li's goodwill mission that propels his recent personality dominates his virtually self-hosted Facebook Page, whereas other Pages run by ordinary users fail to emphasise that charitable presence. The second and third ranked Pages generated from Facebook searches for 'Jet Li' both share the same title 'Jet Li'. By the last survey of the site on 24 August 2015, the second-ranked page had earned 244,942 'likes' and the third-ranked page had earned 52,667 'likes'. Different from the '李连杰 Jet Li' Page, the majority of postings on these two Pages focus on Li's cinematic presence rather than his charitable persona. Timelines on the two Pages generally consist of news items and updates about Li's latest film appearances, movie stills, and clips, photographs of premiere screenings, publicity events, and a wide range of movie stills from Li's pictures, promulgating Li's multi-faceted personality. Many of these stills exhibit fight scenes centring upon Li's acrobatic physique and martial arts dexterity. Local and international fans alike continue to hail, admire, and consume Li's forceful physical presence. Attracting countless 'likes' and the laudatory comments from users, the posts constitute a constellation of texts highlighting Li's movies as well as his martial arts personae. These user-made fan pages serve as extensions of Li's screen personality, while hardly mentioning his equally momentous philanthropic status.

Unsurprisingly, these Facebook Pages seldom mention the ambiguous, yet intriguing, aspects of Jet Li's onscreen masculinity, let alone the public rancour concerning his screen roles. David Bordwell argues that Li is an impassive actor, specialising in roles that demand 'stoic heroism mixed with a boyish awkwardness around women' (2000: 139). Mary Farquhar notes that Li's adolescent image of asexuality and romanticism appears as early as his debut film *Shaolin Temple* and persists throughout his filmography (2010: 116). This holds true for his performance in *Once Upon a Time in China* (1991), wherein the young protagonist Wong Fei-hung often absconds from all romantic situations (Wen Hui 1994, quoted in Yu 2010: 230). While filming *Swordman II* (1992) director Tsui Hark asked Li, 'How come filming you in a romantic scene feels like you are being assaulted?' (ibid.). This inability to credibly convey intimate relationships with the heroines in movies continues in Li's Hollywood films. Some Western critics complain about Li's lack of chemistry with the heroines in his movies, deeming him 'sexually unattractive' (Yu 2010: 230) in *Romeo Must Die* (2000) and *Kiss of the Dragon* (2001). The chaste image, manifested alongside a lack of onscreen sexual play, appears problematic for some Asian American audiences (Stringer 2003: 281–8). His 'uncharismatic' sexuality, or in Yu's words, 'sexless' (2010: 229) image in movies not only casts doubts on his screen masculinity but also diminishes his marketability as an action star. Hollywood-style action heroes such as Bruce Willis, Matt Damon, Harrison Ford, and Arnold Schwarzenegger are much more emotional and rough-hewn than Li; their romantic relationships tend to be bittersweet, and thus interesting even though not necessarily successful.

While scholarly, critical, and popular attention has been directed to Jet Li's problematic masculine screen image, the Pages this chapter examines lack comparable commentary. This illustrates a kind of human capital of favour, leading to an affective fan–celebrity relationship infused with pleasures, desires, and identities. Disputes as a result of fan rivalry and fan loathing are rare due to a lack of varying interests and contrasting viewpoints among users. Unity and harmony rather than arguments and conflicts typically define fan interaction. This, too, creates a discursive space advantageous to Li's humanitarian advocacy. Effortlessly, Li's goodwill persona becomes the locus in which this discursive power is concentrated, attracting the attention from his supporters without challenge. One might expect the open and interactive format of Facebook to catalyse greater public scrutiny of Li than ever before, but instead the fan group dynamics formulated on the platform reifies these strong identificatory ties connecting celebrities and fans.

Negotiating the structuring contradiction of nationalism vs cosmopolitanism in Li's persona

The above analysis shows how a star's screen persona persists alongside his philanthropic profile, illuminating the connections of cosmopolitan stardom to nationalistic nuances that continue to circulate in the global context of cyberculture. Jet Li's national-yet-cosmopolitan personality, which is incessantly and forcefully reinvented by the dialectical tensions, comes to incorporate complex interactions between nationalism and cosmopolitanism, between onscreen and offscreen personae. From his acrobatic body to his philanthropic presence, Jet Li's public image oscillates in the ambivalent space fuelled by these tensions and this space is jointly constructed and engineered by publicity and fans together using a global-cyber-network.

Jet Li's cinematic roles invoke nationalist vigour while his charitable appeal is a sign that transcends any national or ethnic boundaries, representing cosmopolitan consciousness. From his beginnings as an entertainer, Li's popularity is derived from his authentic martial arts skills and underlines an attempt to shape an image of the Chinese hero. Authenticity dominates scholarly discussions about Li's celebrity status, synthesising martial arts and film acting. Notions of authenticity serve as a nexus of accordance and conflict between stars' public presences and private lives, deemed necessary for audience belief in modern stardom (Hinerman 2006: 457). Li's early career as a martial arts champion and a sports ambassador was a source of national pride for his compatriot, laying the ground of his authentic martial arts personality. His talent for martial arts was discovered at the age of eight. He began practising this form of acrobatics on the Beijing Wushu Team, a state-organised group that performs martial arts at The National Games of the People's Republic of China ('Jet Li biography' n.d.). Martial arts, or *wushu*, is a term employed by the PRC government to designate a national sports-health scheme of sundry martial arts techniques, becoming 'a people's sport' since the 1950s (Farquhar 2010: 106). Li ascended to national eminence as a teenaged martial arts idol at eleven years old. He was, furthermore, selected as one of China's top thirty athletes to tour the United States. The tour involved a performance at the White House for President Richard Nixon. When President Nixon asked Li to be his personal bodyguard when he grew up, Li replied, 'No, I don't want to protect any individual. When I grow up, I want to defend my one billion Chinese countrymen!' (Li n.d.a). As Li's biographer Christy Marx writes, Li's response made him a national hero and a celebrity when he returned to China (2002: 33). Furthermore, Li gained national championship and ambassadorship in the 1970s, the era of Maoism. As Mary Farquhar (2010: 21) elucidates, celebrity status in Maoism equates to the revolutionary worker-peasant-soldier model, manufactured by the Chinese Communist Party and distributed by the state-run press (2010: 21–44). The state-oriented framework orchestrated and developed Li's martial arts personality.

Jet Li's filmic career followed a similar nationalist model. His *Shaolin Temple* series had already started to shape his authentic martial arts persona as well as the imagined Shaolin-specific martial arts space. In the celebrated *Once Upon a Time in China* series (1991–3), Tsui Hark re-imagines a young Wong Fei-hung, propagating and celebrating a cultural piety predicated upon an essentialist vision of the national culture and a set of cultural mythologies. Li's subsequent embodiment of legendary Chinese heroes who are also kung fu masters, such as Zhang Sanfeng in *Tai Chi Master* (1993) and Fong Sai Yuk in *The Legend of Fong Sai Yuk I and II* (both 1993), perpetuates the ideology that martial arts are imbued with nationalistic virtues. Although not particularly memorable, some of Li's later modern roles, like the People's Liberation Army (PLA) security official in *The Bodyguard from Beijing* (1994), also feature Li as China's loyal civil servant, furthering his strong associations with the national identification. To many fans, Li was a genuine martial arts star whose onscreen persona embodied nation-based identity and culture.

Contrastingly, Jet Li's charitable persona bespeaks a 'worldly' awareness of universal humanistic concerns extending beyond his martial arts identity and its nationalist connotations. The analysis of Li's self-hosted Facebook fan page illustrates the ways his public persona shifts towards global humanitarianism as he transitions from martial arts actor to philanthropist. Such benevolent endeavours align with Immanuel Kant's conception of perpetual peace, as reiterated by Pheng Cheah, which refers to 'nothing less than the regulative idea of "a perfect civil union of mankind"' (Cheah 1998: 23). This idyllic cosmopolitan view echoes the founding concept of One Foundation. Li explains this philosophy in relation to his concern to provide disaster relief: natural disasters know no boundaries. Nobody on the planet is immune. Because we share this common vulnerability, let us unite across national borders, race, religion, age, and politics. In other words, let us transcend traditional boundaries and unite as one . . . As we all know, the world has five major continents. It is how we are geographically divided. However, if you take a bird's-eye view of the planet, there is only one Earth. Everyone belongs to the planet (Li n.d.c). The One Foundation sees peoples in the world as 'one nation', echoing its slogan, 'One Foundation, One Family', in which individuals transcend national boundaries. Human compassion and decency should extend to everyone, notwithstanding differences in ethnicity, language, gender, religion, and political views. Cosmopolitanism is a signature idea of One Foundation 'whose allegiance is to the worldwide community of human beings' (Nussbaum quoted Robbins 1998: 2).

Jet Li's cinematic presence reflects his cosmopolitan-conscious image. The name 'One Foundation' references Li's Hollywood science-fiction film *The One* (2001), which elaborates upon the multiverse theory of an infinite number of parallel universes existing in the same space. In the film, directed by Chinese American film-maker James Wong, bridges form between these parallel universes and must be policed by a futuristic United Nations-like coalition called the Multiverse Authority. Li plays dual roles as both Gabe Law (the 'good' guy) and Yu Law (the 'bad' guy), culminating in a series of battles between the 'selves', or as Craig Reid phrases it, 'Jet fights Jet' (Reid 2011). The conceptual and eponymous similarities between the film and his philanthropic mission demonstrate how Li's movie persona bleeds into his advocacy work, as discussed above.

Jet Li's online persona is a successful amalgam of the star's connectedness to the world and a fixation with nationalistic consciousness. His persona reconciles the seemingly opposite meanings of nationalism and cosmopolitanism, giving way to a compelling and legitimate global star image. As Dyer argues, representations in any society always involve contradictions between ideologies. Yet Li's online presence signifies cosmopolitan goodwill sensitivity without abandoning Li's nationalistic persona 'construct[ed] out of its own contradictions', Li's online image reveals collaborative effort from cyber fans to 'mask' or 'displace' those contradictions, although perhaps unconsciously. The implication of this stellar presence in cyberspace is that a nationalistic persona requires a foil of cosmopolitanism in order to yield a viable global Chinese celebrity-philanthropist. Suffice it to say, Li's philanthropic presence, as a result of celebrity publicity and packaging, reveals 'a consensual ideology' in the capitalistic entertainment arena. It heightens his market value and social capital of the celebrity, propelling him towards global stardom (1979: 3).

Star construction in the global social networks poses challenges for the meaning of Chinese martial arts star personas in the age of global entertainment. Li's celebrity-philanthropist image becomes the locus where star power, martial arts skills, cinephilia, and charity are intersected and anchored to formulate a multi-dimensional persona. It, moreover, unfolds a changing role of philanthropy in the age of Web 2.0. In addition to forging a favoured persona, philanthropy also provides an aperture for fans to participate in the image building and meaning-making processes in the open cyber-network. The participatory logic in cyberspace allows multiple strategies and approaches to understanding Li's star image, which is a text of linked significations opened up for users' relentless (re)making, revisiting, and interrogating, complicating the meaning of Chinese celebrities. In this sense, the meaning of Jet Li as a star becomes destabilised with the plurality and openness embraced in the cyber-networked setting. Fans from diverse cultural and ethnic backgrounds interact and connect with one another by negotiating their own relations to Li's persona and arguing among themselves as to what his star image is about, consequently formulating new patterns of star–fan dynamics.

Chapter 4

YouTubing Zhang Ziyi: Chinese female stardom in fan videos on video-sharing sites

Introduction: Chinese fame on the rise

Whereas fans and critics recognise Jet Li for his explicit endeavour of relief work of the Sichuan earthquake in 2008, Zhang Ziyi gains a bad name by the charity fraud she commits in this disaster. The calamity spawns a phenomenal upsurge in individual and corporate philanthropy in China (Jeffreys 2011: 4). Countless famed figures and celebrities join the goodwill effort, including Zhang Ziyi who promised to donate one million yuan to the disaster-relief fund – but the donation was eventually forfeited. Dubbed 'donation-gate', Zhang's failed pledge resulted in public discontent, exploding on bilingual blogs and through online videos, accusing the actress of bringing ignominy to the philanthropic causes and to the Chinese nation (Alexandra099tianya 2010; Dogonfire2005 2010). The ruthless public responses coerce Zhang to offer an exclusive interview to a state-run English-language newspaper *China Daily*, employ a team of US-based lawyers, and devote to rehabilitated philanthropic attempt so as to clear her bad name (Zhou 2010a, 2010b). It is not difficult to find a range of videos pertaining to Zhang's abortive endowment posted from 2008 through 2010 on YouTube, one of the most high-volume and predominant video-sharing sites (Burgess and Green 2009: 5). The entries, in both English and Chinese languages, are either the copy-and-paste or edited versions of the discourses in other media conduits such as television and Internet sites. The clips attract thousands of views and dozens of comments, imparting illegitimacy to the Chinese star on the global visual circuit. The presence of these user-generated texts also signifies that when an internationally known Chinese actress achieves certain notoriety like such, this is no longer simply a personal issue. Rather, it is an honour-or-shame issue of the ethnic Chinese, alongside the notion of the rising China in the global arena. In other words, the phenomenon entails the issue of ethnicity that cannot be forgotten but is ready to reappear at any moment in the fan discourse even long after the incident happened.

As an A-list celebrity in China, Zhang Ziyi has been one of the few figures who attains global fame while having her public personality so frequently tainted by scandals and so intensely scrutinised by the public. Zhang rose to international stardom with her appearance in *Crouching Tiger, Hidden Dragon* (2000). Playing a spirited, headstrong swordswoman who is 'active, mobile, physically strong' (Cai 2005: 448) in the film, Zhang displays fight and flight and eventually impresses the audience with her personality. As a global cinematic phenomenon, the film earned more than US$200 million worldwide, becoming the most successful foreign-language picture in the film history in America (Klein 2004a: 18). The success of the film has won Zhang subsequent appearances in a number of Hollywood and Chinese-language star vehicles such as *Memoirs of a Geisha* (2005), *Hero* (2002), and *House of Flying Daggers* (2004), in which Zhang's choreographed presence noticeably continues. In addition to the realm of commercial cinema, she is increasingly active in world-renowned film festivals like Cannes and Venice. For instance, she joins the jury at Cannes in 2006 as its youngest member ever, which has been perceived as an accomplishment (IndieWire 2006). Myriad celebrity and fashion magazines as well as entertainment websites vote Zhang as one of the 'most beautiful Chinese women in the world', or similar titles. She, moreover, earns the contracts from the huge brands such as OMEGA Watches and Maybelline to be a spokesperson. On *Forbes's* (mainland) China Celebrity List in 2009 and 2010, Zhang is ranked number two, immediately followed by basketball player Yao Ming, of China's top 100 power-ranking celebrities ('2010 Forbes China celebrity list' 2010). In this fashion, Zhang epitomises the mounting significance of Chinese stars in global cultural markets.

Being arguably the most celebrated female stars of the nation, at the same time, Zhang Ziyi's transnational profile is challenged by a series of scandals, notably about her linguistic incapability and alleged sexual promiscuity. As an ethnic Chinese actress, Zhang gives the impression that in some attention-grabbing occasions like the Oscars and film festivals' press conferences, she is unable to eloquently communicate in English. Even if she manages articulating English speeches, she has elicited inappropriate words and peculiar accents. For example, in the meet-the-press event at the 57th Cannes Film Festival on Wong Kar-wai's movie *2046* (2004), an attendee asked Zhang Ziyi about the differences between Wong Kar-wai and her debut filmmaker Zhang Yimou. In the midst of answering the question in English, Zhang Ziyi suddenly becomes incapable of continuing and asks for a translator to help, resulting in an abrupt, embarrassing pause. This gossip-like incident is reported by Shanghai's 'OpenV', a leading Chinese interactive web television platform, and is transposed to Youku, a video hosting platform in the PRC, and is then relayed to YouTube by another user. Besides, one may recall the well-documented event of Zhang's award presentation for the best editing at the Oscars in 2006. While some media in Taiwan and the PRC assume that Zhang's 'Oscars' appearance could have been 'an ethnic Chinese pride-pumping moment' (*China Daily* 2006), Hong Kong mainstream media are notorious for making fun of Zhang's broken English. For example, *Apple Daily* from the Next Media Group of Hong Kong elicited a headline, 'Zhang Ziyi presents awards with Beijing-accented English' (*China Daily* 2006). The story elaborated, 'She still can't change her English with a Beijing country accent. She didn't pronounce the "r" in the winning movie "Crash" properly.' Another Hong Kong newspaper, *Sing Tao Daily*, similarly disparaged Zhang's pronunciation of 'Crash' that sounded like the toothpaste brand 'Crest' (ibid.). These enunciatory moments, which potentially augment the mediated visibility of the star in front of the international public, now promote the actress's name in a derogatory sense.

Zhang Ziyi has also been involved in a cluster of sexuality-themed scandals that has placed her under the negative, particularly domestic, publicity. Rumours reveal that she has been sleeping with Zhang Yimou, the well-known Chinese filmmaker who discovers Zhang in her screen debut *The Road Home* (1999) and cast her for the subsequent blockbuster *Hero* (2002) and *House of Flying Daggers* (2004). She is also under reprimand due to her role in Hollywood's *Memoirs of a Geisha* (2005) in the context of an intense anti-Japan ethos that stemmed from the constant refusal of the Japanese Government to offer a formal apology for the military mayhems in World War II. This not only causes the cancellation of the film's original release in China but also results in the open reproach of Zhang's depiction of a woman selling her virginity to the top Japanese contestant as a national insult (Bezlova 2006; 'China cancels release of "Memoirs of a Geisha"' 2006). Intertextual and extratextual knowledge explain how Zhang's personality is under wide observation, unpacking the dynamics of star making against the backdrop of transnational cultural politics.

As Zhang Ziyi's fame is interwoven to the paradox of reverence and condemnation, fan-made videos become an emergent vehicle for fabricating fame, or notoriety, in the interactive cyberspace. Both legitimate and 'unofficial' materials go viral online, insinuating that Zhang's debatable persona probably holds more appeal for users than the institutionalised persona. Users recycle footage related to Zhang Ziyi, including press conferences, commentaries, and innuendoes culled from mass media and represent in the form of fan-made videos, suggesting YouTube's 'textual and metatextual dimensions' (Uricchio 2009: 24). Fan-made video events have the root of media fandom that began in the mid-1970s with the use of slide projector stills, grew through the 1980s and 1990s with the development of VHS and DVD technology, and by the 2000s attained near-universal feasibility via the Internet (Russo 2009). A proliferation of fan sites now allows audiences to post and distribute news of their idols with enormous speed and spread. The mid-2000s witnesses the development of high bandwidth and the manageable editing software, giving way to the eruption of video-sharing sites. Video files are now downloadable and directly transferable between devices such as television and computer. Fans readily search, cull, copy, and post movie clips, trailers, and interviews from digital sources like DVD and Internet websites. In addition to the appropriation of materials, they also edit the images and mix them with other texts. They eagerly post the selected and edited works on video-sharing sites in order to show their fondness of and to make comments on the stars, soliciting feedback and support from other members in the user community. YouTube's 2005 launch signposts the maturation of the fan-based culture in generating star discourse. Under-regulated and unruly in its own right, YouTube is a crucial venue of 'cultural aggregation' in which images, voices, and modes of address amass and 'all combine into a dynamic and seamless whole' (Uricchio 2009: 24). Without logics of hierarchisation, thus, the platform has made popular texts promptly available for fan appropriation and manipulation, gathering fans' momentum in reimagining stars in the global visual circuit.

Then, what is the image of Zhang Ziyi on YouTube? How is such image responsive to the cultural and ethnic politics of Chinese performers in the global visual network? This chapter will analyse how YouTube users enthusiastically represent and interrogate the star identity of Zhang as a Chinese actress in fan-made videos. My identification of the corpus of video texts begins with the installed search facility of YouTube, which is very much like the search engines Google and Yahoo. I keyword-searched the site, by using the phrases that point to two categories of controversies that chiefly dogged Zhang's publicity: (1) 'Zhang Ziyi, interview', which directly denotes the celebrity's language capacity, and (2) 'Zhang Ziyi, sex scandal', which suggests the transgressive star image. On 1 August 2017, the day I researched the site, altogether 4,650 results were generated, organised, and displayed in twenty-six web pages. Along the two axes of search, I have identified the most-viewed entries as the key object of enquiry, supplemented by the analysis of a couple of entries that contain high reference values. On top of the video entries, I will also probe the user commentary to consider the elaborate dynamics between users. By focusing on the user-generated materials, I will argue that Zhang's poor English-speaking performances and sex scandals valorise yet contend her transnational appeal, intermingling diverse fan-based discourses in the star construction. The narrative of hard work, nonetheless, proves that she is a flexible icon in global capitalism that is able to oscillate between the cultural articulations made in English and those made in her mother-tongue. By so doing, this chapter will unravel the nuanced ways that users participate in the lingua- and cultural-crossing star construction of Zhang as part of the global visual exchange.

Two methodological clarifications are necessary here. First, I am well aware of the fact that the web has always been a suspect method for obtaining the 'truth' of any kind, especially with regard to celebrities. With respect to the salient feature of the web of its ability to conceal identity markers like ethnic, cultural, and linguistic background, the users are 'invisible' and anonymous. Yet this exactly serves to grant recognition to the new technology, giving liberty to voice one's opinions regardless of social and cultural privileges, while acknowledging that not all comments are level-headed or useful to the analysis. Second, I employ the keywords in English to conduct the search. Yet, due to the hyperlinked and polyglot nature of YouTube, the search results are not exclusively in the English language. In my study, I will also take consideration of the significant entries in Chinese, in addition to the English-language ones (but not other languages), referencing the two cultures and tongues that Zhang as a star has crossed over, negotiated, and connected across. In addition, regarding Zhang's persona centring on sex scandals, which are mainly the interest of the actress's domestic media, I will locate certain Chinese-language materials as the vantage points of investigation.

Not speaking English? Hollywood's anglophone hegemony and the linguistic-based persona of Zhang Ziyi

Given the importance of English skill for international stars, perhaps it is phenomenal that Zhang Ziyi first won global acclaim with a Mandarin-language film, *Crouching Tiger, Hidden Dragon* (2000), which also inaugurated her Hollywood acting career. Shortly after her name was established on the world screens through the film's success, Zhang's inability to speak fluent English increasingly became a point of public notice. Some global audiences consider Zhang's early public instances of speaking 'imperfect' English as charming and 'forgivable', resonating with her traditionally 'Chinese' screen image in *Crouching Tiger, Hidden Dragon* (2000), *Hero* (2002), *House of Flying Daggers* (2004), and *The Banquet* (2006). However, when Zhang gains her roles in Hollywood, an Anglophone yet global cinema, her proficiency of articulating a foreign tongue becomes an issue. Playing a minor role named Hu Li in *Rush Hour 2* (2000), Zhang recycled the 'dragon lady' image and spoke only three lines of dialogue in English (Leung 2014: 68), displaying her physical vigour that can fight with equal footing with male counterparts.

Although Zhang Ziyi becomes internationally celebrated with *Crouching Tiger, Hidden Dragon* (2000), she had not had her first English interview until September 2004 at the Toronto International Film Festival for the promotion of Zhang Yimou's Chinese martial arts epic, *House of Flying Daggers* (2004). After more than two years following the interview being broadcast on CityTV, the largest independent television station in Canada, the dialogue was uploaded on to YouTube by a user – 'xuchuanqi' – on 5 April 2008, attracting in total 20,068 views by 1 August 2017. The caption insinuates the weight of language in Zhang's speaking persona, reading bilingual as: 'Ziyi Zhang talks about her role in House of Flying Daggers, and about her fame in both Chinese and English. She's so cute. 章子怡双语接受采访谈《十面埋伏》，十分可爱。[Zhang Ziyi shuangyu jieshou caifang tan *Shimian Maifu*, shifen keai].' The uploader points out the fact that the interview is bilingual, followed by commendation of the actress, insinuating the significance of language, as perceived by audiences, for the stars who emerge in the global arena. However, close scrutiny of the clip uncovers that the 'bilingual' is not something intentional but is an inadvertent outcome of Zhang's inability to handle a conversation fully in English. The interview chiefly stresses Zhang's performance in *House of Flying Daggers*, with questions of her role and her experience of working with celebrated Asian actors Andy Lau and Takeshi Kaneshiro. The interviewer addresses Zhang at a relatively slow pace. Zhang's diction codes the exchange as one between a native English speaker and someone who does not possess sufficient English skill for a public interview. Viewers will not miss the fact that the interview, both in terms of content and delivery, is driven by linguistic concerns.

As the clip reveals, Zhang Ziyi strived to be a speaking subject in the verbal exchange, trying to communicate equally with the interviewer, but failed. The interview opens with the question, 'You are such a huge star here in North America [an Anglophone area]. How are you dealing with all of this attention?' Listening to the interviewer, she ponders for a while. Yet the interpreter immediately translates the question for her into Mandarin before she elicits an answer, leading her to respond in her mother tongue. While Zhang attempts to seek subjectivity in her language (Benveniste 1971: 225), her expression of self is only accomplished in a mediated discourse signalled by the interpreter's translation of her first answer since the very beginning. After hearing the English translation of Zhang's reply, the interviewer chuckles while Zhang presents a friendly yet embarrassed smile. Both of these non-verbal cues suggest the linguistic misfit of Zhang to the context of the interview and, in a wider sense, to an English-speaking, Anglo-American world.

For the rest of the interview, a lack of eloquence further obscures Zhang's position as a (quasi-)English speaker. Zhang attempted to alter the initial impression of not being able to speak English by making English utterances herself rather than relying on an interpreter. When asked the second question about her handling of the film, she began her answer in Mandarin, "Because this film . . . [*yin wei zhe ge dian ying*因為這個電影 . . .]' and then abruptly switches to English to continue the response, 'You know . . . Zhang Yimou gave me a lot of space in this movie . . . ' Nonetheless, the remaining part of the interview is marked by the heavily accented pronunciation, syntactically peculiar expression, and limited range of vocabulary. Examples are ubiquitous: Mandarin-tinged words like 'months', 'with', 'everyday', 'difference', 'pretend', 'feeling', 'friendly', and 'nervous'; odd English syntax in sentences like 'Before we start, I live with her, just *watch her everyday* . . . and all the details . . . ' (my emphasis),[1] '*I love to eat*, you know, *meat*, you know, all the things . . . ' (my emphasis);[2] repetition of words and phrases such as 'I', 'just', 'the', and 'that's hard'. About a third of the way into it, the hostess asks Zhang about the most difficult part of her performance, and Zhang recalls her experience of playing the role of a blind girl in the film. She attempts answering in broken English, 'For me, I think, the most part was ... when I play blind, I know I can see; I can see Andy's knife just next me, you know, but I ... I ... I need to pretend I didn't see it. I just ... y[ou] ... sometime ... I ju ... ust, you know, the ... the ... the feeling I can see it, but I ... I try to pretend. But that's hard. And sometimes, you know, um ..., you have to act and ... but you should be a blind. I think that's hard.' Zhang Ziyi has to expose her limited English capacity once again. The reiteration of the words 'I', 'just' and 'the' shows a non-native speaker's hesitation turning into the impression of a lack of eloquence. The expressions 'sometimes' and 'you know' help fill the elocutionary gaps, allowing Zhang to search for words to express herself. Repetition of words and phrases such as 'pretend' and 'that's hard' can expose her limited vocabulary.

The syntactic ellipses and shortage of articulateness mar Zhang's discursive clarity, questioning the plausibility of her speech to the widest audience. Near the end, Zhang appears fairly humbled and embarrassed, apologising to the hostess with a light bow, 'Hope you can stand my English.' It signals Zhang's awareness of her poor command of the English language, which is a potential encumbrance to communication with international press.

The same user, on the same day, has uploaded another video of Zhang Ziyi's interview for her appearance in Hollywood's *Memoirs of a Geisha* (2005) with a focus on the actress's extra-diegetic publicity. The issue of Zhang Ziyi's English-speaking competence becomes further palpable yet complicated in this Hollywood picture, in which Zhang, as an ethnic Chinese actress, earns her 'most visible global role' (Willis and Leung 2014: 11). The movie is an adaptation from Arthur Golden's novel of the same title (1997), a fictionalised memoir of a geisha's life story set in the Gion district of Kyoto in the period of the 1930s to the 1950s.[3] The Cinderella-like story presents a subject that is an exotic, mysterious figure even in her native country, bringing its readers to the 'secret world of the geisha', a phrase widely adopted in sundry media texts, including travel blogs, documentary footages, and online newspapers (Cloutman 2015; Waterlow 2015; Kolinovsky n.d.). Director Rob Marshall retells the story in cinematic terms that both the film text and the filmmaking provide a specific context for star-making. While it is a Hollywood project using American capital and an American filmmaker, its cast involves Chinese, Chinese-American, Japanese, and Caucasian actors and actresses, enacting a Japanese-based story. With respect to the movie's multi-ethnic and multilingual cast, English seems to be the common language for people to communicate in. Five years later than Zhang's Hollywood debut, *Rush Hour 2* (2001), the Chinese-speaking actress seemed to learn enough English to take on a major role in *Memoirs of a Geisha* (2005), a film casting the three biggest female stars in the Chinese-speaking world. Alongside Michelle Yeoh and Gong Li, Zhang Ziyi plays the character of Sayuri, a young lady from a humble background who matures to be a celebrated geisha. Zhang speaks the lines with her own voice but her English rivets disapproval and contempt. For example, writer and translator Anne Ishii (2005) criticises the movie in light of the actress's English speeches: 'The worst part of *Memoirs* is still that Ziyi Zhang speaks slow and crude English that she learned in half a year.' Likewise, *Sight & Sound*'s Leslie Felperin (2006) described that the trio of leads speaks 'a ridiculous brand of movie-English throughout' (71). Zhang's English-speaking capacity comes under spotlight as she begins developing her transnational profile.

This time, the clip shows Zhang Ziyi's co-appearance with Michelle Yeoh, the other key actress in *Memoirs of a Geisha*. Attracting 561,085 views on 1 August 2017, the entry is a replication of an interview entitled 'Mystery Women: Inside the Life of a Geisha' of MSNBC, an American cable and satellite television network for the movie's promotion. The uploader gives his/her own title to the post as 'Ziyi Zhang and Michelle Yeoh talk about *Memoirs of A Geisha* on NBC's Today show' (Figure 4.1). The video opens with the introduction of the movie by a presenter, followed by an interview in English between the experienced American television reporter Jamie Gangel and the actresses Michelle Yeoh and Zhang Ziyi. The exchange is intersected by sequences of the movie that serve as illustration and supplement to what the conversation pertains to. Furthermore, the interview incorporates the well-recalled sword fight scene between Yeoh and Zhang in the martial arts hit *Crouching Tiger, Hidden Dragon* (2000), of which the two actresses are famously in the main cast. This leads to Gangel's question about the difficulty of performing action in front of the camera, foregrounding the interest to and significance of the choreographic spectacle. In this fashion, the focus of discussion seems to waver between the personalities of Japanese geishas and Chinese martial arts heroines.

Ethnicity emerged as a point of notice, as the interview develops, through not only appearance but also enunciation. Zhang wears light

MYSTERY WOMEN
INSIDE THE LIFE OF A GEISHA

0:53 / 4:07

Figure 4.1 'Ziyi Zhang and Michelle Yeoh talk about *Memoirs of a Geisha* on NBC's *Today* show'

make-up and has straight hair, echoing her coquettish, girlish image in her early career. Gangel asks questions in a slower pace than normal conversation, accommodating to the purportedly insufficient English proficiency of the stars. In a soft-spoken, amicable yet timorous, unconvinced fashion, Zhang gives brief, simple answers with exceptional discretion in accented English. Her speech is, not surprisingly, marked by unnatural stress, simplistic diction, and equivocal use of vocabulary. In contrast, Yeoh manages to speak eloquent English with minimal grammatical errors and evident humour. She also gestures in a natural, reflexive way while talking. As the clip indicates, when the hostess enquires about the intensive, 'boot camp'-type geisha training, Yeoh instructs Zhang, although in a casual manner, 'Tell them about your dancing,' referring to an outstanding scene of Zhang-as-Sayuri dances on extremely high-heeled shoes. Gangel jokingly adds that she was nervous for Zhang who needs to perform the graceful yet challenging steps, showing how impressive the scene appears to her. The highly stylistic and exotic scene displays the actress's dancing adroitness. Grounded in dance training since the age of eleven at the Beijing Dance Academy, Zhang develops her kinetic image with a small body-build and a flexible skeleton. Her bodily movements often appear natural. Accredited to her ballerina-type physique, some of her screen fights arguably resemble dances. Consider the bamboo fight scene between

Li Mu Bai (Chow Yun-fat) and Jen (Zhang Ziyi) in *Crouching Tiger, Hidden Dragon* that the heroine flies over and stands at treetop with the seemingly weightless body. Her choreographic style seems distinctive to the dominant paradigm in the Hong Kong action genres that emphasise either hard-fighting aerobatics or weapon-wielding violence, which is also the one Yeoh's screen persona best typifies. Zhang's dancing kineticism occasionally recycles in her subsequent movies such as *House of Flying Daggers* and *Memoirs of a Geisha* that provoke the Orientalist imagination. Therefore, Zhang's kinetic body constantly reemerges in media discourse.

It is obvious that in the interview, Michelle Yeoh dominates the verbal responses and exhibits certain discursive agency over Zhang Ziyi. In this light, Yeoh showcases a more viable image than Zhang of Chinese stars who can survive and negotiate her power in Hollywood. Her culturally diverse upbringing helps her develop not only proficient spoken English but also her transnational image. As a Malaysian-born Chinese in an émigré family of the Hokkien ancestral connection, Yeoh learned English and Malay as her first languages. In her teenage years, she learnt ballet at the Royal Academy of Dance in London, which can help to explain her British-accented English. She is one of the few Hong Kong actresses who successfully earns a foothold in Hollywood. After she began establishing her fame in the role of the Bond Girl named Wai Lin in her first English-language film *Tomorrow Never Dies* (1997), she gained contracts for films such as *The Mummy: Tomb of the Dragon Emperor* (2008) and *The Lady* (2011) in which she found no problem in speaking fluent English.

In the context of increasingly border-crossing cinema and international media hysteria, transnational stars are located in the Anglophone culture. Hollywood dominates the globalised media presence by becoming the producer of imperialist texts and images (Jameson 1991; Mattelart 1994). It overly determines the US cultural production and inexorably seeks new markets and larger audiences (Marchetti 2012: 2). Importing foreign talents, packaging, and selling them as international stars (Negra 2001: 60) is one of the ways to fulfil such ambition. Hollywood perpetuates the English-speaking hegemonic project and the assimilative tendencies (Ang 2001: 30–1) that lucidly express the pervasiveness of Western arbitration (Ang 2001: 30–1; Davis 2001: 179). The language-based domination of Hollywood can be viewed through two lenses: competence and accent. According to Sabrina Yu (2012), being *able* to make films in a different language is one of the ways to define the transnational quality of a star (2). In most cases, moreover, an actor who wants to become a transnational star needs to move to Hollywood to make English-language films. Under this logic, Juliette Binoche and Penelope Cruz, whose native tongue is not English, are more likely to be considered as 'transnational' than Nicole Kidman and Kate Winslet who come from the English-speaking countries of Australia and England respectively (ibid.).

History witnesses a plight of transnational Chinese performers in Hollywood like Anna May Wong, Nancy Kwan, Keye Luke, Joan Chan, Lucy Liu, D. B. Wong, and Maggie Q who may or may not speak various dialects of Chinese while they manage performing English-speaking roles. Not only is the ability to speak English at issue here, what is noteworthy, too, is to speak accent-free English. In 1930s Hollywood, some performers from Europe could not get parts in films due to their heavy accents, considering that accents 'muddle actor, star, and role' (Jarvie 2004: 175). Greta Garbo, Sonja Henie, and Ingrid Bergman, who were usually cast as European and Soviet characters with their long-kept Scandinavian accent, seldom get native-born American roles or attain the same intelligibility as their native counterparts. Similarly, British-born star Cary Grant, who acquired a 'transatlantic accent', was readily understandable but is also 'hard to place' (ibid.). With no exception, contemporary transnational stars who are not (native) English speakers like Yeoh and Zhang need to confront the hegemony of Anglo-American culture in Hollywood. Whereas the volubility of Yeoh's English is comparable to that articulated by her white counterparts, Zhang's accented, broken English highlights her Chinese ethnicity. Although Zhang intends to establish her English-speaking image in media publicity, as a consequence, she presents herself as a less flexible actress in the politics of the Anglophone world market.

'Shame on her!': the sex scandals and cultural nationalism

There have been hearsays that Zhang Ziyi's English has improved due to her relationship with her white boyfriend Vivi Nevo in 2008. Since she became famous, Zhang has frequently been piqued by gossip about her love life, one of the Chinese female celebrities whose love life seem to be constantly a focus of paparazzi attention. She is rumoured to have had affairs with a cluster of famous men across geographical, cultural, and professional coordinates, including Chinese filmmaker Zhang Yimou, American filmmaker and music video director Brett Ratner, Hong Kong-Hollywood actor Jackie Chan, and the grandson of the Hong Kong tycoon and philanthropist Henry Fok Ying-tung, Eric Fok Kai-shan. But her better-known controversial relationship was with Vivi Nevo, an Israeli multi-millionaire and venture capitalist, who is twelve years older than Zhang. Tabloids revealed that Zhang was to be engaged to him in 2008, after an approximately one-year relationship (Arango 2008). Subsequent to Zhang's acknowledgement of the romance, media callously speculated on the actress's intentions with regard to the potential benefits for her career since Nevo was a key shareholder in Time Warner and a previous patron of The Weinstein Company with whom Zhang was claimed to have a multiple film deal. Some critics went further, charging that for Zhang to offer herself to a white man was a form of disgrace to Chinese women, or even to Chinese people. The popular discussion surrounding their relationship, hence, exposed tensions over Chinese identity, cultural integrity, and national honour.

The censure reaches its peak with the exposure of the semi-nude photographs of the couple sun-baking on a private beach at St Barts in January 2009. The scandal, coined by Chinese-language media as 'sex photo-gate' (Tan 2009) has expanded the parameters of Zhang's public persona from actress to sexualised celebrity. Its coverage is emblematic of a culture that 'privileges the momentary, the visual and the sensational over the enduring, the written, and the rational', as Graeme Turner (2004: 4) states in discerning the upsetting cultural shift signalled by modern celebrity. The paparazzi blow-ups of Zhang's beach photos, explicated by entertainment news reports, originally released in other media, went viral on the web, including YouTube. On 6 January 2009, user 'jackiezhang1989' posted an approximately two-minute video encompassing the photographs and certain specific opinions from audiences, poached and replicated from www.ku6.com, one of the prevalent video-sharing sites in China[4] (Figure 4.2). The clip is entitled, in Chinese characters, '章子怡 对在海滩被偷拍感到很愤怒' (Zhang Ziyi: Enraged about being spied on the beach), written in simplified Chinese, implying that the uploader was probably a Chinese-speaking user from mainland China. Moreover, the entry has riveted Chinese-language comments as many as English-language ones, vindicating to the manifest attention of the Chinese public to this scandal. The issues that stemmed from this set of scandalous imagery include not only celebrity nudity, public–private dialectics and voyeurism-surveillance polemics but also morality and cultural nationalism.

Figure 4.2 The YouTube video encompassing images of Zhang Ziyi's 'sex photo-gate' copied from the video-sharing site www.ku6.com

Although the violation of Zhang's privacy is perhaps worthy of sympathy, a more common response is to ridicule her for her 'misdeeds', insinuating that she must be held responsible to society's moral expectations (Lull and Hinerman 1997: 21). According to Lull and Hinerman's typology of media scandals, the star scandals are marked by moral contextualisation (20–1). The private deeds enter the public sphere, lying outside the parameters of the star's control and the deeds then become evaluated by the dominant moral code. Public condemnation frames Zhang's nakedness on the beach as immoral. Such moral violation is situated in the image system that the particular transgression is constructed and deciphered against an image in circulation. Whereas the image evokes curiosity (McDonald 2003: 36), it unfolds the 'hidden star', designating the 'intimate transgressions' (ibid.) that permit Internet users to see not just anybody naked but this particular star naked. Portrayed as erotic and fetishised, Zhang becomes an object sexually exploited in the media world and the real world alike. This echoes Richard DeCordova's explication, adopting a Foucauldian framework, that scandal narratives function to make sexuality the ultimate reality of stars' identity (1990: 141). Image reproduction in the cyber world can further loosen and even transgress the borders of (il)legitimacy. As mentioned, the web is generally a less regulated form of media than other traditional mass media like television and print except in certain countries like the PRC. 'Unauthorised' images are readily distributed beyond the control of studios and agents.

Akin to some responses of Zhang's insufficient English, her moral transgressions are read as an honour-or-shame issue related to her status as an ethnic Chinese. The nationalistically charged criticism assails Zhang Ziyi for devoting herself to a man of another race: in January 2009, 'DeeLoveTw' disdains, 'Shame on you Ms. Zhang, a Chinese slut?' In March, 'toyyou2jp' explains, 'She is a hardcore bitch for all Chinese guys but she becomes a puppy dog for western billionaire!!! What a shame to all China.' The same month, 'denisefan' echoes, 'she has become another embarrassment for China'. Users accuse and deride Zhang as a sign of disgrace of the Chinese populace, actively taking part in the construction of her sexualised persona while questioning her status as a Chinese star. As Lull and Hinerman postulate, 'the disgrace of scandal lies in the collective willingness of others to impose shame and even bring damage upon the scandaliser' (1997: 25). It is true that shame demeans the 'integrity of the self" (Giddens 1991: 65). Yet shame is not only about self-respect but is also a quintessential social and cultural construct (Lull and Hinerman 1997: 26). The shame inflicted by scandals exemplifies a specific type of social accountability (ibid.). According to Eric R. Dodds (1951), in a shame culture, individuals are conditioned by the pressure of social conformity because the estimation of oneself is equated to other people's conceptions (28). Here what Zhang does – having intimate exchange with a boyfriend in semi-nudity in a public place – does not conform to the social standard. Moreover, it violates the Confucian values *li* (propriety) that lie at the kernel of the Chinese culture. Popularly framed as a representative of China, as in the aforementioned user comments, Zhang shows her conduct evoking feelings of anxiety and embarrassment on a collective level. It can be inferred that these users are of Zhang's own Chinese identity, evincing worry that the entire ethnic group will be stereotypically dishonoured. Users' narratives of defence of their national honour becomes a response to the unwanted, disrespected shamed celebrity and an avenue to exude their discursive power within the world.

The public denigration does not show a sign of fading in recent years, with the latest rumor being that Zhang Ziyi was paid for sex by Bo Xilai, the former Communist Party leader in Chongqing, China. As the senior party official, Bo has been disgraced by a series of scandals, including a murder of a British man who develops espionage ties with his wife, and his 'playboy' son taking out Jon Huntsman's daughters in an unspecific

Porsche, the enormous overseas fortune, and wiretapping of the Chinese President. Sources allege that from 2007 to 2011, Zhang slept with Bo ten times in exchange for more than 700 million yuan. The anecdote seems to have brewed for some time, but it was first exposed by a controversial US-based Chinese news website called Boxun.com (Taylor 2012). Coined as 'prostitution', the controversy with Bo repositions Zhang within the potentially detrimental repercussions that public visibility can inflict on individuals.

Material about the controversy regarding to Bo do not become invisible on YouTube. One example is the video called 'Zhang Ziyi scandal: Zhang denies she slept with officials for money', which is animated footage produced by Tigerwood Animation, a Taiwan-based news animator that also provides service to the Next Media Group in Taipei, posted on 1 June 2012 by user 'Tomonews Funnies'.[5] The entry shows the Chinese-subtitled, animated version of the news, which is sonically wrapped by the Mandarin-speaking voiceover. The animation portrays Zhang as her iconic female warrior figure in *Crouching Tiger, Hidden Dragon*, proving the fame of her screen personality. In this fashion, Zhang Ziyi's star image suddenly oscillated between the realms of martial arts film star and sex symbol. Her body not only suggests a choreographic spirit but also a multitude of desires and fantasies in a highly sexualised sense. The scandalous images objectify Zhang for a direct voyeuristic appeal to users, making her a spectacle for exchange in the popular image circuitry facilitated first by paparazzi and then by the public dwelled in cyberspace.

My investigation indicates a correlation between the categories of sexuality and gender in the star–fan interactions in participatory cyberspace. As far as sexual difference goes, cyber fans readily engage with Zhang Ziyi's sexualised images and the romance narrative while no such response appears in the cyber discourse of male celebrities. Zhang's star image has been given critical scrutiny holding her to the normative standard of what a Chinese woman should look like and act like in personal and public life. Fans' responses to Jackie Chan have been much more lenient. Certainly, Chan's forays about his amorous encounters, as indicated in the earlier comparison between Jackie Chan and Donnie Yen on the 'family man' image in Chapter 1, have been the interest of Chinese-language tabloids from time to time but it is fair to say it is probably not an enduring topic of cyber fan discourse. It is known that Chan married a Taiwanese actress, Lin Feng-Jiao, in 1982 but did not make it public until 1998 when he published his autobiography, *I Am Jackie Chan* ('Jackie Chan biography' n.d.). A former studio executive Du Huidong mentions in his book *Little Stars* the 'secret' love story between Chan and the famous Taiwanese singer Teresa Tang prior to his marriage to Lin. Except for the public anger and denunciation provoked by Chan's imprudent confession of 'wrongdoing' respective to Elaine Ng's pregnancy, no hints show that cyber fans are critical or fervent about pursuing the gossips. Rather, news about Chan's movies and his philanthropic acts occupy a more central place than the star's public visibility in the cyber-fan conversation. This amounts to an implicit acceptance of the normative notion of men having the freedom to pursue affairs while the women who do so are criticised for their hypersexuality.

The unequal weight of cyber fans' derisive responses to Chinese actors and actresses extends to the instance of the ethnic stars' English-speaking capacity. The lack of English skill of male Chinese stars such as Jackie Chan and Jet Li seldom becomes a focus of reprimand in public discourse. As audiences may easily recall, Chan often makes fun of his broken English and the bloopers become a point of highlight at the end of a range of his movies. This means his English inadequacy is not unnoticed by the public, yet it is rarely disparaged. Likewise, Jet Li's English, which is of approximate fluency to Chan's, is obviously accented. But not sufficient evidence shows that cyber fans elicit reproof to the language of Li.

Based on these differences, it can thus be argued that the female Chinese star has been prone to fan criticism more strongly than the males. Zhang Ziyi enjoys the limelight, yet when it comes to public reception, she has less of the same representational privilege as that relished by Chan and Li when it comes to the linguistic accents and racialised negative publicity. This indicates the divergent assumptions of the public presentation of the two genders. The sexual difference turns out to be more lenient to the male stars than the female star. In this respect, the gender hierarchy largely accepted in the culture is being perpetuated, recirculated, and buttressed in cyber fan communities.

The paradigm of hard work

Counteracting the scandals and gossips surrounding Zhang's persona, narratives of self-transformation redeem her notorious status, negotiating her discursive space in Hollywood as well as in world cinema. Respective to Zhang's 'problem' of speaking broken English, it is not difficult to note that both English- and Chinese-language media show a tendency to promote and glorify Zhang's attempt of fixing such a 'problem' through her hard work. The Chinese website www.people.com.cn reports that for an entire year, Zhang was embarrassed over the loss of chance to communicate with foreign media at the 2010 Oscar ceremony due to her poor English. The report reads: 'Since that Oscar, Zhang Ziyi *painfully* makes up her mind to seriously learn English' ('One-minute performance on-stage costs four-year hard work off-stage: The secret of learning English of Zhang Ziyi' 2005; my emphasis). Zhang hired an American private tutor to coach her closely almost every day (ibid.). In addition, her agent sent her to suburban New York to learn English. 'Dark Horizon', a movie-centric website, frames speaking 'English as a second language' as the 'toughest challenge' to Zhang (Fischer 2005). In one of its interviews, the actress expresses, 'I've been learning English very hard... Actually, I'm doing a Chinese movie right now in Beijing and just every day I try to find five hours to study outside at the hotel as I just try to learn more' (ibid.). The progress of her English was 'rapid' and she was able to speak proficient English after only one year. *World Film Report's* Shen Jian expressed astonishment at the degree of Zhang's English improvement when they met again. Shen writes, 'In 2001, Zhang's English was still poor. Out of my expectations, in 2002 she can speak fluent English' ('One-minute performance on-stage costs four-year hard work off-stage: The secret of learning English of Zhang Ziyi' 2005). He opines that such rapid English acquisition usually comes at the cost of vast quantities of time and energy. Said so, *Memoirs of a Geisha* becomes a showcase of the result of Zhang's effort:

> Because a long time ago, some friend from the film business who is Chinese, told me that it's impossible to act in a second language because that would be a barrier as you just cannot get into your character deeply enough. But after filming this movie, I have to say that's not true as I felt that I could get into Sayuri's mind. What the person said to me *made me really push the work extra hard* and I think I should thank him of my efforts show in my performance. (Fischer 2005; my emphasis)

Zhang assimilates herself to the linguistically hegemonic culture by learning English. Through attending vigorous language training, Zhang evolves from a monolingual actress to a bilingual international star by neither fate nor fortune but hard work. She is, hence, a telling example of how pain is transformed into triumph (Farquhar 2010a: 181).

In the milieu of cyber-fanfare, user-generated videos and commentary serves as the operative discourse of Zhang Ziyi's story of success. YouTube shows users' recognition of Zhang's improved English. In the category of results under the search 'Zhang Ziyi, interview', the third most-viewed entry 'interview Ziyi Zhang English berlin' uploaded by user 'Wk L' on 14 February 2013 can serve as a telling example of the outcome of Zhang's effort.[6] Garnering 162,734 views, this entry displays Zhang's interview in a different context than the first two most-viewed interviews that centre on *Memoir of a Geisha*. Originally posted on Youku and then copied to YouTube, the clip reveals an interview of Zhang at Berlin International Film Festival, one of the prominent events in the circuit, in 2009 upon the international premiere of her movie *Forever Enthralled* for the competition of the Golden Bear Award. *Forever Enthralled* is a 2008 costume drama directed by Chen Kaige, the fifth-generation Chinese filmmaker who makes *Farewell, My Concubine* fifteen years earlier. His later oeuvre is also a biographical film, followed the life of Mei Lanfang, an eminent Peking opera performer in the 1930s and 1940s. In the film, Zhang plays the role of Meng Xiaodong, Mei's lover. In the YouTube video, which is a one-cut, twelve-minute entry, the camera basically remains static to give a medium-close-up of Zhang throughout the conversation, with only occasional and slight zoom-ins and zoom-outs. The interviewer whose face is never shown asks a range of questions regarding Zhang's training in acting school and experiences of movie-shooting. The questions, too, cover a repertoire of Zhang's movies in China, Asia, and Hollywood, including *The Road Home* (1999), *Crouching Tiger, Hidden Dragon* (2000), *2046* (2004), and *Memoirs of a Geisha* (2005), unfolding the potential reach of her personae and reception beyond origin. Distinctive from Zhang's first interview in English analysed earlier, this interview uncovers Zhang's articulate, well-paced English, which is acknowledged by web users. Led by the male voice of the interview who sounds like a fluent, if not native, English speaker, Zhang, as a Chinese female, does not show a clue of nervousness or indeterminacy. Rather, she is able to provide extensive, level-headed answers with clarity and eloquence. In addition, she offers responses with an impressive range of vocabulary, for example, 'tremendous', 'incredible', and 'thrilled', terms that unlikely appear in her previous interview. Both the re-posting of this clip and the comments testify cyber users' awareness of Zhang's improved English. This video rivets sixteen entries of comments. In such a limited number, about half of it devotes to the aspects of her linguistic articulation whereas the other mainly exhibits general adoration from enchanted fans. User 'cici long' elicits a response in March 2013, 'her grammar improved a lot'. One month later, user 'gryphon50c' proffered a similar opinion, 'wow she's really been working on her English'. The comment given by user 'radiant1020' also reads, 'she's learning english.. great'. In May 2013, user 'Dorothy2295', likewise, expresses, 'her english has gotten really good'. All of these entries of annotation unfold recognition to her articulate appeal, propagating the Asian femininity that is readily imagined and scrutinised by YouTube users.

In addition to the English upgrade, Zhang Ziyi also unveils ambition to extend her profession from onscreen performance to back-screen presence. The discourse of Zhang's assiduousness cements her star status in a visibly proliferating cultural exchange within and outside East Asia (Joo 2007: 84). The increasing significance of pan-Asian co-productions can be considered as a way to counter Hollywood's power in view of its potential economic benefit, compatible to the benefit the US market has provided to Hollywood (Joo 2007: 84, 88). Zhang's self-improvement epitomises regional stardom while her industriousness works to expand the reach of her films and personae. Capitalising on the success of *Crouching Tiger, Hidden Dragon*, Zhang affords a newer and more visible profile in the transnational film scene than other personalities such as Donnie Yen, a Hong Kong action star who co-starred with Zhang in *Hero* (2002), who is virtually anonymous outside the East Asian market (Martin 2014: 27). In 2009, Zhang works as a producer for the romantic comedy *Sophie's Revenge*, a Chinese-Korean collaboration, and its prequel, *My Lucky Star*, in 2013. In 2010, she reveals her plans to produce the film *Snow Flower and the Secret Fan*, an English-language film based on Lisa See's novel of the same title. Unexpectedly, Zhang withdrew from the project. The withdrawal is, as Zhang self-claims, due to a busy schedule whereas a mainland Chinese newspaper unfolds that it is perhaps caused by Zhang's affair with a married man, reiterating her controversial private life (Xie 2010). Moreover, Zhang's improved linguistic skill and aspiration in film helps promote her films internationally. An example is the 2012 Chinese film, *Dangerous Liaisons*, directed by Korean filmmaker Hur Jin-ho, loosely based on the novel of the same title written by Pierre Choderlos de Laclos. The film's multi-ethnic cast comprising of the A-list Hallyu star Jang Dong-gun, Hong Kong movie actress Cecilia Cheung, and Zhang Ziyi, has readily placed the actors' language issue under limelight (Jung 2012). For example, an article of *Korea Joongang Daily* entitled 'Language no barrier to Jang's appeal' discusses Jang Dong-gun's challenge of memorising and speaking the lines in Chinese language (2012). The film was screened in an array of international film festivals in Cannes, Toronto, and Busan (IndieWire 2012; Sunwoo 2012), observing Zhang's capability in handling foreign press. An article in *The Korea Herald* (English version) reported at the press conference of the movie at Busan's Festival includes a photograph capturing a moment where Zhang Ziyi listens conscientiously to a reporter's question (Lee 2012).[7] The instance portrays Zhang as, not a coveted, shallow appearance, but a motivated film talent who establishes a persona in the international film circuitry, competently mapping her career across various geographical and cultural coordinates. Suffice it to say, Zhang's diligence and expertise makes her entry to the alternative film scene in East Asia.

Zhang Ziyi's self-improvement makes her qualified to be a star, as Richard Dyer analyses in his ground-breaking book, *Stars* (1979). Dyer explains that the element of 'hard work and expertise' is one of the four cornerstones of the 'myth of success', alongside the other three, which are the ordinariness as the trademark of the star, the talents and 'specialness' approved by the star system, and the luck that seems to work at random but can characterise one's career (Dyer 1979: 48). Diane Negra (2001), in her discussion of ethnic female stars, also suggests a similar idea of myths of meritocracy, reinvigorated by discourses on hard work and sacrifice (3). Some may attribute Zhang's accomplishment to luck, another pillar of the myth in Dyer's quadric-dimensional postulation – say, working with top talents in the field since the inception of her career. Nevertheless, some fans refute such a view. A biography on a fansite called 'ziyi forever' enthuses, 'With a little luck and a lot of hard work and perseverance, Zhang Ziyi's career has since taken off, making her one of the most successful and popular actors in her native China today and an ever-growing presence and celebrity to watch for on the international stage' ('ziyi forever' n.d.). Recalling, too, a quote of presumably Zhang Ziyi herself on the fansite, 'Except for all the luck, I think I'm quite tough, you know? I just work very hard. I don't care if I get injured. I just keep going.' Zhang demonstrates to and seeks approval from the viewing public that those who cannot work hard to conform to the norms of production and reception in Hollywood are doomed to fail in the professional world of cinema. Her transformation legitimises the fantasy of the resolvable tension between Chinese-speaking stars and Anglophone media culture.

Through establishing her expertise, Zhang Ziyi has demonstrated herself as a lucrative flexible asset that is compelled to accommodate transnational energies and the commercialised global order. Hard work can overcome the notoriety and ignominy that threatens her reputation as an otherwise well-accepted and viable star, packaging her as a favoured commodity for exchange in the global market. Her marketable narrative of self-transformation precisely epitomises the ideology of the rise of China. The columnist Lionel Seah (2001) calls Zhang Ziyi 'China's best export' or 'China's hottest export', portraying her as being sent out by her nation to the world. Consider the 9 May 2005 issue of the internationally known news magazine *Newsweek*, headlined 'China's Century' and featuring Zhang Ziyi on the cover. Obviously, Zhang is not expected to vie in the same category of her Asian American counterparts whose competence of performing is almost equivalent to the white cast. For example, Lucy Liu is famously cast in *Charlie's Angels* (2000) as Angel Alex Munday, alongside two white 'sisters', played by Hollywood's high-paid actresses Cameron Diaz and Drew Barrymore. Enjoying a rapid rise to transnational superstardom, Maggie Q is cast in English-speaking roles in films primed for the international market attributed to her multi-racial background. In her English-language films such as *Mission Impossible III* (2006), Q is co-starred with Tom Cruise for the character of a secret agent, showcasing her physical agility. Albeit that Lucy Liu and Maggie Q impress the audience by speaking as proficiently and performing as professionally as their white counterparts, their personalities are hyper-sexualised and racialised (Funnel 2014: 114–17, 187–9), perpetuating the 'model minority' myth that dominates the history of Asian/Asian American cinematic representation (Hamamoto and Liu 2000: 10; Feng 2002b: 2). Although they may enjoy some threads of linguistically and culturally defined white privilege, their screen personalities, which are the result of the hegemonic strategy employed by Hollywood, do not escape from the stereotyping of Chinese diaspora. Distinctive to Lucy Liu and Maggie Q, Zhang is not precisely in a diasporic position. Rather, Zhang is *situated* (Wang 2014: 29) in a lingua- and cultural-crossing setting, where the boundaries are porous. She negotiates her status through neither naive acceptance nor direct negation but through adoption with diversity. Arguably, Zhang's performance resulted in her determined pursuit of expertise does not show abstract autonomy, nor is it reduced to complete alignment with Anglo-American interpellation. While the global media and web users place Zhang's hard work under the spotlight, the discourses do not abandon her ethno-cultural origin, or her story of success would be irrelevant. In this fashion, Zhang's persona resides in the interstices between China/Asia and Hollywood, the Chinese-speaking and the English-speaking cultures. Her position is embedded in a contingent, capricious context of enunciation, global audience address, and fan interaction. Therefore, Zhang manifests a timely and flexible star persona, which unpacks the possible dynamics of Chinese female stardom in the cyber-global network.

Notes

1. In talking about her preparation for the film, Zhang reveals that she lived with a blind girl for two months before shooting to prepare herself for the role of a blind character. This is what she utters to describe her close observation of the girl.
2. This is her reply to a question about maintaining her figure, Zhang describing herself as a big eater.
3. After its publication, the book was a sensational hit and became the best-seller in the United States (Allison 2001: 381).
4. Available at <https:www.youtube.com/watch?v=LKGqj2dZjnQ> (last accessed 1 August 2017).
5. Available at <https:www.youtube.com/watch?v=tIy7daxL3jY> (last accessed 1 August 2017).
6. Available at <https:www.youtube.com/watch?v=kY3SxFoAHs8> (last accessed 1 August 2017).
7. The exact caption of the photograph is, 'Chinese actress Zhang Ziyi listens to a reporter's question during a press conference promoting her latest film "Dangerous Liaisons" at Centum City Shinsegae in Busan, Friday' (Lee 2012).

Chapter 5

Discussing Takeshi Kaneshiro: the pan-Asian star image on fan forums[1]

The half-Taiwanese, half-Japanese film actor Takeshi Kaneshiro once offered an anecdote regarding his name, 'I feel weird sometimes ... When people call me Mr. Kam, I'm like, who is Mr. Kam? Or they call me Mr. Kim, and I have to remind them that I'm not Korean' (Drake 2003). The varying readings of Kaneshiro's name in disparate regions in Asia reflect his pan-Asian appeal: it is pronounced Kam Shing Mo in Cantonese, Jin Chengwu in Mandarin (written as金城武in Chinese) and Kim Sung Woo in Korean.While it was the success of Wong Kar-wai's *Chungking Express* (1994) that first introduced him to Japanese and international audiences, it is the Japanese form of his name, Takeshi Kaneshiro, which has been most widely circulated. Although the name evokes Japaneseness, it could be considered as a 'misnomer' in that he does not seem as culturally attached to Japan as is often assumed. His face may also easily confuse the public about his ethnic origins, with its seeming mixture of both Eastern and Western facial features (Wang 2001: 92). His star image is notable for a screen cosmopolitanism bridging cultures and regions. He presents himself as a fashion icon, characterised by a rich sense of modernity. As a frequent subject of advertisements and magazine covers, he is often depicted as an introvert yet charismatic urbanite. He has been the target of celebrity endorsement of some huge brands in Europe and Asia, such as Emporio Armani, Prada, CITIZEN, Toyota, Pocari Sweat, Sony, JAA, and, BioTherm, traversing diverse categories of products such as fashion, automobiles, food, telecommunications, airlines, and skincare (Figure 5.1). This cosmopolitan appeal entails a reticent and unobtrusive public persona that leaves space for the audience's imagination. As such, it also suggests a certain degree of universality, enabling his cinematic image to become transnational currency. As a bi-ethnic star, Kaneshiro, therefore, evokes cultural

Figure 5.1 Takeshi Kaneshiro as the subject of celebrity endorsement of CITIZEN in 2012 (source: www.citizen.com.hk)

and symbolic associations that inform and complicate the meanings attributed to transnational stars of Chinese or semi-Chinese heredity.

The emergence of Web 2.0 facilitates the manipulation of Takeshi Kaneshiro's persona not only in films but also in cyber discourse. In cyberspace, fans re-articulate and re-negotiate his bi-ethnic, multi-dimensional appeal with regard to their personal identities and agendas. What aspects of Kaneshiro's star narratives become accessible to cyber users? To what extent does his ethnic identity become a focus of the fan-based exchange? In this chapter, I explore these questions by analysing Kaneshiro as an emblem of pan-Asian star presence on Internet forums. I locate four forums, as embedded in fan sites, and one discussion board as the primary loci for analysis. The justification of the choice of fan forums lies in the more prolific and robust star presence of Kaneshiro and a more interactive fan discourse than that appears on the popular Web 2.0 sites, such as Facebook, Flickr, and YouTube, according to my survey conducted in February 2013. The fan sites, all simply named after the actor, include http:takeshianiki.forumotion.com/, http:www.freewebs. com/takeshikaneshiro/takeng.htm, http:tkfanclub.do.am, and http:www. takeshikaneshiro.org/, which are selected on the basis of degree of user participation and the frequency of updates. In addition to the fan sites, my analysis includes the 'Takeshi Kaneshiro' discussion board at The Internet Movie Database (IMDb) (http:www.imdb.com/name/nm0437580/ board/threads/). As a subsidiary of Amazon, IMDb is a wide-ranging and rapidly growing online database of information pertaining to films, television, video games, production crew personnel, performers, and characters. In terms of traffic, it ranks fifty-seven globally (Alexa n.d.). It is also a substantial database system. Up to June 2017, IMDb contains nearly 4.5 million titles (including episodes) and more than 8 million personalities in its database (IMDb Database Statistics n.d.). The IMDb message boards are among the sites most heavily used areas, allowing users to create and engage in the exchange on the topics that interest them. The 'Takeshi Kaneshiro' IMDb discussion board began in October 2007 and remains active today.

In this chapter, I identify five key themes that cyber fan discourse revolves around to illustrate the polysemic, as Richard Dyer (1979: 3) innovatively terms, star image of Takeshi Kaneshiro, rendering a diversity of meanings and affects in the persona. The themes are: (1) versatile screen performance and the persona's capacity of bridging various cultural audiences; (2) duality of appearance and acting (by comparing with Hollywood actors Johnny Depp and Keanu Reeves); (3) criss-crossing the popular and critical realms (by comparing with Hong Kong actor Tony Leung Chiu-wai); (4) the ambivalent star presence residing between Hong Kong-ese and Japanese; and (5) revival of Kaneshiro's Japanese identity through fans' charity-aimed artworks. By employing these analytical categories, I probe how cyber fans establish, represent, and negotiate Kaneshiro's pan-Asian persona, which oscillates between Chineseness and Japaneseness.

The appeal that sells: Kaneshiro's capacity of bridging various cultural audiences

Takeshi Kaneshiro's transnational star narratives are the vouchers for casting and packaging, plotting the routes of production and consumption of border-crossing personalities. At the age of sixteen, Kaneshiro was signed by a transnational talent agency, Fulong Production Company, which established him as a pop singer and actor in Taiwan and Hong Kong. He was engineered in a boyish, light-hearted image, breaking into the mass culture of pop idols with his record debut in 1992. The Taiwanese press noted the issue of Kaneshiro's mixed identity, but it quickly marginalized the issue as it positioned the actor in parallel to other local pop idols. Together with Jimmy Lin, Nicky Wu, and Alec Su, he formed a boys' group called the Four Little Heavenly Kings ('*Si xiao tianwang*'), named by making a play on the Four Big Heavenly Kings of Hong Kong Cantopop. During that period, Kaneshiro's celebrity image was heavily local, despite the fact that the entertainment business in Taiwan incorporated talents from Hong Kong, Japan, and some overseas communities. In the late 1990s, with the increasing popularity of Japanese dramas on the island, Kaneshiro promoted his music as part of the Japanese drama programming on Star Television, giving his persona a new encoding source that led to a relatively cosmopolitan, confident, and mature image. After *Chungking Express* (1994), Kaneshiro began to work in extra Hong Kong films and then a number of Japanese dramas. In the midst of the rise of Japanese popular culture in Asia, his Japanese works were reimported, elevating him from an adorable local idol to a sexy international star in the eyes of the Hong Kong and Taiwanese press and public. His stardom that inhabits many regimes of historical imaginations and various circuits of cultural production gives merits to the entertainer to demonstrate his commercially valuable persona.

Kaneshiro has performed a diverse range of roles over the course of his career in films, encompassing mainstream genres such as urban action thrillers (*Downtown Torpedoes* (1997); *Sleepless Town* (1998)), romance (*Anna Magdalena* (1998); *Tempting Heart* (1999); *Lavender* (2000); *Turn Left, Turn Right* (2003)), historical epic (*Red Cliff* and *Red Cliff* II (2008 and 2009)), martial arts (*House of Flying Daggers*, (2004)), and science fiction (*Space Travelers* (2000); *Returner* (2002)). In addition, Kaneshiro has appeared in some 'auteur' films such as *Chungking Express* (1994) and *Fallen Angels* (1995). The versatility of Takeshi Kaneshiro's cinematic presence is a common theme in cyber fan discourse. On the fan site of Takeshi Kaneshiro (http:takeshianiki.forumotion.com/), the subforum called 'Takeshi Kaneshiro as an actor' contains a thread on the subject 'discussions of his acting'. A fan called 'Ognyana', one of the active users, offered his/her viewpoint on Kaneshiro's acting style on 29 November 2008:

> By the way, many actors let mannerisms and gestures of their own get into the behavior of their characters. How do I know? Watching films I can see the same gesture repeated, a peculiar way of tossing one's head, etc. What amazes me TK ALMOST NEVER lets this happen. He doesn't repeat himself or his characters. AMAZING! Every role is unique and the best.

In comparing Kaneshiro with other talents, this user discerns Kaneshiro's performance as free of typecasting, able to exhibit unique personalities. In a similar vein, Kaneshiro himself seems to consciously seek distinctness in his roles, once confessing in an interview, 'I don't let myself follow in anyone else's footsteps . . . Let other people do what has been done before. All I want is to do something special' (Drake 2003). 'Not repeating himself' appears to be the crux of Kaneshiro's screen performance.

'Ognyana' makes a parallel point in an earlier thread from the same subforum. On 17 June 2008, she writes:

> As for me, I'm sure that TK [Takeshi Kaneshiro] was great in 'The House of the Flying Daggers', but frankly speaking, I haven't seen a single film with him where his acting is disappointing. He's marvelously different every time, but at the same time in each role he is kind of 'sincere'. Paraphrasing the famous Stanislavsky's quote, 'I do believe'.

Following up on previous threads about *House of Flying Daggers* (2004), this user praises Kaneshiro's performance as versatile and spirited and is marked by variation rather than by mundane uniformity.[2] This comment echoes Kaneshiro's own in regard to *House of the Flying Daggers* in an interview: 'I would like to try out many kinds of films but I don't think that there are a lot of parts for me in certain movies particularly in Hollywood.' This rejoinder was appropriated and uploaded on an entry entitled 'House of Flying Daggers', on an unofficial fan site of Takeshi Kaneshiro by the user 'butterfly' in August 2006. Kaneshiro's answer unmistakably unveils his awareness of significance of conveying a versatile screen personality. It also alludes to the Asian orientation of his acting career.

In the same thread, 'Ognyana' also quotes from Constantin Stanislavski, a Russian actor and theatre director, who developed Method acting, a system based on the naturalistic movement, and described Kaneshiro's acting as 'sincere', corresponding precisely to Stanislavski's advocacy of 'essential notions of the human spirit' (18). According to Kaneshiro's profile, he in fact did not receive formal training in acting. His performance style belongs to neither naturalistic acting nor Method acting, the two models dominating the philosophy of performance. Yet he, as an actor, can 'live the part' (Stanislavski 1991: 18), conveying depth and unveiling the spiritual life and inner life of a distinctive array of characters. Despite Kaneshiro's lack of acting training, 'Ognyana' continues:

> I've been looking for films with his participation, and here in Russia I've found 'Chung King Express', 'Fallen Angels', 'Downtown Torpedoes', 'Ritana', 'House of Flying Daggers', and 'The Warlords'.

> Through channels of my own I've also found 'Lavender' in Chinese
> with English subtitles.
>> It's even difficult to say where he is best. Everywhere.

Here he or she refers to his/her location in Russia, confirming what his/her names already suggested about his/her ancestry as well as her gender: 'Ognyana' is a feminine Bulgarian personal name ('Behind the Name: Ognyana' n.d.). Therefore, we can assume that this user comes from, or identifies him/herself as a member of, European Russia and/or its cultural sphere. In addition to North America and Europe, Russia is included in the overseas distribution networks for Kaneshiro's films. Among the films the user mentions, only *House of Flying Daggers* and *Returner* are available to theatre-goers, according to the IMDb website.[3] Presumably, the user's comment refers to the availability of Kaneshiro's films (except *Lavender*) in Russia's DVD markets, reflecting the growing importance of movie delivery through new media devices such as DVDs and the Internet, as supplementary to the limited cinematic screening in Russia. Furthermore, the movies listed here are productions of various origins (Hong Kong, Japan, and the PRC) and languages (Cantonese, Japanese, and Mandarin). They, by and large, are well-known in international commercial and critical circles, corroborating Kaneshiro's transnational star appeal.

'Ognyana' ends the post by quoting several lines of lyrics from Vladimir Vysotsky, a Soviet singer, songwriter, actor, and poet:

> As Vladimir Vysotsky once wrote,
> In these days, too, the poets
> Walk on razors barefoot
> And – slash to ribbons
> naked hearts and souls

This song is called 'On Fatal Days and Figures', and it was composed in 1971 by Vysotsky, an influential singer in Russian popular culture, gaining his fame in the 1960s. Coined as 'voice for the heart of a nation', the poet-singer develops unique singing styles and thought-provoking lyrics as his signature ('Vladimir Vysotsky: the official site' n.d.). He is, furthermore, remembered for his intrepid confrontational stance against institutions and the government. His works was largely ignored by the official Soviet cultural establishment that his music was banned at the national radio station and his poems were barred from publication (Jaffé 2012: 301). He becomes an icon of defiance and the youth rebellion that swept the world in his era. The inclusion of Vysotsky's song in 'Ognyana's' post may reflect her recognition with the youth spirit and the countercultural predilection disseminated in popular culture. The post-Soviet Russia has opened up to the West as well as to the Western cultural practices since the1990s (Tsipursky n.d.), and, through globalisation, has been exposed to the Asian film culture as well. Here 'Ognyana' has put together Kaneshiro's acting and a Russian popular song, hybridising Russian culture and Asian film culture and, thus, demonstrating the cross-cultural potential that Kaneshiro's image entails. Although without addressing Kaneshiro's bi-ethnic status, she frames Kaneshiro's Asian cinematic presence with shades of Russian balladry, creating a culturally diversified star text of Kaneshiro that extends beyond his already-transnational appeal. Fandom 'offers ways of filling cultural lack and provides the social prestige and self-esteem that go with cultural capital' (Fiske 1992: 33). Therefore, 'Ognyana's' diction not only displays her cultural capital, but also indicates the convergence of the Westernised Russian pop culture and globalised Asian film culture, testifying to the potential of Kaneshiro's image to bridge and sell to various national and cultural audiences.

Good looks and bad acting? The duality of appearance and talent

In Takeshi Kaneshiro's stardom, considerable fans' gaze rests on the issue of 'how he looks' more noticeably than 'how he acts', uncovering the dialectics of appearance and talent. As appearance is one of the core dimensions of Kaneshiro's screen image, the fans' impressions of his looks not only reflect the impact of stardom on the public – the awe, adoration, and ecstasy – but also shapes his presence in which his star power rests, similar to how Carmel Giarratana discusses Keanu Reeves (2002: 68). For some film actors and actresses, the display of physical beauty can attain the level of dramatic impact, too. This corresponds to what Michaela Krützen argues, 'The basis of the work of a film performer is appearance [rather than performance]' (1992: 94).

Beauty is 'an element of the surface splendor of the star' (15), and the affinity of film for representing beauty, together with the technical possibility of close-ups, formulates and exhibits that splendour. Film becomes 'the representative form for Beauty' (v). In this light, Krützen has identified a close link between human beauty and the particularities of the film medium. Film, defining itself as an art form, becomes more proper than any other medium in visually representing physical reality (4). Put another way, the shaping of the star construct is achieved through features inherent in the film medium itself (ibid.). The cinematography of Kaneshiro's films often clearly emphasises the actor's attractive face. For example, Johnnie To's *Turn Left, Turn Right* provides numerous scenes of prolonged close-ups and medium close-ups of both protagonists: to cite a few, the opening rainy scene, the first re-encounter in the park, the recorded telephone conversation before their assumed departure of Taipei, and the futile hide-and-seek scene in the city centre. Krützen observes, 'By means of the close-up, the human face acquires new and special meaning' (ibid.). Johnnie To exhausts the capacity of close-ups to reveal physical reality in great detail. The repetitive use of close-ups not only shows Kaneshiro's facial expressions as part of his performance but also, and equally importantly, strategises the cinematic display of his physical beauty.

Takeshi Kaneshiro's photogenic face is a constant object of the camera. His thick eyebrows, oval-shaped eyes, straight nose, and thin lips, which constitute his superbly chiseled facial features, becomes a key point of visual interest that carries weight in the imagery and narrative space of cinematic representation. Take *Tempting Heart* (1999) as an instance. Framed in discontinuities and multiple layers, the narrative is a romantic tale revolving around a couple of 1970s high-school sweethearts (played by Takeshi Kaneshiro and Gigi Leung, a Hong Kong actress and Cantopop singer famous for her beautiful face and model-like figure) who re-encounter each other in their middle ages. Oftentimes, the camera rests on their faces, capturing subtle facial expressions that are crucial in triggering emotions (Figure 5.2). Their nearly perfect prettiness makes real for the audience the predictable teen and adult romance narrative, inviting their identification. The cinematographic focus on the beauty of the actors unfolds the power of the star presence – the power of the display of physical beauty to facilitate a dramatic act. This presence corresponds to Krützen's (1992: v) description of Greta Garbo's 'non-acting', and to film critic Shelley Kraicer's review of Kaneshiro's performance in *Tempting Heart* – 'at his least expressive' (1999). With respect to the 'non-acting' or 'least expressive' performance, these films allow Kaneshiro to 'look good' rather than to 'act well'.

Figure 5.2 The camera focuses on the 'beautiful' faces of Takeshi Kaneshiro and Gigi Leung in *Tempting Heart* (1999)

A longstanding notion reveals that good looks and convincing acting are two contrasting strands of star presence. Stars who look handsome tend to be interpreted as poor in acting skills, and vice versa. This tension is a major theme in Takeshi Kaneshiro's star phenomenon, attracting media and public attention. The actor has once expressed, 'Even today, the media still like to put a lot of emphasis on my appearance . . . Sometimes, I feel as if my looks have overshadowed my performance and the hard work I put into my characters. They can be an obstacle for me' (SCMP 2008). An evident part of Kaneshiro's fans' cyber-discourse positions him as a celebrity star rather than as a serious star. Consider a fan site established under the name of Takeshi Kaneshiro, http:takeshianiki.forumotion. com/. The subforum 'fan art' features users' creative works relevant to the actor, including pictures, poetry, short stories, and song lyrics, expressing adoration and thoughts. A piece of poetry under the thread title 'new verse for TK' indicates the focus on Kaneshiro's physical appearance. Uploaded on 4 August 2008 by the user 'mikomijade', the poem reads:

> Thy smile makes need of no light shining
> For this is smile of the most beautiful of men.
> When you do that I need no sunshine smiling:
> I only disappear in thee forever and again.

'mikomijade' adopts a couple of archaic English words, 'thy' and 'thee', that are equivalent to 'your' and 'you' in contemporary English. The use of 'I' and 'you' implies a conversation between him/her and Kaneshiro, attempting to demonstrate a direct, close star–fan relationship. In some sense this type of cyber text substitutes for the traditional form of fans' letters to stars, personally expressing and, concomitantly, publicising fans' identification with the idol in the electronically mediated space. In this poem, the star's smile is portrayed as powerful and passionate enough to replace sunlight, proffering warmth and contentment to this user. This vividly signifies the charisma of Kaneshiro, 'the most beautiful of men' in 'mikomijade's' phrase.

Cyber-fan discourse further recognises Takeshi Kaneshiro's enormous visual appeal by paralleling him with certain Hollywood actors who are famous for their good looks. On the IMDb discussion board, under the thread topic 'This guy is the asian Keanu Reeves', user 'Sophitia36' praises Kaneshiro's matinee-idol look in the context of arguing against the assumption that charismatic young actors must have provided soulless acting. His/Her comment demonstrates familiarity with both Hollywood and Asian cinemas. On 7 April 2010, he or she writes:

> I truly believe that being gorgeous (I'm making a difference here between handsome and gorgeous, I think Kaneshiro and Depp both qualify for the latter category), while being a huge advantage in the film business, is also a big obstacle when it comes to critical recognition. Being too beautiful just seems to make you suspect. It makes people jealous, and they denigrate your talent, and assume your looks are all you've got. Of course it doesn't help when you have an array of silly fangirls to make you look even less credible.

Here Takeshi Kaneshiro is compared with Johnny Depp (dissonance to the thread topic that proves the flexibility and openness of cyber texts), one of the most bankable actors in Hollywood. Beginning his acting career in television in 1987, Depp acquired the image of a popular teen idol. He then moved to film and gained his best-recalled picture personalities in *Edward Scissorhands* (1990), *Charlie and the Chocolate Factory* (2005), and *Sweeney Todd* (2007), created by his long-collaborating director, Tim Burton. His role as Captain Jack Sparrow in *Pirates of the Caribbean: The Curse of the Black Pearl* (2003) also impressed fans of Disney's big-budget adventure fantasy films. While the public generally acknowledges his acting technique in the eclectic roles he plays, Depp also relies heavily on his appearance in constructing his persona, proven by the accolade of being selected as 'the Sexiest Man Alive' in 2003 and 2009 by *People* magazine. His screen-idol image is the suggestive mark of his claimed Native American inheritance, too. In an interview with *Entertainment Weekly*, Depp talked about his great-grandmother who grew up Cherokee or Creek Indian, without concealing his pride regarding his possible Indian lineage (Breznican 2001). Like Kaneshiro, Depp's racially equivocal, attractive appearance functions to interrogate his position as a serious actor and a mere celebrity star.

In the quoted thread, the user 'Sophitia36' points out a disadvantage of being 'gorgeous', namely critical neglect of one's acting talent. While 'Sophitia36' recognises the marketing advantage of having considerable 'handsomeness', he or she also articulates the 'obstacles' it poses. Another user, 'jordamarks1', writes, in February 2010, that many people 'accuse' Kaneshiro of being a terrible actor because he has such modest yet delicate facial composition. In saying that 'being too beautiful' may lead to an assumption of shallow performance, 'Sophitia36' implies that Kaneshiro and Depp are actually talented actors whose acting skills are conveniently denied, ignored, or maligned by viewers. His/Her opinion defies any perceived correlation between good look and bad acting.

Similarly, certain scholars defend against the claim about the superficiality and lack of worth associated with a star's appearance. Michaela Krützen (1992) argues that the surface functions as the shell of the centre, of the vital reflection that can tread through and beyond the surface itself. Always being merely 'a totality of edge points' (285), the surface shows minuscule solidifications, yet is a venue where 'film finds medial fulfillment in the depiction of the external – the cinema seems to come into its own when it clings to the surface of things' (quoted in Krützen 1992: 285). Charles Affron (1991), likewise, argues that the primary function of some stars is the embodiment of frivolity: 'An almost total absence of analytical approaches to screen acting reflect the belief that screen acting is nothing more than the beautiful projection of a filmic self, an arrangement of features and body, the disposition of superficial elements' (92). These arguments intriguingly suggest that the foundation of the actor's work is not performance but appearance (94). In this sense, Takeshi Kaneshiro's stardom is by no means diminished by his mesmerising countenance.

Although Takeshi Kaneshiro's acting may not seem convincing to everybody, his performance is sufficient to generate satisfactory box-office returns. In the 1990s and early 2000s, a series of Hong Kong productions starring Kaneshiro achieved quite remarkably in the domestic box-office record. For example, *Downtown Torpedoes* (1997) grossed nearly HKD 12 million, *Tempting Heart* (1999) almost HKD 12.5 million, and *Lavender*

(2000) approximately HKD 14.5 million ('The annals of box office of Hong Kong Films 1969–2016' 2016). Since the mid-2000s, a number of Hong Kong-based, Asian co-produced films such as *House of Flying Daggers* (2004), *Confession of Pain* (2006), *The Warlords* (2007), *Perhaps Love* (2005), and *Red Cliff I* and *II* (2008 and 2009) have generated vast revenues, with box-office sales from mainland China being particularly noteworthy.[4] This bankability of his celluloid image may compensate for his allegedly bad acting technique, securing his stardom in Hong Kong and Asian film industries.

Takeshi Kaneshiro is often compared with Hollywood actor Keanu Reeves, whose image is marked by lack of acting skill and his ambivalent ethnicity. Like Kaneshiro, Keanu Reeves receives both praise for his handsome look and critical reception for his roles of minuscule density. Reeves is well known for his exuberant physicality and racially hybrid charisma and Carmel Giarratana (2002) argues that it is Reeves' performance of beauty rather than the act of performance that seem most attractive to directors. Reeves began his acting career in Hollywood in the 1980s. Besides his early minor roles, he manages to give a convincing performance in a diversity of early roles like the clown in *Bill and Ted's Excellent Adventure* (1989), an angst-laden adolescent in *River's Edge* (1987) and *My Own Private Idaho* (1991). *The New York Times'* critic has also lauded him as able to 'display considerable discipline and range' (Maslin 1991). Yet not until the 1994 action-adventure film *Speed* (1994) did Reeves first become famous, and it was his subsequent appearance as Neo in the sci-fi *The Matrix* trilogy (1999, 2003, 2003) that continued to showcase his allure to both American and international audiences. Notwithstanding his meteoric rise in stardom, many critics and viewers have assessed him as possessing 'no real acting range' (Giarratana 2002: 67). In a blunter manner, Karen Schneider, in her *People's* article 'Much Ado in Keanu' (1995), describes Reeves' celerity and star quality as 'unlikely'. Reeves' 'acting inability' has made his stunning success in film a topic of debate and bewilderment. One may ask why then do audiences still wish to see him? Schneider continues in her critique, 'Reeves's acting style – a detached deadpan somewhere between artful and awful – has never been the primary reason for his success . . . Three reasons why Reeves may be the biggest thing to happen to Brooding Boys since James Dean: beautiful dark, brown eyes, perfect white teeth – and a soul that whispers the blues' (Schneider 1995). Schneider's argument here particularly points to the counter-hegemonic screen masculinity that Reeves embodies that domesticated, sensitive and ethnically diverse. This also draws our attention to Reeves's multi-racial lineage, of which Giarratana (2002) has associated with the celebrity image, in addition to the 'good looks and poor acting' dialectics. Born in Beirut to a family whose mother is English and father an American of mixed Native Hawaiian, Chinese, English, Irish, and Portuguese roots (69), Reeves bears his ethnoracial identity, which is not so easily identified, although he is Canadian by nationality. His co-star in *Speed* (1994), Sandra Bullock, once commented, 'Everything about him is laced with mystery – that's his charm' (quoted in Bassom 2006: 74). Not a few esteemed critics and film theorists have been caught up in the actor's 'mystery' and still seem mystified (Giarratana 2002: 72).

As much as Giarratana suggests at Reeves's multiracial-based 'mysterious' image, Hong Kong filmmaker Johnnie To made a similar observation about Takeshi Kaneshiro's image. Through his collaboration with Kaneshiro in *Turn Left, Turn Right* (2003), To comments on the actor's screen appeal and personal magnetism: '[Kaneshiro is] mysterious ... He doesn't belong to Hong Kong, Taiwan or anywhere' (Drake 2003). To identifies perhaps the most intriguing part of Takeshi Kaneshiro's stardom: the absence of belonging to a specific location or place and a border-crossing capacity. This precisely explains a kind of indeterminate and, in Drake's term, 'unpredictable' quality (2003) of Kaneshiro's image that casts a vital challenge in analysing the star text (Tsai 2005: 103).

Reeves's fame is evident of the decentring of a purist Anglo-American whiteness as the passport to Hollywood A-list male stardom (Everett 2014: 240). His 'slippage' relationship to racial 'purity' (Nishime 2008: 292) and 'malleable features' (ibid.) are what filmmakers find well-suited for constructing certain personae. In 1993, for example, Italian director Bernardo Bertolucci, who has given the allegedly Orientalist portrayal in the earlier *The Last Emperor* (1987) and *The Sheltering Sky* (1990), has made a big-budget epic *Little Buddha*, starring Reeves in the character of Prince Siddhartha who evolves to become the Buddha or the Enlightened One. Film critic Janet Maslin (1991) described Reeves as 'truly a thing of beauty' with the portrayal in the movie '[b]ronzed, painted and bejeweled, with a head covered with luxuriant ringlets'. Reeves incarnates a sort of new exoticism that makes him 'the new face of globalisation' according to the March 2006 issue of *Wired* (Deveraux 2006: 303). Reeves's success proves the era's expanding global media audiences and their increasing fascination with non-white stars and multi-racial celebrity (Everett 2004:

237–8). Said so, it does not mean that the progressive development of the mixed-race heroic representation completely overrides the normative discourse of the representation of race. Leilani Nishime (2008) has called for our awareness that, to many critics and viewers, Reeves's 'Neo's destined to save, and lead the battle against the machines because of his whiteness' (293). Along a similar thread, Reeves reportedly describes himself as white whereas some Asian-American audiences identify him as an Asian American passing as white (Feng 2002: 155).

Reeves's instance of 'passing' can provide some clues for the 'spectatorial perception' of Kaneshiro's screen persona and his ambiguous identity, although some important differences should be acknowledged. First, Kaneshiro is not multi-racial; rather, he is bi-ethnic, having both Japanese and Taiwanese (Chinese) descent. Second, most Hong Kong viewers are themselves Chinese, an ethnicity partly shared by Kaneshiro; his 'passing' is a cultural rather than a racial one, partly illustrated by his accent. Similar to Reeves in Hollywood, Kaneshiro is so well assimilated into Hong Kong's film industry that the linguistic discrepancy is put aside. Interestingly enough, Hong Kong filmmakers do not mind featuring him in roles that require him to speak Cantonese, underscoring the degree of assimilation. *Chungking Express* (1994), *Fallen Angels* (1995), *Lost and Found* (1996), *Downtown Torpedoes* (1997) and *Anna Magdalena* (1998) are some examples. Echoing Peter X. Feng's (2002) argument, audiences who are Cantonese speakers accept Kaneshiro as 'Cantonese' in the sense that they notice yet tolerate the actor's accented Cantonese. Media often note his multilingualism as a speaker of Japanese, Taiwanese, and Mandarin, but rarely include Cantonese on the list, as his Cantonese articulation sounds far from authentic. Nonetheless, Hong Kong audiences do not seem to mind accepting Cop #223 talking over the phone in accented Cantonese in *Chungking Express*, or the smart Jackal negotiating with the 'G team' in broken Cantonese about the plot to steal printing plates from a secured area in *Downtown Torpedoes*, or the local neighborhood piano tuner Chan Kar-fu narrating the fantasy from his pulp novel 'XO Pair' with an 'inaccurate' Cantonese accent in *Anna Magdalena*. Hong Kong audience's reading of Kaneshiro's ethnic identity resonates with Nella Larsen's 1929 classic, *Passing*: 'We disapprove of it and at the same time condone it', quoted by Elaine Ginsberg (1996: 9).

Takeshi Kaneshiro's cinematic assimilation through his accented persona is further corroborated by 'WU XIA – SentieriSelvaggi meets Peter Ho-sun Chan' (2011) that such a persona serves as a contending plane of his appearance and acting. In this film, Kaneshiro plays the role of an eccentric detective called Xu Baijiu who is obsessed with seeking the truth behind the murder and the real identity of the paper-maker Liu Jinxi (Donnie Yen). In an interview with Chan ('WU XIA – Sentier-iSelvaggi meets Peter Ho-sun Chan' 2011), the director confessed that Xu is, in fact, not a character well suited for a good-looking actor like Kaneshiro to perform. Instead, it is more like the roles played by Takeshi Kitano, a Japanese actor-director who is famous for his idiosyncratic, deadpan cinematic works and performance style. A making-of video circulated on YouTube elaborates in detail Kaneshiro's performance in the film ('《武俠》花絮 – 金城武篇 Wu Xia – Making Of (Takeshi Kaneshiro)' 2011). As the clip reveals, the character of Xu goes beyond the type of roles that Kaneshiro used to play. Kaneshiro strove to explore the interiority and complexity of the character so that during the process of filming, he kept questioning Chan about the parts of the screenplay related to Xu. In order to highlight the peculiarity and the exoticism of the character, as Chan recalls, Kaneshiro one day proposed to him that Xu speak in dialect (Sichuan) rather than Mandarin. The linguistic tactic of applying a different language to the role to make it appear more convincing reinforces the limits to personification imposed by Kaneshiro's good looks. On the set, furthermore, the director asked a crew member from Sichuan to coach Kaneshiro on the accent. As Kaneshiro confessed in an interview with TVB, a Hong Kong television channel, speaking another dialect of Chinese becomes a challenge for him and his Sichuan dialect is far from fully authentic. But, interestingly, audiences and critics seldom criticise Kaneshiro's accent. Compare to the case of Zhang Ziyi speaking English, yet the public seems more tolerant of Kaneshiro's inauthentic dialect. Could this be attributable to gender, with audiences tending to be kinder to male than female stars? Is it perhaps a matter of public image with Zhang's relative notoriety inviting gossips and controversy while Kaneshiro's more agreeable image placates audiences? Might the perceived identity stakes be lower for a Japanese-Taiwanese speaking a Chinese dialect than for a Chinese speaking English? These questions warrant future exploration.

In a nutshell, comparing Takeshi Kaneshiro with Hollywood counterparts who are not purely white also underscores the transnational yet ethnic status of Kaneshiro. Such comparison appears in both critical and popular English-language discourses with labels of Kaneshiro like 'the Asian film industry's Johnny Depp' and 'the Asian Keanu Reeves'

(Drake 2003). His protean good look and sinuous physique embody a kind of racialised masculinity, making him an unintimidating Other to the Hollywood stars as objects of fantasy. While Kaneshiro's allure, choice of roles, and romantic chemistry with female counterparts draw parallels to white American actors like Depp and Reeves, his ethnicity still positions him in a fundamentally disparate category from the hegemonic white-star discourses. Such parallels elevate Kaneshiro's stardom to a global level yet place him explicitly in an ethnic category, thus reinforcing the paradigm of Asian masculinity Kaneshiro incarnates.

Straddling the commercial cinema and the festival circuit: the Takeshi–Tony duo

Takeshi Kaneshiro's debatable acting skill makes him an intriguing co-star to Tony Leung Chiu-wai, who holds general acclaim for his talent in acting. The screen collaboration of the two stars prominently figures in *Chungking Express* (1994), *Confession of Pain* (2006), and the *Red Cliff* series (2008 and 2009). Both of them have engineered personae distinct from the classic filmic paradigm of Chinese masculinity, which emphasises virility, invulnerability, and physical toughness. Their subtle, reticent, and versatile screen personalities present alternative star personae from other transnational Chinese stars such as Jackie Chan, Jet Li, and Chow Yun-fat. Even their performance in martial arts films appears to be passive and sometimes hesitant, conveying romantic melancholia instead of macho agility. Consider *Hero* (2002) and *House of Flying Daggers* (2004), both Zhang Yimou movies, as examples. In *Hero*, Tony Leung plays the role of a swordsman-cum-calligraphy master named Broken Sword. He is an assassin who is capable of approaching the emperor and killing hundreds of guards in the palace. However, as an anti-imperialist revolutionary, he embodies a kind of pacifism, making his masculine image ambivalent. In *House of Flying Daggers*, Takeshi Kaneshiro plays a police captain called Jin who is trapped in a love triangle with Mei (Zhang Ziyi) and Leo (Andy Lau). Initially, Jin is aggressive in his love toward Mei but becomes hesitant, especially after his knowledge of Mei's underground romance with Leo. The closure of the plot portrays Jin as a poignant lover in the loss of Mei. Jin is disparate from the conventional masculine image of heroes. Instead of emphasising the physical prowess, both films underline the emotional expressions of the roles, deploying facets of the actors' complex star personae.

With the sensitive, gentle masculinity they incarnate, both actors carry a foothold in both commercial cinema and the festival circuit, engineering a versatile, cosmopolitan personality. Beginning his acting career in Hong Kong television in the early 1980s, Tony Leung is famous for his reticent yet profound acting style that transcends standard acting protocols and adapts well to 'transnational circulation' (Gallagher 2010: 108). The limited dialogue, monologues in voice-over, and acting through body language and facial expression convey an onscreen personality readily comprehended by audiences across different cultures. Since the late 1980s, his screen presence encompasses a broad array of dramatic roles in films of internationally acclaimed auteurs in Western critical circles, for example, the Taiwanese New Cinema's Hou Hsiao-Hsien for *A City of Sadness* (1989) and *Flowers of Shanghai* (1998), Vietnam's Tran An Hung for *Cyclo* (1995), Hong Kong's Wong Kar-wai for *Chungking Express* (1994), *Ashes of Time* (1994), *Happy Together* (1997), *In the Mood for Love* (2000), *2046* (2004), and *The Grandmaster* (2013), the Taiwanese-American Ang Lee for *Lust, Caution* (2007), and PRC's Zhang Yimou's *Hero* (2002). Leung's performance in these films riveted the attention of festival programmers and art-house cinephiles. Throughout the years, Leung retained his art-house currency, notwithstanding his infrequent forays into Hong Kong and Asian mainstream productions like *Tokyo Raider* (2000), *Fighting for Love* (2001), *Chinese Odyssey 2002* (2002), the *Infernal Affairs* trilogy (2002 and 2003), and *Confession of Pain* (2006). Likewise, Takeshi Kaneshiro's diverse characters have also straddled both the commercial cinema and festival circuits. He plays the roles that fit readily into an array of multiple mainstream genres such as urban action thrillers (*Downtown Torpedoes* (1997); *Sleepless Town* (1998)), romance ((*Anna Magdalena* (1998); *Tempting Heart* (1999); *Lavender* (2000); *Turn Left, Turn Right* (2003)) and science fiction (*Space Travelers* (2000); *Returner* (2002)). In addition, many of Kaneshiro's films have had premieres and screenings at various film festivals; for example, *House of Flying Daggers*, *Red Cliff* and *Wu Xia* at the most well-known, Cannes; *Confession of Pain* at the film festivals in Seattle, Philadelphia, and Stockholm; *Temping Heart* at the World Film Festival in Bangkok and *The Warlords* at the film festivals in San Francisco and Stockholm. Both actors steer the twin vehicles of the star texts in mainstream genres and on the art-house circuit that validates their adaptable, polysemic screen personae.

The casting for the role of Zhuge Liang in *Red Cliff* (2008) further illustrates the resemblance between the screen personalities of Tony

Leung and Takeshi Kaneshiro. The Guangdong-born, Hollywood-based director John Woo returned to his homeland to take charge of this historical epic war movie series, *Red Cliff* I and II (2008 and 2009) after sixteen years in America. Referencing the beloved and familiar Chinese novel, *Romance of the Three Kingdoms*, the movie is set in a turbulent epoch in China's warlord history, spanning the collapse of the Han Dynasty and its aftermath. China was split into three major kingdoms led by Cao Cao (Zhang Fengyi), Liu Bei (Yong You), and Sun Quan (Chang Chen). Takeshi Kaneshiro plays the role of Zhuge Liang, the chief military strategist in Liu's leadership, while Tony Leung takes the character of Zhou Yu, Sun Quan's most trusted advisor. Rather than championing only the Zhuge Liang character, Woo also portrays Zhou Yu as an ideal heroic figure who has musical talent and humility, albeit with a mean-spirited personality in the novel version. Both the Zhuge Liang and Zhou Yu characters embody a fair balance of fighting strategy and intellect that speculate proximity in personification. An anecdote about the casting foreshadows such proximity. Media trivia have revealed that John Woo originally cast Chow Yun-fat and Tony Leung, but both of them then announced their departure from the project. Leung later returned to acquire Chow's role while Kaneshiro joined the cast to take over the role vacated by Leung (Jingles 2015). This 'musical chairs' casting indicates that Tony Leung and Takeshi Kaneshiro present similar versions of Chinese male personae and star image, albeit it is Leung who takes the more central role in the film, competent at conveying the rigour and fascination of the character.

Despite the parallel screen image of the two talents, it has been widely perceived that the acting of Leung seems more convincing than that of Kaneshiro. Consider *Confession of Pain* (2006), a character-driven film where the performance of the main actors carries gravity in conveying the plot and the themes. This urban crime thriller portrays a murder investigation story exploring how the injustice and absurdity of life changes people. The cop-turned-private-eye, Bong (Kaneshiro), investigates the death of Chow, the father-in-law of Hei (Leung), his former boss, and eventually discovers that the murderer is Hei. Taking the role of antagonist, Tony Leung has a complex performance as a masquerade killer. Besides the suspense of the investigation, the narrative is marked by a lengthy, philosophical conversation between the protagonists. The camera noticeably shows more close-ups of Leung than Kaneshiro, exposing the profundity of his gaze and sophisticated facial expressions. Take the hospital conversation scene in which Bong reveals the truth of the murder as an example. Lasting more than seven minutes, the dialogue takes place on the outdoor balcony of the medical institution where Hei's dying wife is hospitalised. Bong begins by unfolding the story of the orphan Keung whose family was killed by Chow and his butler two decades ago. The narration is intercut with flashback segments of Keung's childhood experience. Although it is Bong who narrates, Hei becomes the centre of the camera lens; every fleeting expression of his sombre face is captured by medium close-ups and close-ups. As Bong uncovers Hei's real identity, as the orphan Keung, Hei shows restrained surprise yet with subtlety and solemnity, confessing his family trauma and emotional pain. The posture of each character also affects the degree of exposure of his acting technique. Whereas Bong leans forward with his face down, Hei sits relatively straight, leaving his facial expressions visible to the viewers. In this gritty nihilistic thriller, Tony Leung's performance is more effective than Takeshi Kaneshiro's in delivering psychological tension and ecstasies. He employs a range of facial expressions best captured in medium shots and close-ups (Gallagher 2010: 100). In contrast to Leung, Kaneshiro plays a somewhat clichéd role as an alcoholic private investigator. Although he suffers from the loss of his wife, potentially providing sufficient material to work with, Kaneshiro fails to compellingly demonstrate what feelings he has for his wife and what consequences the pain of loss has for him, perhaps due to the chaotic narrative and unpersuasive editing.

Some online chatter also perceives disparities in the acting skills of Tony Leung and Takeshi Kaneshiro. The forum 'Takeshi Forum', embedded in the fan site takeshi-kaneshiro.com, encompasses a number of subforums and one of them is themed as 'Chinese Space'. Copious threads concerning Tony Leung and his filmic performance appear under the subject 'Re: tony leung'. On 5 March 2005, the forum administrator, presumably a female residing in southern California, posted:

> He is like . . . widely accepted as one of the best actors or something. His fan base is perhaps larger than Takeshi . . . I mean most people (especially females) love Takeshi for his looks not that he isn't a good actor but Tony is known for being one of the best actors around and good-looking too. I personally am not a fan of Tony, but I know a hell lot of people (guys and girls; Asian and non-Asian) that are his die-hard fans.
>
> Tony won 'best actor' in Cannes in 2003 (the year could be off . . . I don't remember exactly which year) for 'In the mood for love'.

This user compares the acting skills of the two stars, implying that Tony Leung is the better actor of the two. She characterises Leung as 'one of the best actors', citing his Cannes award to validate her stance. According to this user, Leung also displays solid star power by possessing both tremendous visual appeal and professional acting capacity. She strongly suggests that her affection for Kaneshiro is due more to his appearance than his acting. For her, Takeshi Kaneshiro occupies an ambiguous middle ground between the entertaining films and serious films, rather than being affirmed by his footing in the art-house arena that is often perceived as demanding greater profundity in acting.

Perhaps the 'good looks' argument can also explain why Takeshi Kaneshiro often takes supporting roles in films involving other major actors. *Confession of Pain* (2006), *The Warlords* (2007), and *Wu Xia* (2011) are examples. In these films, the primary roles are played by male stars who either can act more persuasively or have an image better suited to conveying macho, gallant hyper-masculinity. In *Confession of Pain*, Tony Leung receives the primary role to exhibit his commendable acting techniques. *The Warlords* is a heroic tale of brotherhood in times of war and political upheaval. As one of the three co-stars, Kaneshiro plays the character of the youngest brother while the characters of Jet Li and Andy Lau, the elder brothers, embody a more valiant maleness and potency. To a certain extent, Kaneshiro's aura of innocence and lean physique are limiting here. In *Wu Xia*, his secondary status to Donnie Yen is due to his inferior martial arts physique and dexterity. By contrast, for the romance films, which demand the hero be handsome-looking enough to play the heroine's 'Romeo', Kaneshiro receives leading roles. These roles do not require tremendous manly quality, but a subtlety and gentleness that Kaneshiro's refined image can afford. The exceptions to these trends are *Sleepless Town* (1998), *Space Travelers* (2000), *Returner* (2002), and *K-20: Legend of the Mask* (2008), where Kaneshiro was selected to play the lead. All of these films are Japanese productions that capitalise on Kaneshiro's Japanese ancestry, indicating the power of an established star image to delimit the characters one may personify.

Neither Hong Kong-ese nor Japanese: the ambivalent Asian star space

While Kaneshiro's racially wooly appeal interests some web users, it appears to be culturally evasive to some others. Certain fans assert that Kaneshiro lacks a clear identity foothold as either from Hong Kong or Japan specifically. On the IMDb discussion board, the user 'vampypiano' posted a comment on 12 June 2010 that pinpoints this issue. The subject of the thread is 'This guy is the asian Keanu Reeves' (suggesting at the racial ambiguity shared by both Reeves and Kaneshiro) and the comment reads:

> It probably also doesn't help that he isn't the ambitious sort, seeing that he doesn't do a lot of movies and he doesn't pick particularly challenging roles to prove himself as an actor. Xenophobia may not be an issue, but you have to take note that he doesn't just stick to HK films. He will take a break every year or so to do the Japanese roles, most of them being the quirky types. So he's never really a HK actor in HongKongers' eyes and he's never really a Japanese actor in the Japanese's eyes.

In light of Kaneshiro's 'slippery' persona, this comment is able to offer a concise evaluation of the actor's equivocal positioning and the corresponding reception in the cinemas of Taiwan and Japan. Consider the controversial case that Taiwan's Golden Horse Film Awards in 2008 disqualified Kaneshiro from competing for a special prize for local talents with the marital arts epic *The Warlord*. The organiser claims that he was not eligible for nomination because he was a Japanese citizen (Japan Today 2008). Kaneshiro's filming patterns in Japan also reflects the perceived ethnic ambiguity of him. From 2004 to 2012, Kaneshiro only starred in two Japanese movies, *Sweet Rain* (a.k.a. *Accuracy of Death*) and *K20: Legend of the Mask* (a.k.a. *The Fiend with Twenty Faces* on home video in the US) (both 2008). Publicity framed *Sweet Rain* as Kaneshiro's return to Japanese cinema after six years, indicating his gradual loss of attachment to its film industry. In the same year, he was cast in *K20*, an action feature directed and written by Shimako Satō. However, these two films did not serve to expand any dimensions of Kaneshiro's star phenomenon but only continued the confusing Japaneseness of his early roles.

The characters Kaneshiro has played are thus far eccentric, in keeping with his unsettled star status. This has already been observable from the beginning of his acting career in the Japanese television industry. Koiwai Hiroyoshi, the producer of the television dramas *Kamisama, Mosukoshi Dake* and *Love 2000*, has expressed the same view, 'With one look you don't really know where he is from. That's why I want him to do a Japanese TV drama. He is wild and sexy' (Tsai, quoted in Tanaka 2005: 31). In *Kamisama, Mosukoshi Dake*, Kaneshiro plays a pensive songwriter who sleeps with an HIV-positive girl played by Fukuda Kyoko. *Love 2000* portrays him as a terrorist secret agent from a fictional world who falls in love with a system analyst played by Nakayama Miho. In both series,

Kaneshiro is cast in roles that are peculiar and exotic, evading from a lucid category that the Japanese audience can readily identify with.

The vague ethnic identity holds true even when the characters Kaneshiro plays are ethnically Japanese, something that is evident in not only television drama series but also movies. *Sleepless Town* (1998) is a Japan-Hong Kong co-production, made at the time the Hong Kong film industry was mired in the financial crisis, seeking foreign investors and East Asian partners to fund their projects (Kraicer 1998). In the narrative, Kaneshiro personifies a half-Chinese, half-Japanese trafficker named Ryu Kenichi/Liu Jianyi who is an outsider trying to make a living in the mysterious, decadent Shinjuku underworld. Hybridisation is in fact a hallmark of this film in terms of genre, sources of manpower, and finance, and its stars' and characters' ethnic statuses. Kenichi's 'bastard' origin echoes Kaneshiro's Taiwanese-Japanese parentage but is, in Eva Tsai's phrase, 'a denationalised role' (2005: 115). The character embodies the Japanese incorporation of pan-Asian hybridisation. Still, the high-profile distribution of this movie in Japan did not help Kaneshiro clarify his ethnic identity.

Refer back to the aforementioned comment given by user 'vampypiano'. By situating Kaneshiro in the intricate intrigues between the cinematic configurations of Hong Kong and Japan, 'vampypiano''s remark unveils the actor's equivocal ethnic and cultural identity from a fan's point of view. Moving between the two regional film industries, Kaneshiro embodies a kind of cultural rootlessness, belonging to neither Hong Kong nor Japan. In an article entitled 'Kaneshiro Takeshi the incredible 1998 chronicle' from a Hong Kong film magazine, *City Entertainment*, Koji Sogabe (1998) has also discussed what he terms 'the greatest mystery,' of Kaneshiro's star subjectivity interwoven in the labyrinth of his Japanese and Hong Kong star currency, making it difficult to explain Kaneshiro's popularity in Japan and Hong Kong. Sogabe observes:

> Even the Japanese find it odd: why is it that Kaneshiro acquired fame in Japan first and then in Hong Kong? This is because in their minds, they thought Mr. Kaneshiro was a big shot in Hong Kong film industry like Jackie Chan. So do the Hong Kong people like him because of their blind worship of Japan? Or is it simply because he looks especially gorgeous and cool in his hometown? This is the greatest mystery of all. (Sogabe 1998: 20)

Here Sogabe uses the word 'mystery', akin to some uses mentioned in the previous sections in this chapter, referring not only to Kaneshiro's look, as what aforesaid, but also to how Kaneshiro's popularity is borne out in the milieu of the intricate intrigues of cultural production and consumption of stars. A lack of co-identification from the audiences in Hong Kong and Japan further perplexes his star phenomenon in both ethnic and cultural terms.

The situation stems from Kaneshiro's rise of fame via *Chungking Express*. As the introductory part of this chapter mentions, Kaneshiro's name as an actor did not begin in Japanese audienceship until *Chungking Express*, which was released in Japan in 1995 under the title *Koisuru Wakusei* ('Love Planet' – a de-localised title for the sale in Japan). He plays one of the protagonists, a Taiwan-born cop He Qiwu, also known as Cop 223, who postpones the heartbreak from a failed relationship by neurotically collecting canned pineapples with an expiry date of 1 May, one month after the breakup day, hoping for her lover's return on his birthday after consuming the pineapples for thirty days. A major part of the film, set in Hong Kong, shows Kaneshiro speaking accented Cantonese, dubbed in the actor's own voice, albeit that there are some limited Mandarin-speaking scenes. The director Wong Kar-wai not only intends to keep the authenticity of the star presence through the dialogues (or monologues) but also highlights Kaneshiro's 'impure' utterances. As components of pan-Asian storytelling and market integration, Kaneshiro's accented Cantonese and the multi-lingual agency becomes a validating force of the flexible regional distribution system.

Language, which is a source of narrative strategy for mediating Kaneshiro's screen performance and for advancing the movie distribution, is now resurfaced in the cyber-fan discourse. For example, the Korean pop culture forum of Soompi, under the subject 'takeshi kaneshiro' includes a thread concerning whether Kaneshiro's spoken Japanese is authentic. User 'Aisingiorio Nuerhachi' criticises on 14 May 2006, 'His english and japanese sucks. he has that thick mandarin accent.hes english is worser. i saw his interview on CNN? and it sucked.' Another posting from the same user claims, 'trust me,his japanese outside of MOVIE STUDIO has a thick mandarin accent.' While this couple of comments tend to reveal displeasure, another user, 'ilovetakeshi', responded more sympathetically on 25 June 2006 as follows, 'No, actually Takeshi's first language is Taiwanese Hokkien and Mandarin (this being even after Hokkien) ... not Japanese, so it makes sense if his Japanese isn't as fluent.' From disapproval to understanding, diverse enunciations from fans interact and negotiate, which, as a result, offer a spectrum of emotionally laden expressions toward Kaneshiro's Japanese-speaking aptitude.

The feedback reverberates to a type of cultural 'foreign-ness' that Kaneshiro exemplifies in the mediascape in Japan. According to Eva Tsai (2005), Kaneshiro emerges in a 'different' category, not readily identified by the Japanese term *gaijin*, or Asian celebrity groupings (119). *Gaijin*, meaning 'foreign', refers to talents, which Laura Miller describes as 'odd' (1995: 196), who are usually white Westerns and become celebrities through their ability to speak very fluent Japanese on television shows. This fosters Kaneshiro's 'neither here nor there' image, in Tsai's term (2005: 118), as the actor himself expresses, in the English diction that is somewhat ungrammatical, in a CNN interview, 'And maybe it was not so easy to recognise myself, which country person I am' (CNN 2006).

Kaneshiro's ethnically vague stardom and pan-Asian charisma reminds us about the case of Li Xianglan, whose stardom is no less 'mysterious' than that of Kaneshiro. Li is a Manchurian-born Japanese actress with a Chinese stage name in 1940s Shanghai. Born in 1920 with the name Yamaguchi Yoshiko, she uses Li Xianglan, a Chinese name given by her adopted father in 1933, to masquerade as Chinese to foster her wartime fame. Her performance in the early Manchurian film industry and then in Shanghai is regarded as a Japanese cinematic transport to Mainland China (Stephenson 1999: 223). Nonetheless, Shanghai, as the centre of the Chinese filmmaking industry, had proffered a venue that allows a star cult that was realised in the urban audience. This reset Li's position in the already heaving Shanghai-ese star system. The political nuances involved in her stardom marks a noteworthy aperture to explore her instance that her ethnic disguise serves to confirm the Japanese propagandist notion in the occupied Shanghai. Both pro- and anti-Japanese publications adopt the same language to discuss the responsibility of film. They argue the filmic medium is useful to be an unmediated access to human heart, presuming, too, that China not only needs but desires a presence of Japan in the mainland. The phrase of 'Greater East Asia Co-Prosperity Sphere', proposed by Japan in the 1940s, subsumed the interracial unity among nations and peoples in Asia (225). Japan, assuming superiority over other Asian nations, suggested a future Asian community built on interdependence and cooperation, in resistance to the West, particularly after the eruption of the Pacific War in 1941. The operation of such an idea is embodied by Yamaguchi Yoshiko/Li Xianglan, a star presence synthesising cinema and political agenda.

Li's stardom is famous for her 'pretence' of her ethnic Chineseness, both onscreen and offscreen. Her studio employs her role as a Chinese actress as a publicity strategy. Her true nationality was only known to a few executives in her home studio, Man'ei (the Manchurian Film Association), where they endeavoured to keep it secret (233). Accordingly, Li tends to provide evasive answers to the press's questions on her offbeat background (ibid.). For example, in her first trip to Japan in 1940, Li was asked by the press about her life, and she answered, 'My life? What should I say? The false one, or the genuine one?' (ibid). This kind of oblique response could rivet public attention to and evoke mystery about her offscreen life more than her onscreen personality, a condition that defines a star. Arguably, Kaneshiro's complicated hybrid stardom, partly the result of the persona management, is foreshadowed, although obliquely, by Li Xianglan's instance. Unlike Li, nonetheless, his Japanese ethnicity is not hidden from the eyes of the public whereas his Japanese status does not escape from ambivalence. In other words, he fosters an image that does not adhere clearly towards any national culture.

Moreover, instead of the ideology of Asian solidarity that Li's stardom epitomises, what the 'Kaneshiro' Japanese audiences found in *Chungking Express* is emblematic of 'a new Asia' in the age of global capitalism (Tsai 2005: 117). This 'new Asia' persona, as Koichi Iwabuchi (2002: 14) puts it, is 'no longer contained by the image of traditional, underdeveloped, backward neighbors to be civilised by Japan'. Rather, the persona is embodied by a sexy, exotic, mysterious kind of celebrity vigour that fascinates audiences with its novelty. This rise of the 'new Asia' visage reflects Japan's desire to consume mass cultural products and images from Asia as well as the West. Japanese audiences' discovery of Kaneshiro through Hong Kong cinema is reminiscent of the case of Jackie Chan; he appears more as an export than a local, although he can speak the Japanese language. Recall the instance of Li Xianglan. If Li demonstrates the ideology of Asian unity, then Kaneshiro signifies a kind of Asian diversity that coincides with the cosmopolitan picture of seamless flow of capital, people, and images that fits the vision of 'new Asia'. The notion of Asia per se does not indicate a single ethnic identity. Asia is primarily a geographical concept that consists of a multitude of ethnicities, traditions, religions, and cultures. The traditional notion of Asia is chiefly a Eurocentric fabrication that differentiates the West as an advanced subject from the backward, non-Christian civilisations, functioning to channel the Western anxieties about loss of domination and insecurity. The early twentieth century reveals that the pan-Asian resistance against Western powers, alongside the emergence of nationalisms, has further given shape to the so-called Asian solidarity (Lo 2010: 7–9). Nonetheless, this does not mean an exclusion or hostility of Western cultures. Asia, as a region, attempts to integrate 'the contending forces of the global integration and the local autonomy' (Ching 2000: 244). Members of Asian cultures reveal proximity to Western cultures yet simultaneously retain cultural hybridity, which potentially evolves to a kind of irreducible heterogeneity, like what postcolonial theorists suggest, or in Lo's (2005) idea, the 'irreconciliation' of differences (10). Lo argues:

> There is no way to reconcile the difference because it is not an objective difference between two perspectives or positions. Rather, it is 'pure' difference that cannot be rounded in any substantive; the irreconciliation itself becomes the notion of Asia. (ibid.)

Rejecting the notion of Asia as merely a discursive construct of Western hegemony, one can interpret the reality of Asia as 'multiple, active, and antagonistic relations among individuals, groups, and states' (ibid.), rather than something in a certain determined and essential position. It reverberates to the identity of Kaneshiro rendered in cyberspace, represented and contended by diverse intensities in the context of transnational popular cultural flows. Whereas Kaneshiro negotiates a pan-Asian cinematic persona through working on these Asian-oriented projects, Internet users re-negotiate this persona, displaying complex regional and global dynamics in the fan world. Kaneshiro's star phenomenon signifies a growing and vibrant pan-Asian imagination in which his half-Japanese ethnic identity is underplayed, and both the star and his fans are complicit in the star-making process.

Kaneshiro also demonstrates a pan-Asian identity oriented along the Hong Kong–China axis in his recent movies. Since *House of Flying Daggers* (2004), the contours of Kaneshiro's stardom have changed to reveal an affiliation to China and its global market. In subsequent years, he participated in a series of pan-Asian co-productions directed by Hong Kong filmmakers and involving crew members from sundry film industries in the region, for example, *Perhaps Love* (2005), *Confession of Pain* (2006), *The Warlords* (2007), *Red Cliff I* and *II* (2008 and 2009), and *Wu Xia* (2011). These films epitomise the potency of the notion of Asian cinema, which transcends the boundaries of national cinemas. According to Stephen Teo (2008), *Perhaps Love* is a statement that the concept of Asian cinema offers the possibility of making films that share the same sort of universal ideal as Hollywood, insofar as it circulates the message that one should stay in Asia to make films (355). Recall the following line spoken by the heroine, Sun Na (Zhou Xun), in diegesis: 'To make films, you must go to Hollywood.' This is how Hollywood has exhibited its dominance. Pierre Bourdieu remarks that the 'particularity of the dominant is that they are in a position to ensure that their particular way of being is recognised as universal' (2001: 62). One acknowledges Hollywood as the only place to realise the dream of making films, or, in general terms, to realise the universal ideal. But as the plot develops, the actress does not depart for Hollywood. She stays in Beijing for an Asian musical, through which she finds redemption through romance with the dual heroes, Nie Wen (Jackie Cheung) and Jiandong (Takeshi Kaneshiro). The film, thus, challenges the universality revered by Hollywood filmmaking but to acknowledge an Asian version of it.

Kaneshiro, in real life, embodies the ideal of Asian cinema by rejecting to make films in Hollywood. He has overtly revealed that he has no intention of making Hollywood movies while the 'ascendancy to Hollywood' rhetoric dominates the discourse of transnational Chinese stardom. Rather, Kaneshiro's demonstrates consciousness of fashioning links with China, as allegorised in *Perhaps Love* (2005). Kaneshiro's character, Jiandong, is a Hong Kong young man who studies film in Beijing, the capital city of China, and begins his acting career in his homeland. His subsequent return to Beijing to participate in a movie production headed by Nie Wen suggests Beijing as the ultimate locale where he can realise his pursuit in film. Kaneshiro also possesses a similar career trajectory of returning to China, so that his transnational image gradually moves away from the Japan–Western or Asia–global axis. What is meant by 'transnational' is no longer border-crossing ability between East and West but between Hong Kong and mainland China.

'Help for Japan': re-shaping of the Japanese identity

Kaneshiro's pan-Asian star image is capricious on the web because cyber personality is never 'final' as it is always subjected to the incessant (re) construction by fans. Whereas some fan postings emphasise Kaneshiro's transnational yet culturally uncertain status in the context of media consumption, some others revive his Japanese identity, constructing the star meanings in a different setting. In 2011, a fan site called 'TKfanclub' (http:tkfanclub.do.am/) began as a response to the nuclear disaster in Fukushima. A 9.0 earthquake and subsequent tsunami struck Japan in

March 2011, causing vast damage to the Fukushima Nuclear Power Plant and engendering nuclear radiation leaks and a 30-kilometre evacuation zone neighbouring the plant. It purportedly was the world's worst nuclear disaster since the 1986 Chernobyl catastrophe. After the catastrophe, a series of fan-based, mobilising endeavours emerged online in order to garner attention and assistance to the tragedy from the widest possible audience in the globe. The fan site 'TKfanclub' opens a sub-page entitled 'fan-creations' that chronicles a list of postings entitled 'Fan Creations – Help for Japan'. This section compiles artworks produced by an artist called Cheng Lung WS, who self-dubbed as 'Waltraud Schnurr', for fundraising for the relief effort. With the focus on Kaneshiro, these art pieces also function to invoke and re-stage with significance the star's Japanese roots.

Cheng Lung WS produced a special collection of portraits of Kaneshiro, whom she describes as a star 'highly regarded worldwide' (Takeshi Kaneshiro Fan Club) as well as some portraits of Andy Lau, an acclaimed Hong Kong-based film actor and singer. One painting, entitled 'Hope' (Figure 5.3), posted not by the artist herself but by a user named

Figure 5.3 Creative work themed on 'Help for Japan: Hope' by Internet user 'mikomi'

'mikomi' on 22 March 2011, depicts Kaneshiro, dressed in white in the foreground, holding the Earth in his hands, signifying the world-embracing vision of the actor. A flying dove carrying an olive branch in the upper left corner symbolises hope, resonating with the theme of the painting. The red circle in the background denotes the sun, which is also a symbol of hope and warmth, and the national flag of Japan. On the right side of the picture, a pair of praying hands designates a craving of blessing Japan. The top of the painting shows words written in three languages: English, Japanese, and Chinese. The English reads 'Help for Japan', as does the Japanese '日本のための助け', announcing the theme of the campaign. The bilingual text of 'Hope' and '希望', in English and Chinese, moreover, can help the inference that the painting is for a multilingual audience and Cheng seeks to run the charity on a cross-cultural scale.

In the posting, the artist herself provides an exposition of her philanthropic mobilisation through art by capitalising on the star currency. She writes:

> This is the new image from my Takeshi Kaneshiro special art collection I send you, around you and at the same time to ask for your help. At first I was shocked and helpless. Deep sadness in my heart and my soul, and only one thought: You need help! . . . Me with and my goal is with this image and some other objects from my special Fan Art Collection of Takeshi Kaneshiro and Andy Lau (Lau Tak Wah)5 to start an online campaign to auction off these images, coupled with the establishment of a Help – Fund: 'Help for Japan' – 'Hope' to pay to start to assist in with all people do.6

The artist may be a member of the Japanese community, and, as such, readily identifies with the victims, considering the fact that she does not elaborate on the rationale of choosing Kaneshiro and Lau as the subjects of her creative project. Perhaps the artist is a fan of both actors. Perhaps the choice is due to their popularity. In any case, her adoption of Kaneshiro as the subject revitalises the connections between the actor, his Japanese identity, and the Japanese community. Through her medium, she ultimately reclaims Kaneshiro's Japaneseness.

The user 'mikomi' also draws on transnational networks in the service of her goodwill. On 8 April 2011, she posted another message and painting (Figure 5.4) onto the Cheng Lung WS fan site that the link between the visual and the verbal is not overt. The painting depicts Kaneshiro at a public occasion, looking solemn and intently concerned as he speaks into a microphone marked with the Japanese flag icon and the words 'Please

Help Japan'. The backdrop portrays catastrophe-hit Fukushima, as noted in both Chinese and English ('福島渠Fukushima'). The message reads as follow:

> The terrible events in Japan, let me just not come to rest. I have painted the new picture of Takeshi for help to Japan auction.
> Today I have started an online relief campaign with Aktion-deutsch-land-hilft .de,[7] to help for Japan. More information is on my action side found you on my facebook page.
> With this picture called 'Fukushima' This concerns us all 'Please help Japan', I would like to access again all the people in this world: Please help the people of Japan!
> I hope and wish to continue the actions to help Japan with my pictures, but still it is unable to be done!
> Kind regards Your Waltraud Schnurr – Cheng Lung WS[8]

By networking with Germany's Relief Coalition for her advocacy across national borders, the artist taps into the altruistic potential of fan communities in the cyber setting. She, furthermore, directs users who are interested in her paintings to her Facebook page, establishing a network and collaborative outreach for her effort. The structure of Cheng's fundraising campaign typifies the convergence of fan communities, social networks, and charities.

Figure 5.4 'mikomi''s other painting called 'Fukushima', which is used as a means to solicit help from the Internet public for Japan's recovery from the catastrophe

Unlike two famous transnational Chinese stars, Jackie Chan and Jet Li, it is worth noting that no signs show that Takeishi Kaneshiro plays an active role in engineering his philanthropic persona. Li has given high profiles to his contribution in relief work following the earthquake in Sichuan, China, which has been discussed in Chapter 3 of this book. Likewise, Chan has exhibited his altruistic mobilisation in the same disaster. According to The Official Website of Jackie Chan, he has recorded several songs for the earthquake fatalities. A post in the 'Scrapbook' shows a YouTube video of the Mandarin-language song named 'Shengsi Bu Li' (literally meaning 'not leaving, dead or alive'), copied and posted. Below the YouTube link is the lyrics of the song, translated into English (Scrapbook (The Official Website of Jackie Chan) n.d.). Part of the lyrics read:

> No matter where you are,
> I must find you,
> The blood in our veins can create miracles,
> Living is the meaning of life.

The lyrics unfold the underlining of the ethnic origins of Chan and call for his fans to help out. Highlighting the same ethnic origins he shares with the wounded, which he articulates as 'the blood in our veins', Chan positions himself as a comrade of the casualty while an international celebrity. Both Li and Chan, who are mindful to their star-making, have adopted philanthropy as a strategy to escalate fame and to gain a well-respected positioning in the entertainment arena. With a penchant of avoiding repeating what Chan and Li have done, Kaneshiro demonstrates screen cosmopolitanism and he does not unveil any consciousness to the ethnic aspect in his stardom, if not intentionally burying his ethnicity or making it ambiguous so as to appeal to a transnational following. Put another way, charity seems not a field that Kaneshiro intends to involve in his star phenomenon, leaving the endeavours to his fans. In this case, it is Cheng Lung WS, an artist-fan, instead of Kaneshiro himself (or his publicity team) taking such initiatives, epitomising the agency of an artist-fan. One may, therefore, argue that Kaneshiro's fans have the potential to add a new strand to his stardom with the participatory, open, and collaborative features of the web apparatuses, which may not be as well-interwoven to the existing star discourse as Chan and Li embody.

The reinvigorations of Takeshi Kaneshiro's Japanese identity place his star persona in an ambiguous space that vacillates between Japaneseness and Chineseness. Fans in cyberspace engage in the reconstruction of Kaneshiro's image, unstable and polysemic, eliciting neither a clearly delineated national boundary nor a clearly defined Chinese status. The Chineseness Takeshi Kaneshiro embodies is situated within discursive coordinates plotted by the Asian cross-regional imagination. As the notion of Chineseness becomes more expansive and capricious in the current age, Kaneshiro's appeal may be a viable lens to examine the dynamic meanings of Chineseness. It exhibits the possible ongoing interplay and tension between cyber fan discourse and the star text, illuminating the possibilities of pan-Asian star construction in a global cyber context.

Notes

1. This chapter is derived, in part, from an article under acceptance by positions: asia critique that will be published.
2. By adding the phrase 'I'm sure that . . . ' there is the implication that 'Ognyana' has not seen the film. But the context of the thread indeed suggests he or she has seen it. So, that probably reveals a usage error, hinting on her role as a nonnative English speaker.
3. A more recent title, *Red Cliff*, also had theatrical release in Russia. A Kaneshiro fan site relayed the news of the movie's premiere in Russia on 6 August 2009. <http:tkfanclub.do.am/news/2009-08-01-58> (last accessed 24 August 2017)
4. Zhang Yimou's martial arts epic featuring major stars in the Greater China Region, *House of Flying Daggers* (2004), earned nearly RMB100 million in the domestic market (Danwei 2004). *Confession of Pain* (2006) grossed in the territory HKD24 million, while the nationwide revenue totalled about RMB75 million (Box Office Mojo n.d.). It was in intense competition with another blockbuster Zhang Yimou's *Curse of the Golden Flower* (2006), starring Chow Yun-fat, Gong Li, and Jay Chou, during its national release, but managed satisfactory returns. Budgeted on US40 million, Peter Chan's period action movie *The Warlords* grossed nearly HKD28 million in Hong Kong, RMB200 million in mainland China, and RMB300 million in Southeast Asian exhibitions, becoming the second top-grossing Chinese-language picture of the year ('NetEase: The Warlords' n.d.). *Perhaps Love*'s domestic receipt approximated HKD14 million while it earned RMB30 million in mainland China. As premiered on 1 December 2005, the movie set a box-office record in the first week of screening, grossing more than RMB18 million (Boxofficemojo n.d.). Reportedly the most expensive production in Chinese movie history, John Woo's historical epic *Red Cliff* (2008) had box-office earnings of more than RMB300 million (Box Office Mojo n.d.).
5. 'Lau Tak Wah' is the Romanisation of Andy Lau's Chinese name.
6. Available at <http:tkfanclub.do.am/news/fan_creations_help_for_japan/2011-03-22-152> (last accessed 26 August 2017).

7. Literally meaning 'Action-Germany-help', 'Aktion-deutschland-hilft' (in English, Germany's Relief Coalition) is a Bonn-based alliance. It is a consortium for disaster assistance with the purpose of joining forces in order to offer help in a quick and effective way.

8. Available at <http:tkfanclub.do.am/news/fan_creations_help_for_japan/> (last accessed 27 August 2017).

Conclusion

Reimagining Chineseness in the global cyberculture

In the previous chapters, I put the conception of Chineseness in the new frame of participatory cyberspace by examining five cases of transnational Chinese stars. Chineseness becomes a destabilised notion with the plurality and volatility embraced in the cyber setting. I argue that it becomes a kind of imaginary that lies on the verge of cinematic culture and cyberculture, or simply called cine-cyber imaginary, which is a de-essentialised entity resulting from the fan-powered remaking of star personae. Fans gain the capacity to generate or even reinvent stars' virtual bodies by incessantly poaching, copying, editing, and posting images. In this respect, Chineseness, along with the star image, is always on the make, with no closure possible. Moreover, fans from diverse cultural and ethnic backgrounds negotiate their own relations to Chineseness, often arguing among themselves as to what Chineseness is about, and negotiating a blurred space between the virtual and the real. The outcome is a collaborative effort wherein fans participate in the meaning-making process. In this process, Chineseness is an open signifier in which various interests with regard to star power, martial arts skills, and cinephilia may be anchored. It may still evoke ethnicity, albeit with an abstract quality resulting from the abstraction of the cyber image itself. This performative aspect is dissimilar to the outcome shaped by previous conditions in cinema, where Chineseness has usually been fixed in a context, through which viewers come to realise what it is intended to mean. Beforehand, viewers are informed by symbolic referents whose meanings are enclosed within the films. The open signifier in cyberspace is a novelty that does not necessarily endorse previous readings, and thus potentially undermines any hint of hermeneutic directionality. The outcome, I argue, is a peculiar making as if the star body is incapable of being fixed into a definite cultural essence.

My arguments have developed upon David Rodowick's analysis of 'new media' images to inform my discussion of star images and virtual bodies in cyberspace. In his seminal book *The Virtual Life of Film* (2007), Rodowick explores the problematic nature of filmic images that, defined in the visual culture of the twentieth century, has moved from the age of celluloid to the age of digital. There is a dialectics of the digital and the analogue, with replacement of the analogue world by a digital simulation posing an 'allegorical conflict' (Rodowick 2007: 4) in which cinema contends to reassert its identity through a new representational technology that threatens to overwhelm it. While film is considered as 'a clearly defined aesthetic object' and has ontological ground in an aesthetic principle, cyberspace shows loss of such ground and entails the new perceptual and aesthetic order (2). This allows a range of signification and interpretative practices. Elaborating ideas from Stanley Cavell's book *The World Viewed: Reflections on the Ontology of Film (1971)*, Rodowick investigates how one may understand an image after the emergence of so-called new media:

> [A]n idea of cinema persists or subsists within the new media as their predominant cultural and aesthetic model for engaging the vision and imagination of viewers. But this also means that it is difficult to envision what kinds of aesthetic experiences computational process will innovate once they have *unleashed themselves from the cinematic metaphor* and begin to explore their autonomous creative powers, if indeed they eventually do so. (Rodowick 2007: 97–8; my emphasis)

'The cinematic metaphor' is embedded in a complex, highly elaborate, codified system. As Christian Metz defines, a code 'is a constructed rather than inherent unity, and it does not exist prior to analysis' (1974: 12). The plurality of codes already exists in the world of cinematic aesthetics. As Metz insists, the materiality of the cinematic signifiers is heterogeneous. It consists of an array of cinematic and non-cinematic codes, whose very nature is to be conceptually diverse. Nevertheless, in the cyber world, the image is not only heterogeneous but also that the meaning is attached to no specific context of interpretation. Therefore, in film, which is a concrete discursive unity, the codes are virtual but the messages are concrete and singular; differently, the digital imagery refers to a new set of codes, of which the message, or the meaning, is fluid and elusive.

The 'autonomous creative powers', as Rodowick (2007) posits, is something counter to the claim that cinema is an 'auto-destructive' medium because 'each passage of frames through a projector . . . advances a process of erosion that will eventually reduce the image to nothing' (20). In this regard, cyberspace, distinctively, contains the constructive quality medium. Fans' participation is a democratised practice that makes the signification organic and dynamic. Considering the digital as mercurial, simulated expressions, the star phenomenon becomes the 'deterritorised' locus that operates without being attached to any specific time and space. Anytime and anywhere, fans copy-and-paste or rework the choreographed scenes of the Chinese stars, questioning the martial authenticity. It reverberates to the quality of being 'living and changeable' of Chineseness as Gungwu Wang argues:

> I suggest that our understanding of Chineseness must recognise the following: it is living and changeable; it is also the product of a shared historical experience whose record has continually influenced its growth; it has become increasingly a self-conscious matter for China; and it should be related to what appears to be, or to have been, Chinese in the eyes of non-Chinese. (Wang 1991: 2)

Ubiquitous images, interconnected texts, and reciprocal exchange among users facilitate the grassroots engagement to the star appeal as participatory media prosper. The star image is never final but is a case of perpetual remaking, as my previous chapters have shown. As Rodowick (2007) states, the digital image does not 'result in an "end product"' (15), being subjected to 'a state of perpetual change' (19). The 'lack of closure' (15), or what Philip Rosen calls 'practically infinite manipulability' (2001: 319–26), proves how the grassroots forces are synergised in star construction.

By drawing on Rodowick's theory, I here propose a reconsideration of Chineseness for understanding texts of Chinese stars there is the transition from cinematic space to cyberspace. It means an equivocal, amorphous, and pluralistic expression of the Chinese, void of historical substantiality and revealing no clear link between the image and the cultural correlates. It is a new representational order mediated by computer-based technology, not inclined to any established symbolic order such as martial arts cinema and the cinema of Fifth Generation directors of the PRC. It is a synthesised outcome of corporeal, cultural, and technological elements, constituting a new sort of signification in that it points to the absent concrete realities of the Chinese nation and such Chineseness redefines the star body in erratic, multiple, and provocative terms.

As the analysis in this book has indicated, the star texts of the famous transnational Chinese actors and actresses in cyberspace evoke the Chineseness that is virtualised and de-essentialised. When fans transpose

Donnie Yen's nationalistic picture personality to blogs, they de-emphasise its Chineseness, as discussed in Chapter 1. Bloggers juxtapose and blend the Wing Chun body with elements from non-Chinese symbolic spaces such as hip hop and Hollywood sci-fi that obscures the Chineseness he embodies in film. The Chineseness becomes further vague as bloggers reduce Yen's Wing Chun body to the vehicle of carrying out the kung fu technique, as compared to MMA. In addition, bloggers' highlight of Yen's offscreen existence brings his publicity distant from the Chinese heroic, masculine image and towards a feminised, sentimental 'family man' persona.

A shift of emphasis in image construction from choreography to goodwill yields a more cosmopolitan but less traditionally Chinese star persona. In Chapter 2, I have demonstrated that the star construction of Jackie Chan on Flickr that focuses on not only his fighting persona but also his ambassadorial engagement, universalising his public image. As the analysis reveals, Chan and his personnel join ordinary fan networks through Flickr to strategically redress his notoriety and promote the desired image. It remains true that cyber fans show enthusiasm and fervour for Chan's martial arts personae as manifested by the Flickr photographs of the Adelaide flash mob and the fans' visits to the Walk of Fame. However, I have argued that these images constitute an appearance without substance of Chinese nationalism. The Adelaide photographs simply show crowds of flash mob participants filling up the visual space of the pictures. Moreover, the tourism-like images display two types of empty signs: those of Chan and those of the fan imitations of Chan. In addition, Chan's studio and publicity team use Flickr to engineer new star personae as a still-competent martial arts actor, a Chinese patriot, and a cultural ambassador building bridges between China and the world. The 'Official Photos' of *The Forbidden Kingdom*, the 'My Beloved Country' concert, and the UNICEF trip to Myanmar convey border-crossing sensitivity without abandoning Chan's nationalistic consciousness. The implication of this newly diversified star image is that Chineseness requires a foil of universalism in order to yield a viable global Chinese star.

The similar deliberate pursuit of cosmopolitanism is also observed in the instance of Jet Li's star phenomenon on Facebook, as Chapter 3 has shown. While Facebook fans post and share images and news of Li's screen persona as a martial artist, Li himself strategises his goodwill mobilisation by 'friending' others on the platform through his presumably self-hosted Page. His extensive engagement in philanthropy has expanded his appeal from a nationalistic hero fighting for his nation to a global philanthropist serving humanitarian needs. To elaborate, whereas Li's cinematic roles propel nationalist vigour, his charitable appeal transcends any national or ethnic boundaries. His cyber presence is a telling example of the complex interplay between onscreen and offscreen personae, between cosmopolitanism and Chineseness of martial arts personalities.

Video-sharing sites become an important venue for approaching and negotiating the Chineseness of Zhang Ziyi, as investigated in Chapter 4. Users contend Zhang's image in light of her increasing presence on global screens and the contestation stretches beyond the cinema screen to star gossip such as Zhang's broken English and sex scandals. The fan discourse, thus, provokes a vigorous debate on her 'problematic' embodiment of Chinese cultural nationalism. Narratives of hard work, moreover, become significant in the global star-making that her improvement in English becomes an achievement in her film career.

Takeshi Kaneshiro's star presence is noticeably different from that of his Chinese counterparts, which I take note of in Chapter 5. As a half-Taiwanese, half-Japanese actor with a strongly cosmopolitan image, Kaneshiro's Chineseness is elusive and indefinite. Rendering a polysemic, fluid persona, he exhibits versatile performance while users of Internet forums situate him in dialectics of good looks and poor acting, mainstream and art-house cinemas. In addition, fans interrogate Kaneshiro's bi-ethnic identity in ways that complicate his representation(s) of Chineseness. Neither purely Chinese (Taiwanese) nor purely Japanese, the cyber discourse reveals how Kaneshiro personifies a pan-Asian image, as ambiguous and intriguing as possible.

Through a close examination of five ethnic Chinese stars, this book has reconceptualised Chineseness in cyberspace to show that the central issue is not quite about authenticity and stability, instead, towards an open set of possibilities of multiple creative and interpretive intensities. From screen to cyberspace, the star presence of the Chinese performers becomes a virtual entity that can anchor neither substantial historical meaning, nor any stable readings of Chineseness facilitated by their screen representation. A new form of erratic, virtualised Chineseness results as images from disparate symbolic realms merged, ultimately challenging the star's Chinese status. The cyber era has seen an increasing degree of virtualisation in popular images. A new universal space, cyberculture underscores the virtualised aspects of the star appeal, signifying the absence of material embodiment of performers (Lévy 2001: 29). Stars are actualised as visible images but are virtualised as the abstract variable in the cyber network. As Lévy (2001) argues, the digital recording is 'fluid and volatile' and occupies a unique position in the succession of images: implicit in their visible manifestation, it is virtual (36). Lévy continues to argue that the virtualised text is actualised in multiple versions, translations, and editions. The virtualisation of Chinese personae in cyberspace deconstructs the nationalistic foundation upon which traditional readings of the Chinese body are grounded, opening up endless avenues for representing and interpreting Chineseness. Kwai-cheung Lo's argument can work as supplementary to the virtualised outcome of the Chinese star image. In his book *Chinese Face/Off* (2005), Lo has analysed the Chineseness produced by Hong Kong transnational culture, extending the slipperiness and plurality of the quality of being Chinese:

> Chineseness, as examined through Hong Kong culture, is the master signifier of the Chinese nation – nothing but an empty sign standing for an impossible fullness of meaning, insofar as there is no way for its content to be positivised. The pluralism or multiplicity of Chinese identities only presents more choices for a general idea of 'Chineseness,' which, instead of providing anything precise, simply conceals the fact that 'Chineseness' is an empty term. (Lo 2005: 6)

Lo argues that the Hong Kong culture, as signified by the male martial arts body, is marked by formlessness, hybridity, and inconsistency. These characteristics offer no help in constructing a unique Hong Kong identity. On the contrary, they facilitate Hong Kong's reunion with China and its emergence into the global economic system in a manner that disregards its cultural specificity. (6) Therefore, the image of the masculine action body circulated in Hong Kong culture is self-referential and void of historical substance and essential identity. While Lo focuses on the Hong Kong male body in the context of global capitalism, I extend the idea to the bodily construct, which is regarded not as Hong Kong but Chinese, possessing the capacity to represent contestable and unstable national identity. Mediated by cyber technology, Chineseness in cyberspace is hollowed with substantiality, emanating from no historical experience common to all cyber fans. Lacking a sense of historicity, cyber texts are fragmented and sporadic; they may also disappear after a short time, despite the archival functions offered by some websites. Thus, there are no guarantees of continuity in the immaterial or virtual star phenomenon.

What is worth noting is that this Chineseness does not come into existence *ex nihilo* from an entirely new symbolic realm. The grassroots representational forces engaging in cyberspace often lift references from current Chinese symbolic systems in order to reinvent the Chinese bodies. But there is no limit about which symbolic systems to draw upon, as shown in the discussion about the range of interests and issues that are brought into play. I argue that this mixed and unstable connection constitute the basis of a composite, intertextual star discourse that, with its beginnings as a screen artefact of cultural and visual dimensions, is collectively remade to become an irreducibly speculative and aesthetic concoction. The transformation in the Chinese star discourse from a sign of unstable Chineseness to a range of fabrications is not a radical departure from existing cultural elements but a moderation, accommodation, and continuation of them.

The Chineseness of the transnational movie stars readily recurs at all times in the fan discourse in cyberspace. Fans taken as a form of agency is a key part in the realm of stardom. The participatory cyber world renders fans in star construction more visible and noticeable than ever before. Before the era of the popularisation of the web, the fans formed communication networks and circulated news and gossips of stars. With the arrival of interactive cyberspace, fans eagerly poach, post, edit, and share various texts and images of these stars on the web to such an extent that their works now serve as readily available commentary and critique of the stars. Significantly, user-oriented creative effort comes to manipulate the production and circulation of texts, altering the performance of stardom from an industry-based mode to a combined mode of industrial and grassroots forces. As revealed in the analyses of various platforms, fan discourses connect and contest with one another. There exists unprecedented verve, speed, and coverage with cyber connectivity and interactivity. Subsequent to the popular adoption of Web 2.0 technology, fan participation has plotted new contours in the map of martial arts stardom.

The findings and analyses in this book indicate the novel dimensions of fan works that confirm my initial hypotheses, that is, in the cyber era, the collaborative and multi-dimensional fan dynamics make it necessary to take a new understanding of the star phenomenon. This study of the transnational Chinese stars indicates that personae are paraded, remade, contested, defended, queried, and manipulated by such fan texts as blog entries, photographs, and videos. While individual comments and videos are uploaded by individual fans, it is the existence of a global circuit that gives a new digital identity to the fans who are empowered to respond to the stars and to interact with other fans directly and interactively. Within this network, the usual barriers and discrepancies between geographies, classes, and cultures can be said to have virtually disappeared though they can return quickly as well. The cultural impact of fan works appears multi-faceted and diversified, and they often usher in many other topics, as well as other discourses not restricted to a single area. My book shows that the fan discourse about Chineseness and Chinese movie stardom is a complexly formulated type that is marked by a combined mode of forces. The range going from supportive, compliant, oppositional, transgressive, subversive, and counter-cultural is so broad yet they exist concomitantly. The result is an enormously complicated, multiple, and varying matrix of fan narratives in Chinese stardom. The star texts come out of fans and fan groups who collaborate without having to meet in person. The fandom in Web 2.0, even though occasionally revealing the influence of cultural norms and biases, is never singular as the discourses and images remain open in the system for all sorts of changes to take place continually. The web thus provides a space for old and new fan communication circuits, taking fan culture into a technologised stage.

The escalating fan presence and calibre are illustrative of what Henry Jenkins (2010) has described when writing, 'Web 2.0 was fandom without the stigma', propelling the reconsideration of the category of a star's ethnicity in a new framework. The participatory cyberspace has become a prominent site of examining Chinese stardom, of which the conception of Chineseness has evolved after the era of cinema. Transnational capitalism circulates the popular images of cinema and the circulation is made vastly vigorous and extensive on the web. The web gives place to the seamless, networked fans' reworkings of Chinese personalities that first appears in film and then extends to the web. While my book has mobilised to generate a critical rethinking on Chineseness by arguing for an unstable, hybrid construction, further discursive explorations on the notion are called for. The notion of Chineseness is speculated to grow in complexity and diversity as the concept of cyberculture evolves. The extension of Web 2.0's participatory technologies and network culture to a recurrently or increasingly collaborative mode of virtuality will further problematise the Chinese star presence on global screens, unfolding a critical intervention of cyber fans' phenomenon and the cultural construct of Chineseness. In the transnational matrices in which seamless and rapid flows of images, texts, and ideas are found, there is no sign that interactive and networked potency in cyberspace will cease or relinquish. The imaginary of Chinese stars becomes fluid currency in the world of transnational dynamics, subjected to constant re-evaluation and reinvention in the global cyberculture.

Bibliography

1905 Dianying Wang (n.d.), 'The Forbidden Kingdom', <www.m1905.com/FilmInfo/film/2007/5/image67158.html> (last accessed 2 June 2012).

'2010 Forbes China celebrity list' (2010), *China Hush: Stories of China*, 29 April, <www.chinahush.com/2010/04/29/2010-forbes-china-celebrity-list/> (last accessed 9 August 2017).

Adelaide Flashmob (n.d.), <www.adelaideflashmob.com/> (last accessed 2 April 2012).

Affron, Charles (1991a), 'Generous stars', in Jeremy Butler (ed.), *Star Texts: Image and Performance in Film and Television*, Detroit: Wayne State University Press, pp. 90–101.

Affron, Charles (1991b), 'Identifications', in Marcia Landy (ed.), *Imitations of Life: A Reader on Film and Television Melodrama*, Detroit: Wayne State University Press, pp. 98–117.

Alexa: imdb.com (n.d.), <www.alexa.com/siteinfo/imdb.com> (last accessed 23 August 2017).

Alexandra099tianya (2010), 'Earthquake scandal of Ziyi Zhang, Ziyi Zhang donation-fraud', YouTube, 11 February, www.youtube.com/watch?v=jBGhFwq4vm8&feature=related (last accessed 19 August 2017).

Allen, Robert and Douglas Gomery (1985), *Film History: Theory and Practice*, New York: Random House.

Allison, Anne (2000), 'A challenge to Hollywood? Japanese character goods hit the US', *Japanese Studies* 20:1, pp. 67–8.

Allison, Anne (2001), 'Memoirs of the Orient', *Journal of Japanese Studies* 27(2), pp. 381–98.

Allison, Kevin and Aline Van Duyn (2006), 'Google agrees $1.65bn deal for YouTube', *Financial Times*, 10 October, <www.ft.com/cms/s/0/fbe65e70-57fb-11db-be9f-0000779e2340.html> (last accessed 20 July 2009).

Allison, Kevin and Richard Waters (2006), 'Google and Murdoch among the suitors circling YouTube', *Financial Times*, 7 October, <www.ft.com/cms/s/0/1a8d7146-55a0-11db-acba-0000779e2340.html?nclick_check=1> (last accessed 20 July 2009).

Anderson, Aaron (1998), 'Action in motion: Kinesthesia in martial arts films', *Jump Cut* 42, pp. 1–11.

Anderson, Aaron (2009), 'Asian martial-arts cinema, dance, and the cultural languages of gender', in S. Tan, P. Feng, and G. Marchetti (eds), *Chinese Connections: Critical Perspectives on Film, Identity, and Diaspora*, Philadelphia: Temple University Press, pp. 190–202.

Ang, Ien (2001), *On Not Speaking Chinese: Living between Asia and the West*, London and New York: Routledge.

Anheier, Helmut and Diane Leat (2006), *Creative Philanthropy: Toward a New Philanthropy for the Twenty-first Century*, London: Routledge.

Arango, Tim (2008), 'Behind the scenes, a force in the media world', *The New York Times*, 27 July, <www.nytimes.com/2008/07/27/technology/27iht-27viviNEW.14814862. html?_r=1> (last accessed 27 August 2017).

Associated Press (2010), 'Gates, Buffett talk charity with China's super-rich', nbc News. com, <www.nbcnews.com/id/39422689/ns/us_newsgiving/t/gates-buffett-talk-charity-chinas-super-rich/#.U65gnPmSzTZ> (last accessed 20 June 2014).

Austin, Thomas (2003), 'The star system: Introduction', in M. Barker and T. Austin (eds), *Contemporary Hollywood Stardom*, London: Arnold, pp. 25–8.

Bagehot, Walter (1867), *The English Constitution*, New York: Cornell University Press.

Banerjee, Mita (2006), 'The rush hour of Black/Asian coalitions?: Jackie Chan and Blackface minstrelsy', in H. Raphael-Hernandez and S. Steen (eds), *AfroAsian Encounters: Culture, History, Politics*, New York: New York University Press, pp. 204–22.

Barretto, Clyde Erwin (2016), 'Donnie Yen displays MMA skills in "Kill Zone"', *The Underground*, 7 June, <www.mixedmartialarts.com/vault/cma/donnie-yen-displays-mma-skills-kill-zone> (last accessed 2 September 2017).

Barthes, Roland (1972), *Mythologies*. London: Granada.

Bassom, David (2006), *Keanu Reeves – An Illustrated Story*, London: Hamlyn.

Baxter, Joseph (2015), 'Star Wars: Episode 8 wants to cast Hong Kong action star as a Jedi', *CinemaBlend*, August, <www.cinemablend.com/new/Star-Wars-Episode-8-Wants-Cast-Hong-Kong-Action-Star-Jedi-72416.html> (last accessed 9 August 2016).

'Behind the Name: Ognyana' (n.d.), *Behind the Name: The Etymology and History of First Names*, <www.behindthename.com/name/ognyana> (last accessed 20 August 2017).

Benveniste, Emile (1971), *Problems in General Linguistics*, Miami: University of Miami Press.

Berry, Chris (2006), 'Stellar transit: Bruce Lee's body or Chinese masculinity in a transnational frame', in F. Martin and L. Heinrich (eds), *Embodied Modernities: Corporeality, Representation, and Chinese Cultures*, Honolulu: University of Hawai'i Press, pp. 218–34.

Berwick, Stephen (2000), 'Donnie Yen: The evolution of an American martial artist', *Kung Fu Qigong Magazine*, July, <www.kungfumagazine.com/magazine/article. php?article=119> (last accessed 8 July 2017).

Bettinson, Gary (2005), 'Reflections on a screen narcissist: Leslie Cheung's star persona in the films of Wong Kar-Wai', *Asian Cinema* 16:1, pp. 220–38.

Bezlova, Antoaneta (2006), '"Memoirs of a Geisha" lost in political din', *Inter Press Service*, 7 February, <www.ipsnews.net/2006/02/china-memoirs-of-a-geisha-lost-in-political-din/> (last accessed 19 August 2017).

Bishop, Matthew (2009), 'Philanthrocapitalism: Yes we can', *Huffpost*, 3 May, <www. huffingtonpost.com/matthew-bishop/philanthrocapitalism-yes_b_163253.html> (last accessed 27 August 2017).

Blood, Rebecca (2002a), 'Introduction', in J. Rodzvilla (ed.), *We've Got Blog: How Weblogs are Changing Our Culture*, Cambridge, MA: Perseus Publishing, pp. ix–xiii.

Blood, Rebecca (2002b), 'Weblogs: A history and perspective', in J. Rodzvilla (ed.), *We've Got Blog: How Weblogs are Changing Our Culture*, Cambridge, MA: Perseus Publishing, pp. 7–16.

Bordwell, David (2000), *Planet Hong Kong: Popular Cinema and the Art of Entertainment*, Cambridge, MA: Harvard University Press.

Bordwell, David (2001), 'Aesthetics in action: Kungfu, gunplay, and cinematic expressivity', in **E.** Yau (ed.), *At Full Speed: Hong Kong Cinema in a Borderless World*, Minneapolis and London: University of Minnesota Press, pp. 73–94.

Bourdieu, Pierre (2001), *Masculine Domination*, Stanford: Stanford University Press.

Bowman, Paul (2010a), 'Sick man of transl-Asia: Bruce Lee and Rey Chow's queer cultural translation', *Social Semiotics* 20:4, pp. 393–409.

Bowman, Paul (2010b), *Theorizing Bruce Lee: Film – Fantasy – Fighting – Philosophy*, Amesterdam: Rodopi.

Bowman, Paul (2016), 'The intimate schoolmaster and the ignorant sifu: Poststructuralism, Bruce Lee, and the ignorance of every radical pedagogy', *Philosophy and Rhetoric* 49:4, pp. 549–70.

Box Office Mojo: 'Red Cliff' (n.d.), <www.boxofficemojo.com/movies/?id=redcliff.htm> (last accessed 20 August 2017).

Box Office Mojo: 'Ru guo – Ai (Perhaps Love)' (n.d.), <www.boxofficemojo.com/movies/intl/?page=&country=HK&id=_fPERHAPSLOVE01> (last accessed 20 August 2017).

Box Office Mojo: 'Seung sing (confession of pain)' (n.d.), <www.boxofficemojo.com/movies/intl/?page=&country=HK&id=_fSEUNGSINGCONFES01> (last accessed 20 August 2017).

Brady, Robert (1947), 'The problem of monopoly.' *The ANNALS of the American Academy of Political and Social Science* (November), pp. 125–36.

Brennan, Timothy (1990), 'The national longing for form', in H. Bhabha (ed.), *Nation and Narration*, London: Routledge, pp. 44–70.

Breznican, Anthony (2011), 'Johnny Depp on "The Lone Ranger"', *Entertainment Weekly*, 8 May, <http:ew.com/article/2011/05/08/johnny-depp-tonto-lone-ranger/> (last accessed 10 August 2017).

Bruns, Axel (2005), *Gatewatching: Collaborative Online News Production*, New York: Peter Lang.

Bruns, Axel (2008), *Blogs, Wikipedia, Second Life from Beyond: From Production to Prousage*, New York: Peter Lang.

Burgess, Jean and Joshua Green (2009), *YouTube: Online Video and Participatory Culture*, Cambridge: Polity.

Burr, Martha (1999), 'Keanu Reeves in The Matrix. *Whoa is (not) me*', <www.whoaisnotme.net/articles/1999_xxxx_kea.htm> (last accessed 4 August 2016).

Burt, Ronald (1992), *Structural Holes: The Social Structure of Competition*, Cambridge, MA: Harvard University Press.

Butler, Jeremy (ed.) (1991), *Star Text: Image and Performance in Film and Television*, Detroit: Wayne State University Press.

Butler, Judith (1993), *Bodies that Matter: On the Discursive Limits of 'Sex'*. New York: Routledge.

Cai, Rong (2005), 'Gender imaginations in *Crouching Tiger, Hidden Dragon* and the *Wuxia* world', *positions: east asia cultures critique* 13:2, pp. 441–71.

Canclini, Nestor Garcia (1995), *Hybrid Cultures: Strategies for Entering and Leaving Modernity*, trans C. L. Chiappari and S. L. López, Minneapolis: University of Minnesota Press.

Carey, James (1998), *Communication as Culture: Essays on Media and Society*, Boston: Unwin Hyman.

Cavell, Stanley (1981), *Pursuits of Happiness: The Hollywood Comedy of Remarriage*, Cambridge, MA: Harvard University Press.

'Celebrity Jet Li becomes first goodwill ambassador' (2010), International Federation of Red Cross (IFRC) and Red Crescent Societies, 23 September, <www.ifrc.org/en/news-and-media/news-stories/international/celebrity-jet-li-becomes-first-goodwill-ambassador/> (last accessed 24 June 2013).

'Chan faces film boycott over comments' (2009), 23 April, <www.theage.com.au/news/entertainment/film/chan-faces-film-boycott-over-comments/2009/04/23/1240079771109.html> (last accessed 30 August 2017).

Chan, Felicia (2014), 'Maggie Cheung, "une Chinoise": Acting and agency in the realm of transnational stardom', in W. Leung and A. Willis (eds), *East Asian Film Stars*, Basingstoke: Palgrave Macmillan, pp. 83–95.

Chan, Natalia (2010), 'Queering body and sexuality: Leslie Cheung's gender representation in Hong Kong popular culture', in C. Yau (ed.), *As Normal as Possible: Negotiating Sexuality and Gender in Mainland China and Hong Kong*, Hong Kong: Hong Kong University Press, pp. 133–49.

Chan, Stephen (2001), 'Figures of hope and the filmic imaginary of jianghu in contemporary Hong Kong cinema', *Cultural Studies* 15:3–4, pp. 486–514.

Cheah, Pheng (1998), '"The cosmopolitical – today', in P. Cheah and B. Robbins (eds), *Cosmopolitics: Thinking and Feeling beyond the Nation*, Minneapolis: University of Minnesota Press, pp. 20–43.

Child, Ben (2014), 'Netflix's first original movie will be Crouching Tiger, Hidden Dragon sequel', <www.theguardian.com/film/2014/oct/01/netflixs-first-original-movie-will-be-crouching-tiger-hidden-dragon-sequel> (last accessed 6 August 2016).

'China: Alarming new surveillance security in Tibet' (2013), *Human Rights Watch*, 20 March. <www.hrw.org/news/2013/03/20/china-alarming-new-surveillance-security-tibet> (last accessed 27 August 2017).

'China cancels release of "Memoirs of a Geisha"' (2006), *Associated Press*, 1 February, www.usatoday.com/life/movies/news/2006-02-01-geisha-canceled-china_x.htm (last accessed 15 August 2017).

'China – Sichuan earthquake: Facts and figures', International Federation of Red Cross and Red Crescent Societies (2008), <www.sinoptic.ch/textes/communiques/2008/20080820_IFRC_Facts_Figures.pdf> (last accessed 1 August 2017).

'China to mourn quake dead, public entertainment to be suspended' (2010), CCTV, 20 April, <http:english.cctv.com/20100420/107825.shtml> (last accessed 27 August 2017).

Chinatown Los Angeles (official website) <http:chinatownla.com/wp1/> (last accessed 30 August 2017).

Ching, Leo (2000), 'Globalising the regional, regionalizing the global: Mass culture and Asianism in the Age of Late Capital', *Public Culture* 12:1, pp. 233–57.

Chow, Rey (2000), 'Introduction: On Chineseness as a theoretical problem', in R. Chow (ed.), *Modern Chinese Literary and Cultural Studies in the Age of Theory: Reimagining a Field*, Durham, NC: Duke University Press, pp. 1–25.

Chu, Karen (2015), 'Hong Kong star Donnie Yen talks shooting "Star Wars" film "Rogue One," working with Mike Tyson', *The Hollywood Reporter*, 23 December, <www.hollywoodreporter.com/news/donnie-yen-rogue-one-shoot-850941> (last accessed 2 August 2016).

Chu, Yiu Wai (2008), 'The importance of being Chinese: Orientalism reconfigured in the age of global modernity', *Boundary 2* (Summer) 35:2, pp. 183–306.

Chun, Allen (1996), 'Fuck Chineseness: On the ambiguities of ethnicity as culture as identity', boundary 223:2, pp. 111–38.

Ciecko, Anne (1997), 'Transnational action: John Woo, Hong Kong, Hollywood', in S. Lu (ed.), *Transnational Chinese Cinema: Identity, Nationhood, Gender*, Honolulu: University of Hawai'i Press, pp. 221–37.

'CITIZEN's new advertising campaign starring Takeshi Kaneshiro – performing the great power of persistent beliefs' ('CITIZEN推出全新金城武廣告-演繹堅持信念的強大力量') (2012), CITIZEN, 18 July, <www.citizen.com.hk/html/tc/news/what-s-news/citizen%E6%8E%A8%E5%87%BA%E5%85%A8%E6%96%B0%E9%87%91%E5%9F%8E%E6%AD%A6%E5%BB%A3%E5%91%8A-%E6%BC%94%E7%B9%B9%E5%A0%85%E6%8C%81%E4%BF%A1%E5%BF%B5%E7%9A%84%E5%BC%B7%E5%A4%A7%E5%8A%9B%E9%87%8F.html> (last accessed 24 September 2017).

Cloutman, Violet (2015), 'The secret world of Geisha', *Inside Japan*, 6 October, <www.insidejapantours.com/blog/2015/10/06/the-secret-world-of-geisha/> (last accessed 31 August 2017).

CNN (2006), 'Takeshi Kaneshiro Talkasia Transcript', CNN.com, 10 February, <http:edition.cnn.com/2006/WORLD/asiapcf/02/10/talkasia.kaneshiro.script/> (last accessed 26 August 2017).

Cohan, Steven (1997), *Masked Men: Masculinity and the Movies in the Fifties*, Bloomington: Indiana University Press.

Collins, Randall (1998), *The Sociology of Philosophies: A Global Theory of Intellectual Change*, Cambridge, MA: Harvard University Press.

Danwei (2004), 'House of Flying Daggers box office: 110 million yuan', <www.danwei.org/film/house_of_flying_daggers_box_of.php> (last accessed 26 July 2017).

Davis, Bob (2003), 'Takeshi Kitano', *Senses of Cinema*, July, <http://sensesofcinema.com/2003/great-directors/kitano/> (last accessed 17 July 2016).

DeAngelis, Michael (2001), *Gay Fandom and Crossover Stardom: James Dean, Mel Gibson, and Keanu Reeves*, Durham, NC: Duke University Press.

Debord, Guy (1995), *The Society of the Spectacle*, New York: Zone Books.

DeCordova, Richard (1990), *Picture Personalities: The Emergence of the Star System in America*, Chicago: University of Illinois Press.

DeCordova, Richard (1991), 'The emergence of the star system in America', in C. Gledhill (ed.), Stardom: Industry of Desire, London: Routledge, pp. 17–29.

Denson, Shane and Julia Leyda (2016), 'Perspectives on post-cinema: An introduction', in S. Denson and J. Leyda (eds), *Post-Cinema: Theorizing 21st-Century Film*, Falmer: Reframe Books.

Desser, David (2000), 'The kung fu craze: Hong Kong cinema's first American reception', in P. Fu and D. Desser (eds), *The Cinema of Hong Kong: History, Arts, Identity*, Cambridge: Cambridge University Press, pp. 19–43.

Deveraux, Michelle (2006), '10 Reasons Keanu Rules', *Wired*, 1 *March*, <www.wired.com/2006/03/keanu/> (last accessed 10 August 2017).

Dien, Yuen (2008), 'Jet Li, philanthropist & martial arts star', 31 October, <http://www.asianphilanthropyforum.org/jet-li-philanthropist-martial-arts-star/> (last accessed 11 June 2018).

Dirlik, Arif (1997), *The Postcolonial Aura: Third World Criticism in the Age of Globalisation*, Boulder, CO: Westview.

Dodds, Eric (1951), *The Greeks and the Irrational*, Berkeley: University of California Press.

Dogonfire2005 (2010), 'Chinese actress Ziyi Zhang suspected embezzling earthquake relief funds', YouTube, 11 February, <www.youtube.com/watch?v=rlgsBhH0Fo&feature=related> (last accessed 17 August 2017).

Donath, Judith (2007), 'Signals in social supernets', *Journal of Computer-Mediated Communication* 13(1), pp. 231–51.

Donnie Yen (official website) <www.donnieyen.asia/> (last accessed 27 July 2017).

Drake, Kate (2003), 'Pan-Asian sensation', *Time*, 29 September, <www.time.com/time/magazine/article/0,9171,490735,00.html> (last accessed 26 May, 2012).

Dyer, Richard (1979), *Stars*, London: BFI.

Dyer, Richard (1986), *Heavenly Bodies: Film Stars and Society*, London: Routledge.

Ellison, Nichole, Jessica Vitak, Rebecca Gray, and Cliff Lampe (2014), 'Cultivating social resources on social network sites: Facebook relationship maintenance behaviors and their roles in social capital process', *Journal of Computer-Mediated Communications* 19:4, pp. 855–70.

Everett, Anna (2004), 'Johnny Depp and Keanu Reeves: Hollywood and the Iconoclasts', in A. Everett, G. Blasini and M. Donalson (eds), *Pretty People: Movie Stars of the 1990s*, Piscataway, US: Rutgers University Press, pp. 225–48.

Fam, Jonathan (2017), 'Jackie Chan's ex-mistress and mother of his only daughter says he never gave them a single cent', *8 Days*, 31 March, <www.8days.sg/sceneandheard/entertainment/jackie-chan-s-ex-mistress-and-mother-of-his-only-daughter-says-8550346> (last accessed 23 July 2017).

Fanon, Frantz (1963), *The Wretched of the Earth*, New York: Gross Press.

Fanon, Frantz (1967), *The Wretched of the Earth*, Harmondsworth: Penguin.

Farquhar, Mary (2010a), 'Jackie Chan: Star work as pain and triumph', in M. Farquhar and Y. Zhang (eds), *Chinese Film Stars*, London and New York: Routledge, pp. 180–95.

Farquhar, Mary (2010b), 'Jet Li: "Wushu Master" in sport and film', in L. Edwards and E. Jeffreys (eds), *Celebrity in China*, Hong Kong: Hong Kong University Press, pp. 103–23.

Farquhar, Mary and Zhang Yingjin (eds), (2010), *Chinese Film Stars*, London and New York: Routledge.

Felperin, Leslie (2006), 'Memoir of a Geisha', *Sight & Sound* 16(2), p. 71.

Feng, Lin (2011), 'Star endorsement and Hong Kong cinema: The social mobility of Chow Yun-fat 1986–1995', *Journal of Chinese Cinemas* 5:3 (7 November), pp. 269–81.

Feng, Lin (2017), *Chow Yun-fat and Territories of Hong Kong Stardom*, Edinburgh: Edinburgh University Press.

Feng, Peter X. (2000), 'Recuperating Suzie Wong: A fan's Nancy Kwan-diary', in D. Y. Hamamoto and S. Liu (eds), *Countervisions: Asian American Film Criticism*, Philadelphia: Temple University Press, pp. 40–58.

Feng, Peter X. (2002a), 'False and double consciousness: Race, virtual reality and the assimilation of Hong Kong action cinema in *The Matrix*', in Z. Sardar and S. Cubbitt (eds), *Aliens R Us: The Other in Science Fiction Cinema*, Sterling, VA: Pluto Press, pp. 149–63.

Feng, Peter X. (2002b), *Screening Asian Americans*, New Brunswick, NJ: Rutgers University Press.

Fischer, Lucy and Marcia Landy (eds), (2004), *Stars: The Film Reader*, New York: Routledge.

Fischer, Paul (2005), 'Interview: Zhang Ziyi for "Memoirs of a Geisha"', *Dark Horizons*, 23 November, <www.darkhorizons.com/features/425/zhang-ziyi-for-memoirs-of-a-geisha> (last accessed 21 August 2017).

Fiske, John (1992), 'The cultural economy of fandom', in L. Lewis (ed.), *Adoring Audience: Fan Culture and Popular Media*, London: Routledge, pp. 30–49.

Fitzpatrick, Liam (2008), 'The Liberation of Jet Li', *Time*, 27 November, <www.time.com/time/magazine/article/0,9171,1862595,00.html> (last accessed 25 June 2013).

Fore, Steve (1997), 'Jackie Chan and the cultural dynamics of global entertainment', in S. Lu (ed.), *Transnational Chinese Cinemas: Identity, Nationhood, Gender*, Honolulu: University of Hawaii Press, pp. 239–64.

Funnell, Lisa (2013a), 'Fighting for a Hong Kong/Chinese female identity: Michelle Yeoh, body performance, and globalised action cinema', *Asian Popular Culture in Transition*, Abingdon: Routledge, pp. 171–85.

Funnell, Lisa (2013b), 'Hong Kong's It/Ip Man: The Chinese contexts of Donnie Yen's transnational stardom', in R. Meeuf and R. Raphael (eds), *Transnational Stardom: International Celebrity in Film and Popular Culture*, New York: Palgrave Macmillan, pp. 117–38.

Funnell, Lisa (2014), *Warrior Women: Gender, Race, and the Transnational Chinese Action Star*, New York: State University of New York Press.

Furbel, James (2008). 'Jackie Chan honours late parents in Australia', Reuters, 9 March, <https://www.reuters.com/article/us-australia-chan/jackie-chan-honors-late-parents-in-australia-idUSSYD17523720080309> (last accessed 2 May 2018).

Fury, Mike (2011), 'Donnie Yen: The Wing Chun connection', *Jade Screen*, <www.mikefury.net/files/donnie-yen---the-wing-chun-connection---mike-fury.pdf> (last accessed 29 April 2018).

Gallagher, Mark (2004), 'Rumble in the USA: Jackie Chan in translation', in Andy Willis (ed.), *Film Stars: Hollywood and Beyond*, Manchester: Manchester University Press, pp. 113–39.

Gallagher, Mark (2010), '"Would you rather spend more time making serious cinema?": *Hero* and Tony Leung's polysemic masculinity', in G. Rawnsley and M. Rawnsley (eds), *Global Chinese Cinema: The Culture and the Politics of Hero*, Abingdon: Routledge, pp. 106–20.

Gallagher, Mark (2015), 'Tony Leung's thrillers and transnational stardom', in C. Shin and M. Gallagher (eds), *East Asian Film Noir*, New York: I. B. Tauris, pp. 197–214.

Gallagher, Mark (2016), 'Tony Leung Chiu-Wai: Acting sexy in Hong Kong and China', *Asian Cinema* 27:1, pp. 43–58.

Gamson, Joshua (1994), *Claims to Fame: Celebrity in Contemporary America*, Berkeley: University of California Press.

Gateward, Frances (2009), 'Wong Fei-Hung in da house: Hong Kong. Martial-arts films and hip-hop culture', in S. K. Tan, P. X. Feng, and G. Marchett (eds), *Chinese Connections: Critical Perspectives on Film, Identity and Diaspora*, Philadelphia: Temple University Press, pp. 51–67.

Geraghty, Christine (2000), 'Re-examining stardom', in C. Gledhill and L. Williams (eds), *Reinventing Film Studies*, London: Arnold, pp. 183–200.

Gerow, Aaron (2007), *Kitano Takeshi*, London: British Film Institute.

Giarratana, Carmel (2002), 'The Keanu effect – stardom and the landscape of the acting body: Los Angeles/Hollywood as sight/site', in A. Ndalianis and C. Henry (eds), *Stars in our Eyes: The Star Phenomenon in the Contemporary Era*. Westport, Connecticut: Praeger, pp. 61–84.

Gibson, William (1984), *Neuromancer*, New York: Ace Books.

Gibson, Charles (2009), 'China's Facebook status: Blocked', abc News, 8 July, <http:blogs.abcnews.com/theworldnewser/2009/07/chinas-facebook-status-blocked.html > (last accessed 27 August 2017).

Giddens, Anthony (1991), *Modernity and Self-identity: Self and Society in the Late Modern Age*, Cambridge: Polity Press.Giddens, Anthony (1992), *The Transformation of Intimacy*, Cambridge: Polity Press.

Gillis, Stacy (2005), 'Introduction', in S. Gillis (ed.), *The Matrix Trilogy: Cyberpunk Reloaded*, London: Wallflower Press, pp. 1–8.

Ginsberg, Elaine (1996), *Passing and the Fictions of Identity*, Durham, NC: Duke University Press.

Gledhill, Christine (ed.), (1991), *Stardom: Industry of Desire*, London and New York: Routledge.

Gotham, Kevin (2012), 'Make it right? Brad Pitt, post-Katrina rebuilding, and the spectacularisation of disaster', in R. Mukherjee and S. Banet-Weiser (eds), *Commodity Activism: Cultural Resistance in Neoliberal Times*, New York and London: New York University Press, pp. 97–113.

Granovetter, Mark (1974), *Getting a Job: A Study of Contacts and Careers*, Cambridge, MA: Harvard University Press.

Gray, Jonathan, Cornel Sandvoss, and C. Lee Harrington (2007), 'Introduction: Why study fans?', in J. Gray, C. Sandvoss, and C. L. Harrington (eds), *Fandom: Identities and Communities in a Mediated World*, New York: New York University Press, pp. 1–16.

Grusin, Richard (2016), 'Post-cinematic atavism', in S. Denson and J. Leyda (eds), *Post-cinema: Theorizing 21st-century Film*, Falmer: Reframe Books, pp. 65–87.

Guillen, Michael (2006), *The Evening Class: Chinese Cinema – Grace Chang: An Appreciation*, 24 March, <http:theeveningclass.blogspot.hk/2006/03/chinese-cinemagrace-chang-appreciation.html> (last accessed 15 August 2016).

Gurbel, James (2008), 'Jackie Chan honours late parents in Australia', *Reuters*, 9 March, <www.treuters.com/article/2008/03/09/us-australia-chan-idUSSYD1752372 0080309> (last accessed 31 July 2017).

Hamamoto, Darrell and Sandra Liu (2000), *Countervisions: Asian American Film Criticism*, Philadelphia: Temple University Press.

Hannerz, Ulf (1996), *Transnational Connections: Culture, People, Places*, London and New York: Routledge.

Hansen, Miriam (1991), 'Pleasure, ambivalence, identification: Valentino and female spectatorship', in C. Gledhill (ed.), *Stardom: Industry of Desire*, London: Routledge, pp. 259–82.

Harrington, Lee and Denise Bielby (2007), 'Global fandom/Global fan studies', in J. Gray, C. Sandvoss, and C. L. Harrington (eds), *Fandom: Identities and Communities in a Mediated World*, New York and London: New York University Press, pp. 179–97.

Hellekson, Karen and Kristina Busse (eds), (2006), *Fan Fiction and Fan Communities in the Age of the Internet: New Essays*, Jefferson, NC: McFarland & Co.

Hills, Matthew (2002), *Fan Cultures*, London: Routledge.

Hinerman, Stephen (2006), '(Don't) leave me alone; tabloid narrative and the Michael Jackson child-abuse scandal', in P. D. Marshall (ed.), *The Celebrity Culture Reader*, New York: RoutledgeCurzon, pp. 455–69.

Hollinger, Karen (2006), *The Actress: Hollywood Acting and the Female Stars*, New York and London: Routledge.

'Hollywood star learns Wing Chun' (2010), *Daily Kung Fu*, 20 April, <www.dailykungfu.com/2010/04/hollywood-star-learns-wing-chun.html> (last accessed 15 May 2012).

Hood, Johanna (2010), 'Celebrity philanthropy: The cultivation of China's HIV/AIDS Heroes', in L. Edwards and E. Jeffreys (eds), *Celebrity in China*, Hong Kong: Hong Kong University Press, pp. 85–102.

Hsing, Alfred (2010), 'Sister to Donnie Yen, daughter to Bow Sim Mark: Lunch with martial arts star Chris Yen', The Blog of Alfred Hsing, 23 April, <http://alfredrocks.com/blog/sister-to-donnie-yen-daughter-to-bow-sim-mark-lunch-with-martial-arts-star-chris-yen/> (last accessed 2 May 2018).

Hudson, Dale (2006), '"Just play yourself, 'maggie Cheung'": Irma Vep, rethinking transnational stardom and unthinking national cinemas', *Screen* 47:2, pp. 213–32.

Hunt, Leon (2003), *Kung Fu Cult Masters*, London and New York: Wallflower.

Hunt, Leon (2014), 'Too late the hero? The delayed stardom of Donnie Yen', in W. Leung and A. Willis (eds), *East Asian Film Stars*, Basingstoke: Palgrave Macmillan, pp. 143–55.

'I'm too pretty for my career, says Takeshi' (2008), scmp.com, 5 July, <www.scmp.com/article/644042/im-too-pretty-my-career-says-takeshi> (last accessed 11 August 2017).

IMDb: Chi bi (2008), <www.imdb.com/title/tt0425637/?ref_=fn_al_tt_1> (last accessed 23 August 2017).

IMDb Database Statistics, IMDb. <www.imdb.com/stats> (last accessed 23 August 2017).

IndieWire (2006), 'AFP: Chinese actress Zhang Ziyi to join Cannes jury', *IndieWire*, 17 April, <www.indiewire.com/2006/04/afp-chinese-actress-zhang-ziyi-to-join-cannes-jury-76831/> (last accessed 10 August, 2017).

Indiewire (2012), 'Toronto 2012: China's "Dangerous Liaisons" Goes to Well Go USA', *IndieWire*, 8 September, <http://www.indiewire.com/2012/09/toronto-2012-chinas-dangerous-liaisons-goes-to-well-go-usa-241719/> (last accessed 12 June 2018).

'Interview about Web 2.0' (2006), July, <www.paulgraham.com/web20interview.html> (last accessed 12 July 2016).

'Ip Chun (葉準), 84-year-old Wing Chun legend' (2009), *South China Morning Post*, 16 March, <www.youtube.com/watch?v=y6oPgV0tJrM> (last accessed 5 September 2017).

Iwabuchi, Koichi (2002), *Recentering Globalization: Popular Culture and Japanese Transnationalism*, Durham, NC: Duke University Press.

'Jackie attends state dinner for Hu Jintao' (2011), SuperChan's Jackie Chan Blog, 20 January, <http:superchanblog.blogspot.hk/2011/01/jackie-attends-state-dinner-for-hu.html> (last accessed 30 August 2017).

'Jackie Chan at the Australia-China film industry forum (translated)', 2012, YouTube, <www.youtube.com/watch?v=VY34OjtE50Q> (last accessed 31 August 2017).

'Jackie Chan biography' (n.d.), *Encyclopedia of World Biography*, <www.notablebiographies.com/supp/Supplement-Ca-Fi/Chan-Jackie.html> (last accessed on 26 August 2017).

Jacobs, Andrew (2009), 'Jackie Chan strikes a Chinese nerve', *The New York Times*, 23 April, <www.nytimes.com/2009/04/24/world/asia/24jackie.html?_r¼1&> (last accessed 1 August 2017).

Jaffé, Daniel (2012), *Historical Dictionary of Russian Music*, Lanham, MD: Scarecrow Press.

Jameson, Fredric (1986), 'Third World literature in the era of multinational capitalism', *Social Text* 15 (Autumn), pp. 65–88.

Jameson, Fedric (1991), *Postmodernism, or, The Cultural Logic of Late Capitalism*, Durham, NC: Duke University Press.

Japan Today (2008), 'Takeshi Kaneshiro disqualified from Taiwan Film Awards', 1 November, <https:japantoday.com/category/entertainment/takeshi-kaneshiro-disqualified-from-taiwan-film-awards> (last accessed 20 August 2017).

Jarvie, Ian C. (2004), 'Stars and ethnicity: Hollywood and the United States, 1932–51', in L. Fischer and M. Landy (eds), *Stars: The Film Reader*, New York: Routledge, pp. 167– 80.

Jeffreys, Elaine (2011), 'Zhang Ziyi and China's celebrity-philanthropy scandals', *Portal: Journal of Multidisciplinary International Studies* 8:1, <http:epress.lib.uts.edu.au/journals/index.php/portal/article/view/1627> (last accessed 21 August 2017).

Jenkins, Henry (1992), *Textual Poachers: Television Fans and Participatory Culture*, New York: Routledge.

Jenkins, Henry (2006a), *Convergence Culture: Where Old and New Media Collide*, New York: New York University Press.

Jenkins, Henry (2006b), 'Confronting the challenges of participatory culture: Media education for the 21st century', *Building the Field of Digital Media and Learning*, 19 October, <www.macfound.org/press/publications/brochure-building-the-field-of-digital-media-and-learning-october-19-2006/> (last accessed 24 August 2017).

Jenkins, Henry (2010), 'Fandom, participatory culture, and Web 2.0 – A syllabus', 9 January, <http:henryjenkins.org/2010/01/fandom_participatory_culture_a.html> (last accessed 18 April 2013).

'Jet Li biography' (n.d.), imdb.com, <www.imdb.com/name/nm0001472/bio> (last accessed 24 August 2015).

'Jet Li breaks film salary record' (2007), BBC News, 26 November, <http:news.bbc.co.uk/2/hi/entertainment/7112639.stm> (last accessed 2 September 2015).

'Jet Li plays with heart in "Ocean Heaven"' (2010), *People's Daily Online*, 17 June, <http://en.people.cn/90001/90782/90875/7028268.html> (last accessed 20 August 2015).

Jingles (2015), 'Takeshi Kaneshiro shares his views on aging and acting', Jayne Stars, 5 September, <www.jaynestars.com/news/takeshi-kaneshiro-shares-his-views-on-aging-and-acting/> (last accessed 1 August 2017).

Jung, Hyun-mok (2012), 'Language no barrier to Jang's appeal', Korea JoongAng Daily, 8 October, <http://koreajoongangdaily.joins.com/news/article/article.aspx?aid=2960411> (last accessed 12 June 2018).

Kandel, Janine (2012), 'In Myanmar, UNICEF Goodwill Ambassador Jackie Chan visits children affected by human trafficking', 11 July, <www.unicef.org/people/myanmar_65332.html> (last accessed May 20, 2017).

Kato, M. T. (2007), *From Kung Fu to Hip Hop: Globalisation, Revolution and. Popular Culture*, Albany: State University of New York Press.

Kazeniac, Andy (2009), 'Social networks: Facebook takes over top spot, Twitter climbs', *Compete Pulse*, 9 February, <http:blog.compete.com/2009/02/09/facebook-myspace-twitter-social-network/> (last accessed 28 June 2013).

Kearney, Carol (2013), 'Jet Li highest-paid actor in the world', *Mediamass* 28, June, http:en.mediamass.net/people/jet-li/highest-paid.html (last accessed 23 June 2013).

Khoo, Olivia (2010), 'Fifteen minutes of fame: Transient/Transnational female stardom in *Hero*', in G. Rawnsley and M. T. Rawnsley (eds), *Global Chinese Cinema: The Culture and Politics of Hero*, London and New York: Routledge, pp. 121–31.

King, Barry (2003), 'Embodying an elastic self: The parametrics of contemporary stardom', in T. Austin and M. Baker (eds), *Contemporary Hollywood Stardom*, London: Arnold, pp. 45–61.

Kirkpatrick, David (2008), 'Is Facebook worth your time?', *CNN Money*, 18 April, <http:money.cnn.com/2008/04/18/technology/kirkpatrick_facebook.fortune/index.htm> (last accessed 22 June 2013).

Klein, Christina (2004a), '"*Crouching Tiger, Hidden Dragon*": A diasporic reading', *Cinema Journal* 43:4, pp. 18–42.

Klein, Christina (2004b), 'Martial arts and the globalisation of US and Asian film industries', *Comparative American Studies* 2:3, pp. 360–84.

Kolinovsky, Sarah (n.d.), 'Inside the secret world of a geisha', abc News, <http://abcnews.go.com/International/photos/inside-secret-world-geisha-26497343/image-26497516> (last accessed 19 August 2017).

Kraicer, Shelly (1998), 'Sleepless Town', *Chinese Cinemas*, <www.chinesecinemas.org/sleeplesstown.html> (last accessed 29 May 2012).

Kraicer, Shelly (1999), 'Tempting Heart', *Chinese Cinemas*, <www.chinesecinemas.org/temptingheart.html> (last accessed 18 August 2017).

Kritsadaj (2016), 'Happy Birthday Jackie Chan', 7 April, <https:blogs.unicef.org/east-asia-pacific/happy-birthday-jackie-chan/> (last accessed 24 May 2017).

Krützen, Michaela (1992), *The Most Beautiful Woman on the Screen – the Fabrication of the Star Greta Garbo*, Frankfurt: Peter Lang.

LaSalle, Mick (1995), 'Hong Kong icon gets chopped up/ "High Risk" spoofs Jackie Chan', SFGate, 15 December, <www.sfgate.com/entertainment/article/Hong-Kong-Icon-Gets-Chopped-Up-High-Risk-3017710.php> (last accessed 30 August 2017).

Lau, Shing-hon (ed.) (1980), *A Study of the Hong Kong Martial Arts Film, 4th Hong Kong International Film Festival*, Hong Kong: Urban Council.

Lau, Shing-hon (ed.) (1981), *A Study of the Hong Kong Swordplay Film (1954–1980), 5th Hong Kong International Film Festival*, Hong Kong: Urban Council.

Lee, Claire (2012), 'Zhang, Cheung touched by Jang Dong-gun's professionalism', *The Korea Herald*, 5 October, <www.koreaherald.com/view.php?ud=20121005000783> (last accessed 11 August 2017).

Lee, Edmond (2015), 'Donnie Yen talks Ip Man 3, Star Wars spin-off and his final kung fu film', *South China Morning Post*, 21 December. <www.scmp.com/lifestyle/film-tv/article/1892577/donnie-yen-talks-ip-man-3-star-wars-spin-and-his-final-kung-fu> (last accessed 10 August 2016).

Lee, Edmond (2016), 'Hong Kong action star Donnie Yen on how he changed Rogue One: A Star Wars story', *South China Morning Post*, 13 December, <www.scmp.com/culture/film-tv/article/2054237/hong-kong-action-star-donnie-yen-playing-blind-warrior-rogue-one> (last accessed 26 June 2017).

Lee, Maggie (2011), 'Wu Xia (Dragon): Cannes Review', *The Hollywood Reporter*, 14 May, <www.hollywoodreporter.com/review/wu-xia-dragon-cannes-review-188449> (last accessed 31 August 2017).

Lee, Maggie (2014), 'Film review: "The Monkey King in 3D"', *Variety*, 31 January, <http:variety.com/2014/film/global/film-review-chinese-blockbuster-the-monkey-king-1201080253/> (last accessed 28 June 2017).

Lee, Vivian (2011), 'Introduction: Mapping East Asia's cinemascape', in V. Lee (ed.), *East Asian Cinemas: Regional Flows and Global Transformation*, Basingstoke: Palgrave Macmillan, pp. 1–12.

Leonard, Devin (2010), 'What you want: Flickr creator spins addictive new Web service', *Wired*, 28 July, <www.wired.com/magazine/2010/07/ff_caterina_fake/all/>, (last accessed 24 May 2017).

Leung, Wing-Fai (2014), 'Zhang Ziyi: The new face of Chinese femininity', in W. Leung and A. Willis (eds), *East Asian Film Stars*, New York: Palgrave Macmillan, pp. 65–80.

Leung, Wing-Fai (2015), *Multimedia Stardom in Hong Kong: Image, Performance and Identity*, London: Routledge.

Lévy, Pierre (2001), *Cyberculture*, trans. R. Bononno, Minneapolis and London: University of Minnesota Press.

'Li Bingbing UNEP Ambassador in China' (2010), United Nations Environment Programme, 4 July, <http://staging.unep.org/Documents.Multilingual/Default.asp?DocumentID=630&ArticleID=6637&l=en&t=long> (last accessed 20 June 2013).

Li, Jet (1999), 'Mind/essays/to my fans', The Official Jet Li Website, 17 June, <http:jetli.com/jet/index.php?l=en&s=mind&ss=essays&p=2> (last accessed 22 June 2013).

Li, Jet (2000), 'Body/questions', The Official Jet Li Website, 20 October, <http:jetli.com/jet/index.php?l=en&s=body&ss=questions&p=x&date=001020> (last accessed 22 June 2013).

Li, Jet (n.d.a), 'Life/Essays/Part 7', The Official Jet Li Website, <http:jetli.com/jet/index.php?s=life&ss=essays&p=7> (last accessed 24 June 2013).

Li, Jet (n.d.b), 'Spirit/Essays/Jet's personal journey', The Official Jet Li Website, <http:jetli.com/jet/index.php?l=en&s=spirit&ss=essays&p=4> (last accessed 22 June 2013).

Li, Jet (n.d.c), 'Spirit/Essays/The One Foundation project Page', The Official Jet Li Website, <http:jetli.com/jet/index.php?l=en&s=spirit&ss=essays&p=8> (last accessed 21 June 2013).

Li, Jet (2000), 'Body/questions', The Official Jet Li Website, 20 October, <http://jetli.com/jet/index.php?l=en&s=body&ss=questions&p=x&date=001020> (last accessed 22 June 2013).

Lin, Nan (2001), *Social Capital: A Theory of Social Structure and Action*, London: Cambridge University Press.

Lin, Xu (2011), 'Top 100 Chinese celebrities', 23 June, <www.china.org.cn/top10/2011-06/23/content_22845446.htm> (last accessed 27 June 2017).

Liu, James J. Y. (1967), *The Chinese Knight-Errant*, London: Routledge and Kegan.

Liu, Wei (2009), 'Jackie Chan promoted patriotic song in LA', Xinhua/CRIENGLISH. com, <http://english.cri.cn/6666/2009/06/23/1221s495893.htm> (last accessed 31 August 2017).

Lo, Kwai-Cheung (2005), *Chinese Face/Off: The Transnational Popular Culture of Hong Kong*, Urbana: University of Illinois Press.

Lo, Kwai-Cheung (2010), *Excess and Masculinity in Asian Cultural Productions*, Albany: State University of New York Press.

Logan, Bey (2007), 'Eastern thunder down under: Hong Kong Cinema's Aussie Connection', 5 July <www.dragondynasty.com/blog/show/42> (last accessed 28 May 2017).

Lull, James and Hinerman, Stephen (1997), 'The search for scandal', in James Lull and Stephen Hinerman (eds), *Media Scandals: Morality and Desire in the Popular Culture Marketplace*, Cambridge: Polity Press, pp. 1–33.

Lynch, Greg, Jr (2009), 'The Lynch Chronicles: Jackie Chan's beloved country and Tiger Claw's KungFuMagazine.com Championship', KungfuMagazine.com, 24 July, www. kungfumagazine.com/ezine/article.php?article¼4827> (last accessed 27 May 2017).

Mackintosh, Jonathan D. (2014), 'Bruce Lee: A visual poetics of postwar Japanese manliness', *Modern Asian Studies* 48:6 (1 November), pp. 1,477–518.

Magnan-Park, Aaron Han Joon (2007), 'The heroic influx in John Woo's trans-pacific passage', in G. Marchetti and S. K. Tan (eds), *Hong Kong Film, Hollywood and New Global Cinema: No Film is an Island*, London: Routledge, pp. 35–49.

Marchetti, Gina (2010), 'Departing from *The Departed*: The *Infernal Affairs* trilogy', in L. Kam (ed.), *Hong Kong Culture: Word and Image*, Hong Kong: Hong Kong University Press, pp. 147–68.

Marchetti, Gina (2012), *The Chinese Diaspora on American Screens: Race, Sex, and Cinema*, Philadelphia: Temple University Press.

Marchetti, Gina and Tan See Kam (2007), 'Introduction: Hong Kong Cinema and Global Change', in G. Marchetti and S. K. Tan (eds), *Hong Kong Film, Hollywood and New Global Cinema: No Film is an Island*, London: Routledge, pp. 1–9.

Marshall, David (1997), *Celebrity and Power: Fame in Contemporary Culture*, Minneapolis: University of Minnesota Press.

Marshall, David (2006), 'New media – new self: The changing power of celebrity', in David Marshall (ed.), *The Celebrity Culture Reader*, New York and London: Routledge, pp. 634–44.

Martin, Daniel (2014), 'Body of action, face of authenticity: Symbolic stars in the transnational marketing and reception of East Asian cinema', in W. Leung and A. Willis (eds), *East Asian Film Stars*, Basingstoke: Palgrave Macmillan, pp. 19–34.

Marx, Christy (2002), *Jet Li*, New York: Rosen.

Maslin, Janet (1991), 'Review/Film; Surf's Up For F.B.I.,' in Bigelow's "Point Break"', *The New York Times*, 12 July, <www.nytimes.com/movie/review?_r=2&res=9D0C E3D9143EF931A25754C0A967958260&partner=Rotten%2520Tomatoes> (last accessed 17 August 2017).

Mattelart, Armant (1994), *Mapping World Communication: War, Progress, Culture*, Minneapolis: University of Minnesota Press.

Matuszak, Sascha (2015), 'Kung fu film legend Donnie Yen lands role in *Star Wars*', *Fightland Blog*, 8 July, <http:fightland.vice.com/blog/kung-fu-film-legend-donnie-yen-lands-role-in-star-wars> (last accessed 3 May 2018).

Mayne, Judith (1993), *Cinema and Spectatorship*, London and New York: Routledge.

McDonald, Paul (2000), *The Star System: Hollywood's Production of Popular Identities*, London: Wallflowers.

McDonald, Paul (2003), 'Stars in the online universe: Promotion, nudity, reverence', in T. Austin and M. Barker (eds), *Contemporary Hollywood Stardom*, London: Arnold, pp. 29–44.

MDeeDubroff (2008), 'Red: China's color of fire and celebration', *Weird*, <www.weirdasianews.com/2008/10/13/red-chinas-color-fire-celebration/> (last accessed 28 May 2017).

merrick (2008), 'Does Jackie & Jet's FORBIDDEN KINGDOM actually rock?? The Drunken Reviewer says so. . .' *Ain't It Cool News*, 1 February, <www.aintitcool.com/node/35467> (last accessed 1 August 2017).

Merton, Robert (1946), *Mass Persuasion: The Social Psychology of a War Bond Drive*, New York: Harper & Bros.

Metz, Christian (1974), *Language and Cinema*, trans. Donna Jean Umiker-Sebeok, The Hague: The Mouton.

Miller, Laura (1995), 'Crossing ethnolinguistic boundaries: A preliminary look at the Gaijin Tarento in Japan', in J. Lent (ed.), *Asian Popular Culture*, New York: Westview Press, pp. 189–201.

Miller, Vincent (2011), *Understanding Digital Culture*, London and Thousand Oaks: SAGE Publications.

Mislove, Alan, Hema S. Koppula, Krishna P. Gummadi, Peter Druschel, and Bobby Bhattacharjee (2008), 'Growth of the Flickr social network', in M. Steenstrup (ed.), *Proceedings of the 1st ACM SIGCOMM Workshop on Social Networks (WOSN)*, USA: Seattle, pp. 25–30.

Mitra, Ananda and Elisia Cohen (1999), 'Analyzing the Web: Directions and challenges', in S. Jones (ed.), *Doing Internet Research: Critical Issues and Methods for Examining the Net*, Thousand Oaks: Sage, pp. 179–202.

Moore, Malcolm (2009), 'Jackie Chan said Chinese people need to be controlled', *The Telegraph*, 19 April, <www.huffingtonpost.com/2009/04/18/jackie-chan-chinese-peopl_n_188541.html> (last accessed 1 August 2017).

Morin, Edgar (1968), *The Stars*, Minneapolis: University of Minnesota Press.

Morley, Rachel (2003), *Growing up with Audrey Hepburn: Text, Audience, Resonance*, Manchester and New York: Manchester University Press.

Mottram, James (2016), 'Crouching Tiger, Hidden Dragon: Sword of Destiny – more martial arts wizardry', *South China Morning Post*, 12 February, <www.scmp.com/lifestyle/film-tv/article/1909296/crouching-tiger-hidden-dragon-sword-destiny-more-martial-arts> (last accessed 2 September 2017).

'My visit to the White House' (2011), The Official Website of Jackie Chan: JC Diary, 21 January, <http:jackiechan.com/blog/1154189--My-Visit-to-the-White-House> (last accessed 30 March 2012).

Myers, Greg (2010), *Discourse of Blogs and Wikis*, London: Continuum.

Nagel, Joane (1998), 'Masculinity and nationalism: Gender and sexuality in the making of nations', *Ethnic and Racial Studies* 21:2, pp. 242–69.

Nairn, Tom (1977), *The Break-up of Britain: Crisis and Neo-nationalism*, London: NLB.

Negra, Diane (2001), *Off-White Hollywood: American Culture and Ethnic Female Stardom*, London: Routledge, 2001.

'NetEase: The Warlords' (n.d.), <http:ent.163.com/special/00032G7E/The_Warlords. html> (last accessed 17 August 2017).

Nic (2016). 'Top 5 facts you didn't know about Donnie Yen', MMA.TV, <www.mma. tv/best-of/top-5-facts-you-didnt-know-about-donnie-yen/5/> (last accessed 3 September 2017).

Nishime, Leilani (2008), 'The Matrix trilogy, Keanu Reeves, and multiraciality at the end of time', in M. Beltran and C. Fojas. (eds), *Mixed Race Hollywood*, New York: New York University Press, pp. 290–312.

Nishime, LeiLani (2017), 'Reviving Bruce: Negotiating Asian masculinity through Bruce Lee paratexts in *Giant Robot* and *Angry Asian Man*', *Critical Studies in Media Communication* (8 February), pp. 1–10.

NIX (2007), 'Jet Li Talks about the Monkey King in The Forbidden Kingdom', beyondhollywood.com, 9 July, <www.beyondhollywood.com/jet-li-talks-about-the-monkey-king-in-the-forbidden-kingdom/> (last accessed 30 August 2017).

Odendahl, Teresa (1990), *When Charity Begins at Home: Generosity and Self-Interest among the Philanthropic Elite*, New York: Basic Books.

'One Foundation' (n.d.), Global Giving Foundation, <www.globalgiving.org/ donate/15390/one-foundation/> (last accessed 10 September 2017).

One Foundation (n.d.), 'Introduction', <www.onefoundation.cn/en/introduction. html> (last accessed 10 June 2014).

'One-minute performance on-stage costs four-year hard work off-stage: The secret of learning English of Zhang Ziyi' [Taishang yijuhua taixia siniangong jiemi Zhang Ziyi xueyingwen licheng] (2005), 2 March, <http:ent.people.com.cn/ GB/1082/3213896.html> (last accessed 15 August 2017).

Ongiri, Amy (2005), 'Bruce Lee in the ghetto connection: Kung fu theatre and African Americans reinventing culture at the margins', in S. Dave, L. Nishima and T. Oren (eds), *East Main Street: Asian American Popular Culture*, New York and London: New York University Press, pp. 249–61.

Orange, B. Alan (2016), 'Ip Man 3 will star Mike Tyson and CG Bruce Lee', Movieweb, February, <http://movieweb.com/ip-man-3-cast-mike-tyson-cg-bruce-lee> (last accessed 18 August 2016).

O'Reilly, Tim (2004), 'The architecture of participation', June, <http://archive. oreilly.com/pub/a/oreilly/tim/articles/architecture_of_participation.html> (last accessed 2 May 2018).

Pang, Laikwan (2007), 'Jackie Chan, tourism, and the performing agency', in G. Marchetti and T. S. Kam (eds), *Hong Kong Film, Hollywood and the New Global Cinema: No Film is an Island*, London and New York: Routledge, pp. 206–18.

Pomerance, Murray (2012), 'Introduction: Stardom in the 2000s', in M. Pomerance (ed.), *Shining in Shadows: Movie Stars of the 2000s*, New Brunswick, NJ: Rutgers University Press, pp. 1–11.

Prelinger, Rick (2009), 'The appearance of archives', in P. Snickars and P. Vonderau (eds), *The YouTube Reader*, Stockholm: National Library of Sweden, pp. 268–74.

Pring, Cara (2014), 'Facebook Page vs Group: A Facebook marketing dilemma', *The Social Skinny*, 31 January, <http:thesocialskinny.com/facebook-page-vs-group-a-facebook-marketing-dilemma/> (last accessed 27 August 2017).

Pulumbarit, K. E. (2015), 'Donnie Yen avoids bed scenes to please wife Cissy Wang', *China Topix*, 19 August, <www.chinatopix.com/articles/62378/20150819/donnie-yen-avoids-bed-scenes-to-please-wife-cecilia-cheung.htm> (last accessed 24 July 2017).

Putnam, Robert (2000), *Bowling Alone: The Collapse and Revival of American Community*, New York: Simon & Schuster.

'Quote of the day: Photo sharing a "social medium"' (2005), CNET News.com, 16 December, <http:news.cnet.com/Quote-of-the-day-Photo-sharing-a-social-medium/2110-1025_3-5998534.html?tag¼lia;rcol> (last accessed 17 August 2017).

Rafferty, Terence (2006), 'Film; exit kicking: Jet Li's martial arts swan song', *The New York Times*, 17 September, <http:query.nytimes.com/gst/fullpage.html?res=9E05E6DA1531F934A2575AC0A9609C8B63&scp=3&sq=Fist%20of%20Legend&st=cse&pagewanted=1> (last accessed 19 June 2013).

Rahner, Mark (2008), '"Forbidden Kingdom": Martial-arts titans Jet Li and Jackie Chan join forces', *The Seattle Times*, 18 April, <www.seattletimes.com/entertainment/movies/forbidden-kingdom-martial-arts-titans-jet-li-and-jackie-chan-join-forces/> (last accessed 30 August 2017).

Rapoza, Kenneth (2011), 'China's Weibos vs US's Twitter: And the winner is?', *Forbes*, 18 May, <www.forbes.com/sites/kenrapoza/2011/05/17/chinas-weibos-vs-uss-twitter-and-the-winner-is/> (last accessed 24 August 2015).

Rawnsley, Gary and Rawnsley, Ming-Yeh (2010), 'Introduction', in G. Rawnsley and Ming-Yeh Rawnsley (eds), *Global Chinese Cinema: The Culture and Politics of Hero*, London and New York: Routledge, pp. 1–10.

Ray, Kate (2009), 'Reactions to Jackie Chan's views of freedom in China', 20 April, <http:shanghaiist.com/2009/04/20/kung_fu_movie_star_jackie_chan.php> (last accessed 28 May 2017).

Rayns, Tony (1980), 'Bruce Lee: Narcissism and nationalism', in S. Lau (ed.), *A Study of the Hong Kong Martial Arts Film*, Hong Kong: Urban Council, pp. 110–20.

Redmond, Sean and Holmes, Su (2007), 'Introduction: What's in a reader?', in S. Redmond and S. Holmes (eds), *Stardom and Celebrity: A Reader*, Los Angeles: Sage, pp. 1–16.

Reid, Craig, (1994), 'An evening with Jackie Chan', *Bright Lights* 13, pp. 18–25.

Reid, Craig (2011), 'Vintage Jet Lee movies', *Black Belt: World's Leaning Martial Arts Resource*, 19 March, <www.blackbeltmag.com/daily/martialarts-entertainment/martial-art-movies/vintage-jet-lee-movies-the-one/> (last accessed 29 May 2014).

Rein, Irving, Philip Kotler, and Martin Stoller (1997), *High Visibility: The Making and Marketing of Professionals into Celebrities*, New York: McGraw-Hill.

Resnick, Paul (2001), 'Beyond bowling together: Socio-technical capital', in J. Carroll (ed.), *HCI in the New Millennium*, New York: Addison-Wesley, pp. 647–72.

Robbins, Bruce (1998), 'Introduction part I: Actually existing cosmopolitanism', in P. Cheah and B. Robbins (eds), *Cosmopolitics: Thinking and Feeling beyond the Nation*, Minneapolis: University of Minnesota Press, pp. 1–19.

Robinson, Tasha (2016), 'Crouching Tiger, Hidden Dragon: Sword of Destiny shrinks the original in more ways than one', *The Verge*, <www.theverge.com/2016/2/26/11121436/crouching-tiger-hidden-dragon-sword-of-destiny-movie-review-netflix> (last accessed 10 August 2016).

Rodowick, David (2007), *The Virtual Life of Film*, Cambridge, MA: Harvard University Press.

Rodriquez, Hector (1997), 'Hong Kong popular culture as an interpretive arena: The Huang Feihong film series', *Screen* 38:1, pp. 1–24.

Rosen, Philip (2001), *Changed Mummified: Cinema, Historicity, Theory*, Minneapolis: University of Minnesota Press.

Rosenbaum, S. I. (2009), 'Wushu martial arts daughter – Chris Yuen', 13 March, <www.wushukicks.com/chinese-martial-arts/tag/chris-yen/> (last accessed 2 September 2017).

'Row over Jackie Chan deepens' (2009), *South China Morning Post*, 23 April, <www.scmp.com/article/677774/row-over-jackie-chan-deepens> (last accessed 27 August 2017).

Russo, Julie Levin (2009), 'User-penetrated content: Fan video in the age of convergence', *Cinema Journal* 48.4, pp. 125–30.

Russo, Charles (2016), *Striking Distance Bruce Lee and the Dawn of Martial Arts in America*, Lincoln, Nebraska and London, England: University of Nebraska Press.

Sandell, Scott (2010), 'Jackie Chan – Hollywood Star Walk', *Los Angeles Times*, 1 March, <http:projects.latimes.com/hollywood/star-walk/jackie-chan/> (last accessed 24 August 2017).

Sandvoss, Cornel (2005), *Fans: The Mirror of Consumption*, Cambridge: Polity Press.

Saunders, Tim (2008), 'Jet Li speaks at Clinton Global Initiative', *Look to the Stars*, 3 December, <www.looktothestars.org/news/1669-jet-lispeaks-at-clinton-global-initiative> (last accessed 17 June 2014).

Schickel, Richard (2000), *Intimate Strangers: The Culture of Celebrity*, Chicago: Ivan R. Dee.

Schneider, Karen (1995), 'Much Ado in Keanu', *People*, 5 June, <http:people.com/archive/cover-story-much-ado-about-keanu-vol-43-no-22/> (last accessed 10 August 2017).

Schwartz, Missy and Michelle Kung (2005), 'The women of geisha', *Entertainment Weekly*, 9 December, <www.ew.com/ew/article/0,,1138891,00.html> (last accessed 20 August 2017).

Scodari, Christine (2007), 'Yoko in cyberspace with Beatles fans: Gender and the re-creation of popular mythology', in J. Gray, C. Sandvoss and C. L. Harrington (eds), *Fandom: Identities and Communities in a Mediated World*, New York: New York University Press, pp. 48–59.

Scrapbook (The Official Website of Jackie Chan) (n.d.), <http:jackiechan.com/scrapbook/206277--Songs-for-the-Earthquake-Victims> (last accessed 14 February 2013).

Seah, Lionel (2001), 'Zhang Ziyi is China's best export', *The Straits Times*, July, <www.helloziyi.us/Articles/Ziyi_Chinas_Best.htm> (last accessed 1 March 2010).

Seidlhofer, Barbara (2011), *Understanding English as a Lingua Franca*, Oxford: Oxford University Press.

Seigel, Lucas (2016), 'Donnie Yen's son dressed as his Rogue One character again', Comicbook.com, 23 December, <http:comicbook.com/starwars/2016/12/23/donnie-yens-son-dressed-as-his-rogue-one-character-again/> (last accessed 8 July 2017).

Seto, Kit Yan (2010), 'Fighting fit', *The Star Online*, 23 April, <http:ecentral.my/news/story. asp?file=/2010/4/23/movies/6112482&sec=movies> (last accessed 3 July 2012).

Shaviro, Steven (*1993*), *The Cinematic Body*, Minneapolis and London: University of Minnesota Press.

Shaviro, Steven (2010), *Post Cinematic Affect*, Winchester: Zero Books.

Shaw, Jeffrey and Peter Weibel (2003), *Future Cinema: The Cinematic Imaginary After Film*, Cambridge, MA: MIT.

Shih, Shu-mei (2004), 'Global literature and the technologies of recognition', *PMLA* 119:1 (January), pp. 16–30.

Shih, Shu-mei (2007), *Visuality and Identity: Sinophone Articulations across the Pacific*, Berkeley: University of California Press.

Sims, David (2016), '*Crouching Tiger, Hidden Dragon*: The sad sequel', *The Atlantic*, 27 February, <www.theatlantic.com/entertainment/archive/2016/02/crouching-tiger-hidden-dragon-sword-of-destiny-review/471234/> (last accessed 10 August 2016).

Singel, Ryan (2009), 'The future is social, not search, Facebook COO says', *Wired*, 21 October, <www.wired.com/business/2009/10/facebook-social-2/> (last accessed 20 June 2013).

Slack, Jack (2015), 'Wing Chun and MMA: Controlling the center', Fightland Blog, 22 April, <http:fightland.vice.com/blog/wing-chun-and-mma-controlling-the-center> (last accessed 2 July 2017).

Sogabe, Kobi (1998), 'Jin Chengwu '98 nian Riben fengliu shi' (Kaneshiro Takeshi the incredible 1998 chronicle), *City Entertainment* 513, pp. 19–22.

Stacey, Jackie (1991), 'Feminine fascinations: Forms of identification in star-audience relations', in C. Gledhill (ed.), *Stardom: Industry of Desire*, London and New York: Routledge, pp. 141–63.

Stacey, Jackie (1994), *Star Gazing: Hollywood Cinema and Female Spectatorship*, London and New York: Routledge.

Staiger, Janet (1992), *Interpreting Films: Studies in the Historical Reception of American Cinema*, Princeton: Princeton University Press.

Stanislavski, Constantin (1991), 'When acting is an art', in J. Butler (ed.), *Star Texts: Image and Performance in Film and Television*, Detroit: Wayne State University Press, pp. 18–33.

Statista (2014a), 'Top statistics about social networks', <www.statista.com/topics/1164/social-networks/> (last accessed 1 June 2014).

Statista (2014b), 'Number of monthly active Facebook users worldwide from 3rd quarter 2008 to 1st quarter 2014', www.statista.com/statistics/264810/number-of-monthly-active-facebook-users-worldwide/> (last accessed 1 June 2014).

Stephenson, Shelley (1999), '"Her races are found everywhere": Shanghai, Li Xianglan, and the "Greater East Asia Film Sphere,"' in Y. Zhang (ed.), *Cinema and Urban Culture in Shanghai, 1922–1943*, California: Stanford University Press, pp. 222–45.

STORMTROOPERLARRY (2016), 'Exclusive: The latest on Rouge One actor Donnie Yen', 20 June, <https:stormtrooperlarry.com/2016/06/20/exclusive-the-latest-on-rogue-one-actor-donnie-yen/> (last accessed 12 August 2016).

Stringer, Julian (2003), 'Talking about Li: Transnational Chinese movie stardom and Asian American Internet reception', in G. Rawnsley and M. Rawnsley (eds), *Political Communications in Greater China: The Construction and Reflection of Identity*, London and New York: Routledge Curzon, pp. 275–90.

Stringer, Julian (2010), 'Leslie Cheung: Star as autosexual', in M. Farquhar and Y. Zhang (eds), *Chinese Film Stars,* London and New York: Routledge, pp. 207–24.

Studlar, Gaylyn (1996), *This Made Masquerade: Stardom and Masculinity in the Jazz Age,* New York: Columbia University Press.

Sunwoo, Carla (2012), 'Dangerous Liaisons' heads to Cannes', *Korea JoongAng Daily,* 26 April, <https://web.archive.org/web/20120612064445/http://koreajoongangdaily.joinsmsn.com/news/article/Article.aspx?aid=2951994> (last accessed 12 June 2018).

Swale, Alistair (2015), *Anime Aesthetics: Japanese Animation and the 'Post-Cinematic' Imagination,* Basingstoke: Palgrave Macmillan.

Swifty (2006), 'Swifty reviews "Fearless", Jet Li's last martial arts film', 29 January, <www.edmundyeo.com/2006/01/swifty-reviews-fearlessjet-lis-last.html> (last accessed 19 June 2014).

Szeto, Kin-yan (2011), *The Martial Arts Cinema of the Chinese Diaspora: Ang Lee, John Woo, and Jackie Chan in Hollywood,* Carbondale: Southern Illinois University Press.

'Takeshi Kaneshiro' (Facebook) (n.d.), <www.facebook.com/takeshikaneshiropage> (last accessed 17 February 2013).

'Takeshiro Kaneshiro fan site' (n.d.), <www.takeshikaneshiro.org/> (last accessed 17 February 2013).

'Takeshi Kaneshiro message board' (n.d.), Internet Movie Database, <www.imdb.com/name/nm0437580/board/nest/151097310> (last accessed 10 February 2013).

'Takeshi Kaneshiro news: Red Cliff in Russian theatres (short review)' (2012), Takeshi Kaneshiro fan club, 30 May. <http:tkfanclub.do.am/news/2009-08-01-58> (last accessed 12 February 2013).

'Takeshiro Kaneshiro san!: The best role' (n.d.), Forumotion, <http:takeshianiki.forumotion.com/t24-the-best-role> (last accessed 19 February 2013).

'Takeshironline.com' (n.d.), <www.takeshionline.com/index.php> (last accessed 12 February 2013).

Tan, Lili (2009), 'Zhang Ziyi sexy beach photo scandal', *Chinese-tools.com,* 5 January, <www.chinese-tools.com/china/people/2009-01-05-zhang-ziyi-beach-scandal.html> (last accessed 11 September 2017).

Taylor, Adam (2012), 'The latest insane Bo Xilai rumor is that he was paying this Chinese movie star for sex', *Business Insider,* 31 May, <www.businessinsider.com/bo-xilai-zhang-ziyi-hong-kong-apple-daily-2012-5> (last accessed 17 August 2017).

Teo, Stephen (2008). 'Promise and perhaps love: Pan-Asian production and the Hong Kong–China interrelationship', *Inter-Asia Cultural Studies* 9:3, pp. 341–58.

Terdiman, Daniel (2004), 'Photo site a hit with bloggers', *Wired,* 9 December, <www.wired.com/culture/lifestyle/news/2004/12/65958> (last accessed 27 August 2017).

'The annals of box office of Hong Kong Films 1969–2016' (1969–2016年香港電影歷年票房排行總榜 1969–2016 nian xiangang dianying linian piaofang paixing zhongbang) (2016), 30 November, <https:read01.com/QRQQ7D.html#.WZ_MVj4jHIU> (last accessed 24 August 2017).

'The celebrity' (2009), *Forbes,* 28 September, <www.forbes.com/2009/09/25/jet-li-philanthropy-china-leadership-one-foundation.html> (last accessed 27 June 2013).

'The philosophy of Bruce Lee' (n.d.), Becoming, <www.becoming.8m.net/bruce02.htm> (last accessed 21 June 2013).

'The tsunami that changed my life' (2008), *Newsweek,* 27 September, <www.newsweek.com/id/161054/page/> (last accessed 16 June 2013).

'The Yushu, Qinghai earthquake has caused over 400 deaths' (2010), BBC UK China website, 14 April, <www.bbc.co.uk/zhongwen/trad/china/2010/04/100414_qinghai_quake_update.shtml> (last accessed 15 May 2014).

Toffler, Alvin (1980), *The Third Wave: The Classic Study of Tomorrow*, New York: Bantam.

Tolson, Andrew (1996), *Mediations: Texts and Discourses*, London: Arnold.

'Tony Blair and Jet Li launch new climate change partnership for a low carbon future' (2009), The Office of Tony Blair, 25 March, <www.tonyblairoffice.org/climatechange/news-entry/Tony-Blair-and-Jet-Li-launch-new-climate-changepartnership-for-a-low-carbo/> (last accessed 17 June 2014).

'Trafficking in children' (n.d.), International Labour Organization, <www.ilo.org/ipec/areas/Traffickingofchildren/lang--en/index.htm> (last accessed 28 August 2017).

Tran, Maria (2010), 'PEOPLE: Face to face with Bey Logan', Quest for Jackie Chan, <http:questforjackiechan.blogspot.hk/2010/12/people-face-to-face-with-bey-logan.html> (last accessed 31 August 2017).

Tran, Maria (2011), 'Internet R.I.P: Jackie Chan', *Maria Tran: Blogger. Vlogger. Know-it-all*, 10 April, <http:maria-tran.blogspot.hk/2011/04/internet-rip-jackie-chan.html> (last accessed 1 January 2013).

Trope, Alison (2012), 'Mother Angelina: Hollywood philanthropy personified', in R. Mukherjee and S. Banet-Weiser (eds), *Commodity Activism: Cultural Resistance in Neoliberal Times*, New York and London: New York University Press, pp. 154–73.

Truitt, Brian (2016), 'Donnie Yen is the "man" in Hong Kong action scene', *USA Today*, 28 January, <www.usatoday.com/story/life/movies/2016/01/18/donnie-yen-ip-man-crouching-tiger-star-wars/78860818/> (last accessed 1 August 2016).

Tsai, Eva (2005), 'Kaneshiro Takeshi: Transnational stardom and the media and culture industries in Asia's global/postcolonial age', *Modern Chinese Literature and Culture* 17:1, pp. 100–32.

Tsipursky, Gleb (n.d.), 'Russian Youth and "Western" cultural influence, 1945 to the present', seminar, UNC Chapel Hill, <www.unc.edu/world/2011Seminars/Tsipursky_PPT.pps> (last accessed 22 August 2017).

Tu Wei-ming (ed.) (1994), *The Living Tree: The Changing Meaning of Being Chinese Today*, Stanford: Stanford University Press.

Tucker, Nancy (2008), 'China's relations with the West: The role of Taiwan and Hong Kong', *Foreign Policy Research Institute Newsletter* 13:7, 11 May, <www.fpri.org/footnotes/1307.200805.tucker.chinawesttaiwanhongkong.html>, (last accessed 27 August 2017).

Tudor, Andrew (1974), *Image and Influence: Studies in the Sociology of Film*, London: George Allen and Unwin.

Turner, Graeme (2004), *Understanding Celebrity*, London: SAGE.

Turner, Graeme (2007), 'The economy of celebrity', in S. Redmond and S. Holmes (eds), *Stardom and Celebrity: A Reader*, Los Angeles: Sage, pp. 193–205.

'UNICEF Goodwill Ambassador Jackie Chan in Myanmar: "Children are not for sale"' (2012), UNICEF: Press Release, <www.unicef.org/media/media_65216.html> (last accessed 31 May 2017).

'UNICEF in Myanmar' (n.d.), UNICEF: Myanmar, <www.unicef.org/myanmar/overview.html> (last accessed 18 May 2017).

Uricchio, William (2009), 'The future of a medium once known as television', in P. Snikkars and P. Vonderau (eds), *The YouTube Reader*, London: Wallflower Press, pp. 24–39.

Vettorel, Paola (2014), *English as a Lingua Franca in Wider Networking: Blogging Practices*, Berlin and New York: Mouton de Gruyter.

Vladimir Vysotsky: the official site. <www.kulichki.com/vv/eng/> (last accessed 26 August 2017).

Walker, Alexander (1970), *Stardom: The Hollywood Phenomenon*, London: Michael Joseph.

Wang Ying-Shun (2001), 'The Satellite-Style Idol who Carries No Historical Burden' (不背歷史包袱的衛星型偶像*Bubei Lishi Baou de Weixingxing Ouxiang*), *Business Next* (1 March), pp. 90–2.

Wang, Georgette and Emilie Yueh-yu Yeh (2005), 'Globalisation and hybridisation in cultural products: The cases of *Mulan* and *Crouching Tiger, Hidden Dragon*', *International Journal of Cultural Studies* 8:2, pp. 175–93.

Wang, Gungwu (1991), *The Chineseness of China: Selected Essays*, Oxford: Oxford University Press.

Wang, Haizhou and Ming-Yeh T. Rawnsley (2010), '*Hero*: Rewriting the Chinese martial arts film genre', in G. Rawnsley and M. T. Rawnsley (eds), *Global Chinese Cinema: The Culture and Politics of* Hero, London; New York: Routledge, pp. 90–105.

Wang, Yiman (2007), 'A star is dead: a legend is born: Practicing Leslie Cheung's posthumous fandom', in S. Redmond and S. Holmes (eds), *Stardom and Celebrity: A Reader*, London: Sage, pp. 326–52.

Wang, Yiman (2004), 'Anna May Wong: A border-crossing "minor" star mediating performance', in M. Farquhar and Y. Zhang (eds), *Chinese Film Stars*, London and New York: Routledge, pp. 9–31.

Wang, Yiman (2012), 'The palimpsest body and the s(h)ifting border: On Maggie Cheung's two crossover films', *Positions* 20:4, pp. 953–81.

Wang, Ying-Shun (2001), 'The satellite-style idol who carries no historical burden' (不背歷史包袱的衛星型偶像*Bubei Lishi Baou de Weixingxing Ouxiang*), *Business Next* (1 March), pp. 90–2.

Waterlow, Lucy (2015), 'Inside the secret world of the Geisha: Intimate photos reveal how Japanese women maintain 400-year-old traditions in modern world', *Mail Online*, 7 May, <www.dailymail.co.uk/femail/article-3071763/Inside-secret-world-Geisha-Intimate-photos-reveal-Japanese-women-maintain-400-year-old-traditions-modern-world.html> (last accessed 11 September 2017).

Weiss, Amanda (2013), '"Mediated persona" and Hong Kong stars: Negotiating mainland celebrity', *Celebrity Studies* 4:2, pp. 219–32.

Wenn.com Source (2007), 'Jet Li earns record salary for Chinese-language film', Hollywood.com, 26 November, <www.hollywood.com/movies/jet-li-earns-record-salary-for-chinese-language-film-57170391/> (last accessed 20 June 2017).

Williams, Tony (2003), 'Transnational stardom: The case of Maggie cheung Man-yuk', *Asian Cinema* 14:2, pp. 180–96.

Willis, Andy and Wing-Fai, Leung (2014), 'Introduction: Star power from Hollywood to East Asia', in A. Willis and W. Leung (eds), *East Asian Film Stars*, New York: Palgrave Macmillan, pp. 1–16.

Wu, Huaiting and Man Chan, Joseph (2007), 'Globalising Chinese martial arts cinema: The global-local alliance and the production of *Crouching Tiger, Hidden Dragon*', *Media Culture Society* 29:2, pp. 195–217.

Wu, Jiao (2007), 'E'gao: Art criticism or evil?' *China Daily*, 22 January, <www.chinadaily. com.cn/china/2007-01/22/content_788600.htm> (last accessed 20 May 2017).

Wu, Linfei (2013), 'Top ten celebrity charity campaign 2012', All-China Women's Federation, 14 January, <www.womenofchina.cn/html/womenofchina/report/148608-1.htm> (last accessed 25 June 2013).

'WU XIA – SentieriSelvaggi meets Peter Ho-sun Chan' (2011), YouTube, <www.youtube.com/watch?v=a6HfuFEShZU> (last accessed 18 February 2010).

Xie, Tingting (2010), 'Zhang Ziyi quits "secret fan": Report', CRIENGLISH.com, 27 January, <http:english.cri.cn/6666/2010/01/27/1261s545707.htm> (last accessed 23 August 2017).

Xie Xiaoyang (2009), 'A martial arts world that once vanished reappears' *[Chongxiang yidu yanmo de wulin]*, *Yazhou Zhoukan* 23:8 (1 March), pp. 26–33.

Xu, Lin (2011), 'Top 100 Chinese celebrities 2011: #6 Donnie Yen', China.Org.Cn., 23 June, <http://www.china.org.cn/top10/2011-06/23/content_22845446_5.htm> (last accessed 3 May 2018).

Yang, Xiaowen. 楊孝文 (1991a), 'Li Lianjie yanzhong de Huang Feihung' 李連杰眼中的黃飛鴻/'Wong Feihung in the Eyes of Jet Li', *Dianying shuangzhou kan*電影雙周刊/*City Entertainment* 323, p. 23.

Yang, Xiaowen (1991b), 'Wong Feihung in the eyes of Jet Li' [Li Lianjie yanzhong de Huang Feihung], *City Entertainment* 323, pp. 23–4.

Yeo, Edmund (2006), 'Swiftly reviews "Fearless", Jet Li's last martial arts films', *Swifty, Writing*, 29 January, <www.edmundyeo.com/2006/01/swiftyreviews-fearless-jet-lis-last.html> (last accessed 23 June 2013).

Yip, Wai Yee (2013), 'Donnie Yen is best Ip Man, say ST readers', *The Straits Times*, 7 April, <www.straitstimes.com/breaking-news/lifestyle/story/donnie-yen-best-ip-man-say-st-readers-20130407> (last accessed 20 May 2013).

'Your husband is great, but Donnie Yen is even better' (2017), Nextshark.com, 14 January, <https://nextshark.com/donnie-yen-cissy-wang-relationship/> (last accessed 2 July 2017).

Yu, Sabrina (2010), 'Jet Li: Star construction and fan discourse on the Internet', in M. Farquhar and Y. Zhang (eds), *Chinese Film Stars*, London and New York: Routledge, pp. 225–36.

Yu, Sabrina (2012), *Jet Li: Chinese Masculinity and Transnational Film Stardom*, Edinburgh: Edinburgh University Press.

Yue, Audrey and Olivia Khoo (2014), 'Framing Sinophone cinemas', in A. Yue and O. Khoo (eds), *Sinophone Cinemas*, Basingstoke: Palgrave Macmillan, pp. 3–12.

Yuen, Dien (2008), 'Jet Li, philanthropist & martial arts star', *Asian Philanthropy Platform*, 31 October, <www.asianphilanthropyforum.org/jet-li-philanthropist-martial-arts-star/> (last accessed 19 June 2014).

Zhang, Xudong (2001), 'The making of the post-Tiananmen intellectual field: A critical overview', in X. Zhang (ed.), *Whither China?: Intellectual Politics in Contemporary China*, Durham, NC: Duke University Press, pp. 1–78.

'Zhang Ziyi has fans worldwide except in Hong Kong' (2006), chinadaily.com, 17 March. <http:www.chinadaily.com.cn/english/doc/2006-03/17/content_542741. htm> (last accessed 19 July 2015).

Zhou, Raymond (2010a), 'Actress denies charity fraud', *China Daily*, 16 March, <www. chinadaily.com.cn/china/2010-03/16/content_9593921.htm> (last accessed 19 August 2017).

Zhou, Raymond (2010b), 'Clearing her name', *China Daily*, 16 March, <www.chinadaily. com.cn/life/2010-03/16/content_9596922.htm> (last accessed 19 August 2017).

Zhang, Rui (2008), *The Cinema of Feng Xiaogang: Commercialisation and Censorship in Chinese cinema after 1989*, Hong Kong: Hong Kong University Press.

'ziyi forever' (n.d.), <http:ziyiforever.primenova.com/> (last accessed 13 August 2017).

'《武俠》花絮 – 金城武篇 Wu Xia – Making Of (Takeshi Kaneshiro)' (2011), <www. youtube.com/watch?v=yVaXKwilax4&feature=player_embedded> (last accessed 20 August 2017).

Filmography

1911/辛亥革命, dirs Jackie Chan and Zhang Li, PRC and Hong Kong, Beijing Alnair Culture & Media, Changchun Film Studio, China City Construction, Jackie & JJ Productions, 2011.

2046, dir. Wong Kar-wai, Hong Kong and PRC, Jet Tone Films, Shanghai Film Group, Orly Films, Paradis Films, 2004.

14 Blades/錦衣衛, dir. Daniel Lee, Hong Kong, PRC and Singapore, Shanghai Film Studios, Mediacorp Raintree Pictures, Visualiser Film Productions, Western Movie Group, Desen International Media, 2010.

A City of Sadness/悲情城市, dir. Hsiao-Hsien Hou, Taiwan and Hong Kong, 3-H films, ERA International, 1989.

Accidental Spy/特務迷城, dir. Teddy Chan, Hong Kong, Golden Harvest Company, Panfilm, 2001.

Anna Magdalena/安娜瑪德蓮娜, dir. Chung Man Yee, Hong Kong, Amuse Hong Kong, United Filmmakers Organization, 1998.

Ashes of Time/東邪西毒, dir. Wong Kar-wai, Hong Kong, Taiwan, Jet Tone Production, Block 2 Pictures, Scholar Films Company, 1994.

Bill and Ted's Excellent Adventure, dir. Stephen Herek, USA, De Laurentiis Entertainment Group, De Laurentiis Film Partners, Interscope Communications, 1989.

Blade II, dir. Gullermo del Toro, USA and Germany, Amen Ra Films, Marvel Enterprises, Imaginary Forces, Justin Pictures, Linovo Productions GmbH & Co. KG, 2002.

Bodyguards and Assassins/十月圍城, dir. Teddy Chan, PRC and Hong Kong, Beijing Poly-bona Film Publishing Company, Cinema Popular, 2009.

Charlie and the Chocolate Factory, dir. Tim Burton, USA, UK and Australia, Warner Bros, Village Roadshow Pictures, The Zanuck Company, Plan B Entertainment, Theobald Film Productions, Craig Miller Productions, 2005.

Charlie's Angels, dir. McG, USA and Germany, Global Entertainment Productions GmbH & Company Medien KG, 2000.

Chinese Odyssey/大話西遊終結篇, dir. Jeffrey Lau, Hong Kong, Block 2 Pictures, Hakuhodo, Shanghai Film Group, 2002.

Chinese Zodiac/十二生肖, dir. Jackie Chan, Hong Kong and PRC, Emperor Film Production, Huayi Brothers Media, Jackie & JJ Productions, 2013.

Chungking Express/重慶森林, dir. Wong Kar-wai, Hong Kong, Jet Tone Production, 1994.

Come Drink With Me/大醉俠, dir. King Hu, Hong Kong, Shaw Brothers, 1966.

Confession of Pain/傷城, dirs Andrew Lau and Alan Mak, Hong Kong, Media Asia Films, Beijing Poly-bona Film Publishing Company, Avex Entertainment, Sil-Metropole Organisation, Basic Pictures, 2006.

Confucius/孔子：決戰春秋, dir. Mei Hu, China, Beijing Dadi Century Limited, Dadi Entertainment, China Film Group, 2010.

Crouching Tiger, Hidden Dragon/臥虎藏龍, dir. Ang Lee, Taiwan, Hong Kong, China and USA, Asia Union Film & Entertainment Ltd, China Film Co-Production Corporation, Columbia Pictures Film Production Asia, 2000.

Crouching Tiger, Hidden Dragon: Sword of Destiny/臥虎藏龍：青冥寶劍, dir. Yuen Woo-ping, USA and China, China Film Group, Dongyang Paige Huachuang Film & Media Company, Film 44, 2016.

Curse of the Golden Flower/滿城盡帶黃金甲, dir. Zhang Yimou, China and Hong Kong, Beijing New Picture Film Co., Edko Films, Elite Group Enterprises, Film Partner International, 2006.

Cyclo/三輪車伕, dir. Tran Anh Hung, Vietnam, France and Hong Kong, Canal+, CNC, Cofimage 5, 1995.

Danny the Dog, dir. Louis Leterrier, France, USA and UK, EuropaCorp, Danny the Dog Prods Ltd, TF1 Films Production, Qian Yian International, 2005.

Deadly Duo/雙俠, dir. Ching-Chen Yang, Taiwan and Hong Kong, Nine Continents Film Production Co., 1971.

Deep Thrust: The Hand of Death/鐵掌旋風腿, dir. Feng Huang, Hong Kong, Golden Harvest, Hallmark, 1972.

Downtown Torpedoes/神偷諜影, dir. Teddy Chan, Hong Kong, Golden Harvest, 1997.

Dragon Blade/天將雄師, dir. Daniel Lee, China and Hong Kong, Sparkle Roll Media, Huayi Brothers Media, Shanghai Film Group, 2015.

Drunken Master/醉拳, dir. Yuen Woo-ping, Hong Kong, Golden Harvest, 1978.

Edward Scissorhands, dir. Tim Burton, USA, Twentieth Century Fox, 1990.

Empress and the Warriors/江山・美人, dir. Ching Siu-tung, Hong Kong and China, Beijing Poly-bona Film Publishing Company, BIG Pictures, United Filmmakers Organisation, China Film Co-Production Corporation, 2008.

Enter the Dragon/龍爭虎鬥, dir. Robert Clouse, Hong Kong, Warner Bros, Concord Productions, 1973.

Fallen Angels/墮落天使, dir. Wong Kar-wai, Hong Kong, Block 2 Pictures, Jet Tone Production, 1995.

Farewell My Concubine/霸王別姬, dir. Chen Kaige, China and Hong Kong, Beijing Film Studio, China Film Co-Production Corporation, Maverick Picture Company, Tomson Films,1993.

Fearless/霍元甲, dir. Ronny Yu, China and Hong Kong, Beijing Film Studio, China Film Co-Production Corporation, China Film Group, Hero China International, Wide River Investment, 2006.

Fighting for Love/同居蜜友, dir. Joe Ma, Hong Kong, Film Power Company Limited, Singing Horse Productions, 2001.

Fist of Fury/精武門, dir. Lo Wei, Hong Kong, Golden Harvest, 1973.

Fist of Legend/精武英雄, dir. Gordon Chan, Hong Kong, Golden Harvest, 1994.

Five Fingers of Death/天下第一拳, dir. Chang Ho Cheng, Hong Kong, Shaw Brothers, 1973.

Flash Point/導火綫, dir. Wilson Yip, Hong Kong, China, Mandarin Films Distribution, Chang Ying Group, Beijing Poly-bona Film Publishing Company, 2007.

Flowers of Shanghai/海上花, dir. Hou Hsiao-hsien, Taiwan and Japan, 3H Productions, Shochiku Company, 1998.

Flying Swords of Dragon Gate/龍門飛甲, dir. Tsui Hark, China, Beijing Liangzi Group, Beijing Poly-bona Film Publishing Company, Bona Entertainment, China Film Co-Production Corporation, 2011.

Forever Enthralled/梅蘭芳, dir. Chen Kaige, China and Hong Kong, China Film Group, CMC Entertainment, Emperor Motion Pictures, Fat Penguin Pictures, 2008.

Game of Death/死亡遊戲, dirs Robert Clouse and Bruce Lee, Hong Kong and USA, Columbia Pictures and Golden Harvest, 1973.

Give 'Em Hell, Malone, dir. Russell Mclcahy, USA, Blue Rider Pictures, Hannibal Pictures, Malone Productions, Martini Films, 2009.

Happy Together/春光乍洩, dir. Wong Kar-wai, Hong Kong, Japan and Korea, Block 2 Pictures, Jet Tone Production, Prenom H Co. Ltd., Seowoo Film Company, 1997.

Hero/英雄, dir. Zhang Yimou, China and Hong Kong, Beijing New Picture Film Co., China Film Co-Production Corporation, Elite Group Enterprises, Sil-Metropole Organisation, Zhang Yimou Studio, 2002.

High Risk/鼠膽龍威, dir. Wong Jing, Hong Kong, Golden Sun Entertainment, Upland Films Corporation Limited, Wong Jing's Workshop Ltd, 1995.

Highlander: Endgame, dir. Douglas Aarniokoski, USA, Davis-Panzer Productions, Dimension Films, 2000.

House of Flying Daggers/十面埋伏, dir. Zhang Yimou, China and Hong Kong, Beijing New Picture Film Co., China Film Co-Production Corporation, Edko Films, Elite Group Enterprises, Zhang Yimou Studio, 2004.

In the Mood for Love/花樣年華, dir. Wong Kar–wai, Hong Kong, Block 2 Pictures, Jet Tone Producion, Paradis Films, 2000.

Infernal Affairs/無間道, dirs Andrew Lau and Alan Mak, Hong Kong, Media Asian Films, Basic Pictures, 2002.

Infernal Affairs II/無間道II, dirs Andrew Lau and Alan Mak, Hong Kong, China, Singapore, Media Asian Films, Basic Pictures, 2003.

Infernal Affairs III/無間道III終極無間, dirs Andrew Lau and Alan Mak, Hong Kong, China, Media Asian Films, Basic Pictures, Tianjin Film Studio, 2003.

Ip Man/葉問, dir. Wilson Yip, Hong Kong, China, Beijing Shengshi Huarei Film Investment & Management Co., China Film Co-Production Corporation, 2008.

Ip Man II: Legend of the Grand Master/葉問II：宗師傳奇, dir. Wilson Yip, Hong Kong, China, Beijing Shengshi Huarei Film Investment & Management Co., Henan Film & TV Production Group Henan Film Studio, 2010.

Ip Man: The Final Fight/葉問：終極一戰, dir. Herman Yau, Hong Kong, National Arts Films Production, Emperor Film Production, 2013.

Iron Man II, dir. Jon Favreau, USA, Marvel Studios, 2010.

Iron Monkey/少年黃飛鴻之鐵猴子, dir. Yuen Woo-ping, Hong Kong, Film Workshop, Golden Harvest, 1993.

Jackie Chan: My Stunts/成龍：我的特技, dir. Jackie Chan, Hong Kong, The Jackie Chan Group, 1999.

Ju Dou/菊豆, dir. Zhang Yimou, China, China Film Co-Producion Corporation, 1990.

K-20: Legend of the Mask, dir. Shimako Sato, Japan, Dentsu, Imagica, 2008.

Kiss of the Dragon, dir. Chris Nahon, Paris, StudioCanal. O'Brien, B., 2001.

Lavender/薰衣草, dir. Riley Yip, Hong Kong, Golden Harvest (China), 2000.

Legend of the Fist: The Return of Chen Zhen/陳真：精武風雲, dir. Andrew Lau, Hong Kong, China, Media Asia Films, Enlight Pictures, Shanghai Film Media Asia, Basic Pictures, 2010.

Let the Bullets Fly/讓子彈飛, dir. Jiang Wen, China, Hong Kong, China Film Group, 2010.

Lethal Weapon 4, dir. Richard Donner, USA, Silver Pictures, 1998.

Little Big Soldier/大兵小將, dir. Ding Sheng, China, Hong Kong, Beijing Dragon Garden Culture & Art, Jackie & JJ Productions, 2010.

Little Buddha, dir. Bernado Bertolucci, Italy, France, Serprocor Anstalt, 1993.

Lost and Found/天涯海角, dir. Chi-Ngai Lee, Hong Kong, Golden Harvest, UFO, 1996.

Lust, Caution/色，戒, dir. Ang Lee, USA, China, Taiwan, Haishang Films, 2007.

Memoirs of a Geisha, dir. Rob Marshall, USA, Columbia Pictures, DreamWorks, 2005.

Miracle Fighter II/奇門遁甲, dir. Yuen Woo-ping, Hong Kong, Golden Harvest, 1982.

Mission Impossible III, dir. J. J. Abrams, USA, Germany, China, Italy, Cruise/Wagner Productions, 2006.

Mr. Nice Guy/一個好人, dir. Sammo Hung, Hong Kong, Golden Harvest, 1997.

My Lucky Star/非常幸運, dir. Dennie Gordon, China, Bona International Film Group, 2013.

My Own Private Idaho, dir. Gus Van Sant, USA, New Line Cinema, 1991.

New Police Story/新警察故事, dir. Benny Chan, Hong Kong, China, China Film Group, JEC Movies, 2004.

Ocean Heaven/海洋天堂, dir. Xiaolu Xue, China, BDI Films Inc., 2010.

Once Upon a Time in China/黃飛鴻, dir. Tsui Hark, Hong Kong, Golden Harvest, 1991.

Painted Skin/畫皮, dir. Gordon Chan, Hong Kong, China, Golden Sun Film, Mediacorp Raintree Pictures, 2008.

Perhaps Love/如果·愛, dir. Peter Chan, Hong Kong, China, Malaysia, Applause Pictures, Morgan & Chan Films, The Ruddy Morgan Organization, 2005.

Pirates of the Caribbean: At World's End, dir. Gore Verbinski, USA, Walt Disney Pictures, Jerry Bruckheimer Films, Second Mate Productions, 2007.

Pirates of the Caribbean: The Curse of the Black Pearl, dir. Gore Verbinski, USA, Walt Disney Pictures, 2003.

Police Story/警察故事, dir. Jackie Chan, Chi-Hwa Chen, Hong Kong, Golden Way Films, Paragon Films, 1985.

Police Story II/警察故事續集, dir. Jackie Chan, Hong Kong, Golden Way Films, Paragon Films, 1988.

Police Story III: Super Cop/警察故事III超級警察, dir. Stanley Tong, Hong Kong, Golden Harvest, Golden Way Films, 1992.

Police Story IV: First Strike/警察故事4之簡單任務, dir. Stanley Tong, Hong Kong, Golden Harvest, Paragon Films, 1996.

Police Story 2013/警察故事2013, dir. Ding Sheng, China, Hong Kong, China Film Co., China Vision Group, Wanda Media Co., 2013.

Project A/A計劃, dir. Jackie Chan, Hong Kong, Authority Films, Golden Harvest, Paragon Films Ltd, 1984.

Project A II/ A計劃續集, dir. Jackie Chan, Hong Kong, Golden Way Films, Paragon Films Ltd, Towa Productions, 1987.

Protégé de la Rose Noire/見習黑玫瑰, dir. Wong Chun Chun, Donnie Yen, Hong Kong 1618 Action Limited, Universe Entertainment, 2004.

Raise the Red Lantern/ 大紅燈籠高高掛, dir. Zhang Yimou, ERA International, China Film Co-Production Corporation, 1991.

Red Cliff/赤壁, dir. John Woo, Beijing Film Studio, China Film Group, 2008.

Red Cliff II/赤壁：決戰天下, dir. John Woo, Beijing Film Studio, China Film Group, 2009.

Red Sorghum/紅高粱, dir. Zhang Yimou, China, Xi'an Film Studio, 1987.

Returner, dir. Takashi Yamazaki, Japan, Amuse, Fuji Television Networks, 2002.

River's Edge, dir. Tim Hunter, USA, Hemdale, Island, 1987.

Romeo Must Die, dir. Andrzwj Bartkowiak, USA, Silver Pictures, 2000.

Rouge One: A Star Wars Story, dir. Gareth Edwards, USA, Lucasfilm Ltd, 2016.

Rumble in the Bronx/紅番區, dir. Stanley Tong, Hong Kong, Golden Harvest, Maple Ridge Films, Toho-Towa, 1994.

Rush Hour, dir. Brett Ratner, USA, New Line Cinema, Roger Birnbaum Productions, 1998.

Rush Hour 2, dir. Brett Ratner, USA, New Line Cinema, Roger Birnbaum Productions, Salon Films, 2001.

Rush Hour III, dir. Brett Ratner, USA, New Line Cinema, Roger Birnbaum Productions, Arthur Sarkissian Productions, 2007.

Scream, Blacula, Scream, dir. Bob Kelljan, USA, American International Pictures, Power Productions, 1973.

Shanghai Knights, dir. David Dobkin, USA, Hong Kong, Birnbaum/Barber Productions, Jackie Chan Films, All Knight Productions, 2003.

Shanghai Noon, dir. Tom Dey, USA, Hong Kong, Roger Birnbaum Productions, Jackie Chan Films, 2000.

Shaolin/新少林寺, dir. Benny Chan, China, Hong Kong, Emperor Classic Films, China Film Group, Huayi Brothers Media, 2011.

Shaolin Temple/少林寺, dir. Hsin-Yen Chang, China, Hong Kong, Chung Yuen Motion Picture Company, Towa Produtions, Zhongyuan Film, 1982.

Shaolin Temple II/少林寺II：少林小子, dir. Hsin-Yen Chang, China, Hong Kong, Chung Yuen Motion Picture Company, 1984.

Shaolin Temple III/南北少林, dir. Chia-Liang Liu, Hong Kong, Shaw Brothers, 1986.

Shinjuku Incident/新宿事件, dir. Derek Yee, Hong Kong, Emperor Dragon Movies, 2009.

Sleepless Town/不夜城, dir. Chi-Ngai Lee, Hong Kong, Japan, ASmik Ace Entertainment, Hakuhodo DY Media Partners, Kadokawa Publishing Company, 1998.

Snow Flower and the Secret Fan, dir. Wayne Wong, China, USA, IDG China Media, 2010.

Sophie's Revenge/非常完美, dir. Eva Jin, South Korea, China, CJ Entertainment, China Film Group, Sophie Production, 2009.

Space Travelers, dir. Katsuyuki Motohiro, Japan, Fuji Television Network, Robot Communications, Toei Company, 2000.

Speed, dir. Jan de Bont, USA, The Mark Gordon Company, Twentieth Century Fox Film Corporation, 1994.

SPL: Sha Po Lang/殺破狼, dir. Wilson Yip, Hong Kong, Abba Movies, 1618 Action Limited, Greek Mythology Entertainment Company, 2005.

Star Trek, dir. Robert Wise, USA, Paramount Pictures, 1979.

Star Wars, dir. George Lucas, USA, Lucasfilm, Twentieth Century Fox Film Corporation, 1977.

Sweeney Todd: The Demon Barber of Fleet Sheet, dir. Tim Burton, USA, DreamWorks, Warner Bros, 2007.

Sweet Rain, dir. Masaya Kakehi, Japan, Mitsui Bussan, Nippon Television Network, 2008.

Swordman II/笑傲江湖II東方不敗, dir. Ching Siu-Tung, Hong Kong, Film Workshop Co. Ltd, 1992.

Tai Chi Master/太極張三豐, dir. Yuen Woo-ping, Hong Kong, Golden Harvest, 1993.

Tempting Heart/心動, dir. Sylvia Chang, Hong Kong, Media Asia Film, 1999.

The Avenging Eagle/冷血十三鷹, dir. Chung Sun, Hong Kong, Shaw Brothers, 1978.

The Banquet/夜宴, dir. Feng Xiaogang, China, Huayi Brothers Media, Media Asia Films, 2006.

The Big Brawl/ 殺手壕, dir. Robert Clouse, USA, Hong Kong, Golden Harvest, Warner Bros, 1980.

The Bodyguard from Beijing/中南海保鑣, dir. Corey Yuen, Hong Kong, Golden Harvest, 1994.

The Cannonball Run, dir. Hal Needham, USA, Hong Kong, Golden Harvest, Eurasia Investment, 1981.

The Expendables, dir. Sylvester Stallon, USA, Lionsgate, 2010.

The Expendables II, dir. Simon West, USA, Millennium Films, Nu Image Entertainment GmbH, 2012.

The Expendables III, dir. Patrick Hughes, USA, France, Bulgaria, Lionsgate, Millennium Films, Nu Image Entertainment GmbH, 2014.

The Forbidden Kingdom, dir. Rob Minkoff, USA, Lionsgate. 2008.

The Grandmaster/一代宗師, dir. Wong Kar-wai, Hong Kong, China, Block 2 Pictures, Jet Tone Films, 2013.

The Karate Kid, dir. Harald Zwart, Overbrook Entertainment, Sony Pictures Releasing, China Film Group, 2010.

The Lady, dir. Luc Besson, France, UK, EuropaCorp, Left Bank Pictures, France 2 Cinema, 2011.

The Last Emperor, dir. Bernardo Bertolucci, UK, Italy China, France, USA, Recorded Picture Company, 1987.

The Last Tycoon/大上海, dir. Wong Jing, Hong Kong, Mega Vision Pictures, Beijing Enlight Pictures, Bona Film Group, 2012.

The Legend is Born: Ip Man/葉問前傳, dir. Herman Yau, Hong Kong, Mei Ah Entertainment, 2010.

The Legend of Fong Sai Yuk I/方世玉, dir. Corey Yuen, Hong Kong, Eastern Productions, 1993.

The Legend of Fong Sai Yuk II/方世玉續集, dir. Corey Yuen, Hong Kong, China, Eastern Productions, Golden Harvest, 1993.

The Mack, dir. Michael Campus, USA, Harbour Productions, 1973.

The Matrix, dir. The Wachowski Brothers, USA, Warner Bros., 1999.

The Matrix Reloaded, dir. The Wachowski Brothers, USA, Australia, Warner Bros., Village Roadshow Pictures, Silver Pictures, 2003.

The Matrix Revolutions, dir. The Wachowski Brothers, USA, Australia, Warner Bros., Village Roadshow Pictures, NPV Entertainment, 2003.

The Mummy: Tomb of the Dragon Emperor, dir. Rob Cohen, USA, China, Universal Pictures, Relativity Media, 2008.

The Myth/神話, dir. Stanley Tong, China, JCE Movies, China Film Group, 2005.

The One, dir. James Wong, USA, Columbia Pictures. 2001.

The One Armed Swordsman/獨臂刀, dir. Chang Cheh, Hong Kong, Shaw Brothers, 1973.

The Promise/無極, dir. Chen Kaige, China, South Korea, USA, 21 Century Shengkai Film, Capgen Investment Group, China Film Group, Moonstone Entertainment, 2005.

The Protector, dir. Prachya Pinkaew, Thailand, Sahamongkolfilm Co., 2005.

The Road Home/我的父親母親, dir. Zhang Yimou, China, Columbia Pictures Film Production, Asia, Guangxi Film Studio, 1999.

The Sheltering Sky, dir. Bernado Bertolucci, UK, Italy, Recorded Picture Company, 1990.

The Sorcerer and the White Snake/法海: 白蛇傳說, dir. Ching Siu-tung, China, Hong Kong, Juli Entertainment Media, 2011.

The Spy Next Door, dir. Brian Levant, USA, Relativity Media, 2010.

The Stormraiders/風雲：雄霸天下, dir. Andrew Lau, Hong Kong, Golden Harvest Pictures (China), 1998.

The Tuxedo, dir. Kevin Donovan, USA, Blue Train Productions, 2002.

The Warlords/投名狀, dir. Peter Chan, Hong Kong, Media Asia Film, 2007.

*The Water Margin*水滸傳, dir. Chang Cheh, Pao Hsueh Li, Hong Kong, Shaw Brothers, Xian Longrui Film and TV Culture Media Co., 1972.

The Way of the Dragon/猛龍過江, dir. Bruce Lee, Hong Kong, Concord Productions, Golden Harvest, 1972.

Tiger Cage II/洗黑錢, dir. Yuen Woo-ping, Hong Kong, D &D Films, 1990.

Tokyo Raider/東京攻略, dir. Jingle Ma, Hong Kong, Golden Harvest, 2000.

Tomorrow Never Dies, dir. Roger Spottiswoode, UK, USA, MGM, United Artists, 1997.

Transformers, dir. Michael Bay, USA, DreamWorks, Paramount Pictures, 2007.

Turn Left, Turn Right/向左走·向右走, dir. Johnnie To, Wai Ka-wai, Hong Kong, Singapore, Warner Bros, Mediacorp Raintree Pictures Milky Way Image Company, 2003.

Wing Chun/詠春, dir. Yuen Woo-ping, Hong Kong, Peace Film Production, Sil-Metropole Organization, Wo Ping Films, 1994.

Wu Xia/武俠, dir. Peter Chan, Hong Kong, China, Dingsheng Cultural Industry Investment, 2001.

Index

Anglophone, 25, 27, 117, 118
   area of, 113
   cinema of, 112
Anglophone media culture, 127
anti-imperialism, 16
Asia, 11, 33, 53, 56, 57, 74, 78,
      97, 125, 129, 130, 133, 156
Asian femininity, 126
Asian masculinity, 145
Asian solidarity, 154, 155
audience, 9, 20, 21, 30, 38, 44,
      45, 51, 52, 68, 80, 87, 89, 104,
      108, 110, 112, 114, 117, 119,
      123, 128, 137, 143, 144,
      153, 157
   African-American, 40
   American, 65, 66, 141
   as producers of cultural texts, 5
   Asian American, 102, 143
   Australian, 67
   black, 40
   Chinese, 18, 56
   cultural, 132, 136

fan, 21
foreign, 7
global, 1, 6, 11, 13, 29, 53, 70,
      112, 129
global media, 142
Hong Kong, 71, 152
international, 7, 35, 58, 59, 69,
      73, 130, 141
Japanese, 130, 151, 152, 154
local, 35, 53
multilingual, 158
national, 136
Taiwanese, 56
authenticity, 30, 31, 53, 55, 94,
      104, 152, 167
   documentary, 45
   martial, 165
autonomy, 14, 128, 155
   fan, 4

blockbuster, 9, 29, 54, 109
   Hollywood, 35
   martial arts, 84, 87

blog, 4, 20, 24, 30, 31, 32, 35, 37, 43, 45, 46, 47, 52, 64, 107, 166, 169

blogger, 26, 32, 35, 36, 37, 39, 42, 43, 44, 45, 46, 47, 48, 49, 50, 52, 55, 73, 166

blogging, 4, 20, 24, 31

body, 31, 32, 42, 43, 55, 58, 65, 70, 72, 86, 103, 117, 122, 140
  as a site of confrontation and resistance, 34
  Chinese, 26, 37, 54, 168
  female, 48
  kung fu, 61
  male, 38
  martial arts, 16, 18, 19, 26, 32, 35, 36, 37, 42, 43, 52, 54, 62, 82, 168
  reconstruction of, 61
  star, 163, 165
  Wing Chun, 34, 36, 39, 166

bottom-up mode of dissemination, 28n

box-office, 1, 9, 40, 42, 54, 140, 141

capitalism, 78, 89
  global, 9, 10, 11, 18, 19, 77, 111, 154, 168
  transnational, 170

celebrity, 29, 49, 60, 76, 78, 84, 86, 87, 89, 90, 91, 92, 93, 94, 95, 96, 97, 100, 104, 108, 111, 119, 127, 154
  Asian, 153

international, 160
  multi-racial, 142

celebrity activism, 85

celebrity endorsement, 130

celebrity image, 27, 88, 133, 142

celebrity nudity, 119

celebrity philanthropist, 86, 89, 90, 91, 96, 106

celebrity philanthropy, 94

Chan, Jackie, 7, 8, 11, 13, 14, 24, 26, 31, 32, 46, 51, 55, 57, 58, 59, 60, 61, 62, 63, 64, 65, 66, 67, 68, 69, 70, 71, 72, 73, 74, 75, 76, 78, 79, 80, 81, 82, 86, 119, 122, 123, 145, 154, 160, 166

Chen, Kaige, 8, 9, 11, 125

Chen, Zhen, 26, 41, 42, 98, 101

Cheung, Maggie, 9

Chinese martial arts, 6, 7, 33, 37, 38, 58, 82, 98, 101, 106, 112

Chineseness, 10, 12, 13, 14, 15, 16, 17, 18, 19, 25, 26, 27, 28, 32, 34, 35, 37, 42, 45, 52, 54, 60, 62, 66, 70, 82, 132, 153, 161, 163, 165, 166, 167, 168, 169, 170
  cinematic, 43
  cultural imaginary of, 78
  ethnicised, 8
  'fluid', 19
  globalised, 8
  quality of, 165
  racialised, 8
  reconsideration of, 165

choreography, 2, 54, 55, 65, 66,
    68, 86, 87, 97, 166
  martial arts, 101
Chow, Yun-fat, 1, 6, 7, 9, 11, 12,
    13, 54, 55, 117, 145, 147
Chungking Express, 130, 133, 143,
    145, 146, 152, 154
cine-cyber imaginary, 14, 28, 163
computer-generated imagery
    (CGI), 2, 52, 71
cosmopolitanism, 103, 106,
    166, 167
  screen, 130, 160
Crouching Tiger, Hidden Dragon,
    1, 2, 9, 11, 18, 27, 54, 55,
    108, 112, 115, 117, 122,
    125, 126
cultural essentialism, 16
Curse of the Golden Flower, 9, 11
cyberculture, 2, 3, 5, 11, 12, 15,
    19, 20, 28, 103, 167, 170
cyberspace, 2, 3, 4, 5, 6, 12, 13,
    14, 15, 19, 23, 24, 26, 27, 30,
    44, 56, 63, 64, 82, 90, 106,
    110, 122, 131, 155, 161, 164,
    165, 167, 168, 169
  as 'universal without totality', 4
  participatory, 122, 163, 170

Depp, Johnny, 11, 27, 50, 132,
    139
  'the Asian film industry's
    Johnny Depp', 144
diaspora, 8, 16, 18, 41, 76,
    78, 128

diegesis, 156
  nationalist, 44
discourse, 4, 30, 48, 50, 52, 80,
    88, 94, 98, 107, 113, 123,
    125, 126, 127, 128, 143,
    144, 156
  blog, 55
  blogged, 32
  contextual, 22
  cultural, 19
  cyber, 14, 122, 131, 138, 167
  cyber fan, 132, 133, 139,
    152, 161
  fan, 13, 28, 66, 74, 108, 167,
    169, 170
  fan-based, 111
  fan-generated, 13
  white-star, 145
  intertextual, 43
  marketised, 9
  media, 117
  nationalist, 77
  nationalistic, 18
  online, 12
  star, 3, 4, 5, 32, 82, 110,
    160, 169
Dyer, Richard, 21, 45, 127, 132
dynamics, 8, 19, 28, 46, 109,
    111, 129
  fan, 169
  global, 155
  hegemonic, 10
  regional, 155
  star-fan, 32, 90, 96, 106
  transnational, 11, 170

East Asia, 23, 79, 126, 127
Enter the Dragon, 7, 41, 42
ethnicity
  as framework, 30

Facebook, 5, 20, 24, 27, 59, 64,
  74, 89, 90, 91, 92, 93, 94, 95,
  96, 97, 99, 100, 101, 102, 103,
  105, 131, 159, 166
fame, 3, 5, 12, 13, 41, 47, 48,
  49, 51, 52, 54, 57, 58, 59,
  63, 66, 68, 69, 74, 75, 87,
  89, 96, 97, 98, 99, 108, 110,
  112, 117, 122, 135, 142,
  152, 153, 160
  global, 11
  international, 27, 37, 39
fan, 4, 5, 7, 12, 14, 19, 21, 23, 26,
  28, 34, 36, 44, 53, 54, 56, 57,
  59, 61, 62, 63, 64, 68, 70, 72,
  87, 88, 90, 91, 92, 93, 94, 95,
  96, 99, 100, 103, 105, 107,
  127, 131, 138, 139, 149, 151,
  156, 158, 160, 165, 167
  as a discursive position, 23
  as full participants in cultural
    production, 4
  clusters of, 89
  communities of, 159
  cyber, 24, 37, 63, 101, 106,
    123, 168
  Facebook, 101, 166
  gaze of, 136
  international, 102

kung fu, 39
  local, 102
  martial arts, 69
  participation of, 22, 95
  practices of, 24, 25
  presence of, 170
  responses of, 26, 55
  reworking of, 170
  Star Wars, 49, 50
  transnational, 23
  works of, 169
  world of, 155
fan criticism, 123
fandom, 20, 62, 64, 67, 170
  media, 20, 110
fanzine, 8, 13, 89
Fifth Generation, 7, 8, 125, 165
Fist of Fury, 8, 41, 42, 98
Flickr, 5, 24, 26, 59, 60, 61,
  62, 63, 64, 68, 69, 70, 72,
  75, 76, 78, 79, 80, 82,
  131, 166
Forbes, 29, 108
forum, 24, 167
  fan, 24, 27, 148
  Internet, 131
  Soompi, 152
framework, 8, 19, 26, 170
  Foucauldian, 120
  'national cinema', 18
  state-oriented, 104
  transnational, 87
'friending', 4, 24, 166
Fukushima, 27, 156, 157, 159

genre
  Hong Kong action, 117
  mainstream, 133, 146
  martial arts, 8, 14, 15, 16, 54
  science-fiction, 26, 29
genre films, 50
goodwill, 26, 56, 58, 59, 67, 79,
    84, 88, 90, 93, 96, 97, 102,
    106, 107, 158, 166
  activities of, 60
  global, 82
gossip, 20, 123, 144, 167, 169
Grandmaster, The, 11, 34, 146
grassroots, 5, 6, 63, 68, 69, 74, 75,
    82, 168
  engagement of, 165
  forces of, 169

hegemony, 2, 17, 41, 118
  Western, 155
hero, 36, 51, 71, 77, 103
  body of, 37
  Chinese, 37, 52, 104
  Chinese wuxia, 6
  folk, 16
  image of, 145
  martial arts, 72
  nationalistic, 166
  ordinary, 12
  patriotic, 42
Hero, 9, 48, 84, 87, 88, 96, 108,
    109, 112, 126, 145, 146
hierarchy, 5
  gender, 123

Hollywood, 2, 6, 7, 9, 10, 11,
    12, 13, 26, 30, 31, 60, 61, 62,
    65, 66, 67, 69, 83, 86, 87, 97,
    102, 108, 109, 112, 114, 115,
    117, 118, 119, 123, 125, 126,
    127, 128, 129, 134, 143, 144,
    155, 156
  actors of, 33, 50, 132, 139
  an Other to the Hollywood
    stars, 145
  narratives of, 8
House of Flying Daggers, 9, 108,
    109, 112, 117, 133, 134, 135,
    141, 145, 146, 155
hybrid, 141, 170
hybridity
  cultural, 155

'ideal Chineseness', 34
'industrial celebrity', 75
interaction, 31, 63, 82, 89, 90, 91,
    101, 103
  fan, 103, 129
  star-fan, 122
Internet, 1, 3, 21, 23, 25, 90,
    93, 96, 107, 110,
    135, 167
  culture of, 4
  users of, 25, 120, 155
intertextuality, 38
Ip Man, 26, 31, 33, 34, 35, 36,
    37, 43, 47, 48, 52, 55
Ip Man, 11, 26, 33, 34, 35, 37,
    39, 40, 43, 44, 45

Japaneseness, 28, 130, 132, 150, 158, 160

jianghu, 16, 101

Kaneshiro, Takeshi, 9, 13, 14, 24, 27, 32, 53, 54, 113, 130, 131, 132, 133, 134, 136, 137, 138, 139, 140, 141, 142, 143, 144, 145, 146, 147, 148, 149, 158, 160, 161, 167

karateka, 37

kung fu, 7, 30, 31, 33, 46, 47, 52, 54, 61, 62, 66, 70, 166
films of, 33, 40
icon of, 6
masters of, 104
MMA-infused, 37

Lee, Ang, 1, 18, 146

Lee, Bruce, 7, 8, 13, 16, 26, 33, 38, 39, 40, 41, 42, 43, 44, 45, 57, 61, 86, 98

Let the Bullets Fly, 9, 11

Leung, Tony Chiu-wai, 9, 132, 145

Li, Jet, 6, 7, 8, 9, 12, 13, 14, 24, 27, 30, 32, 41, 46, 47, 51, 54, 55, 56, 63, 66, 69, 72, 73, 82, 84, 85, 86, 87, 88, 89, 90, 91, 92, 94, 95, 96, 97, 98, 99, 100, 101, 102, 103, 104, 105, 106, 107, 123, 145, 149, 160, 166

Mandarin, 76, 113, 130, 135, 143, 144, 152

manhood
patriotic, 35

manipulation
fan, 27, 110

marketing, 5, 50, 88, 140
online, 12

martial arts, 1, 33, 34, 44, 47, 48, 49, 57, 63, 71, 73, 76, 87, 89, 98, 100, 104, 106, 149, 163
cinephile of, 69
fighter of, 46, 58, 96
films of, 9, 15, 19, 27, 40, 41, 53, 54, 115, 133, 145, 150
heroines of, 115
image of, 26, 32, 66
imagery of, 11
master of, 38, 91
performers of, 75
philosophy of, 13, 32, 39, 98, 99
representation of, 2

martial arts cinema, 19, 54, 70, 165

masculinity, 34, 49, 58, 72, 146
Chinese, 7, 8, 36, 145
counter-hegemonic, 141
hegemonic, 34
hyper, 149
onscreen, 102
racialised, 145
screen, 103

mashup, 20

Memoirs of a Geisha, 11, 108, 109, 114, 115, 117, 124, 125

Mixed Martial Arts (MMA), 37
mobilisation, 160
　goodwill, 166
　philanthropic, 27, 158
　philanthropist, 83
morality, 119
multi-starrer, 9

nationalism, 16, 34, 36, 42, 74,
　　77, 103, 106
　and narcissism, 42
　Chinese, 26, 32, 39, 78, 166,
　　167
　cultural, 18, 27, 119, 167
　emergence of, 154
　male-chauvinistic, 37
　militarised, 35
　sexualised, 35
nationalistic star presence, 27
network, 3, 10, 59, 89, 92, 94, 96
　calculating, 4
　communication, 169
　culture of, 19
　cyber, 74, 93, 167
　cyber-fan, 101
　cyber-global, 129
　digital, 2
　fan, 8, 166, 169
　fans' communication, 5
　global, 3
　global visual, 110
　global-cyber, 103
　martial arts filmmaking, 46
　online, 49
　overseas distribution, 135

pan-Asian, 9
pan-Chinese, 9
regional, 79
transnational, 158

ordinary user, 68, 69, 102
Orientalised image, 10
Orientalist allure, 11
Orientalist imagination,
　　9, 117
Orientalist portrayal, 142
Orientalist stylistics, 18

participatory culture, 20, 63
performance, 2, 11, 13, 27, 30,
　　31, 62, 66, 70, 71, 87, 102,
　　112, 113, 128, 134, 136, 137,
　　138, 140, 141, 144, 145, 146,
　　147, 148, 153, 167
　box-office, 35
　choreographic, 53
　English-speaking, 111
　filmic, 148
　martial arts, 88
　screen, 68, 69, 126, 132,
　　134, 152
persona
　blogged, 32
　border-crossing, 63
　celebrity, 101
　cinematic, 24, 32, 34, 61, 68,
　　70, 82, 97, 101, 155
　goodwill, 99, 103
　management of, 14
　manipulation of, 5, 131

persona (*cont.*)
  martial arts, 30, 31, 32, 36, 49,
    50, 55, 62, 82, 90, 97, 102,
    104, 166
  martial arts star, 70
  offscreen, 12, 103, 167
  onscreen, 26, 31, 34, 45, 47, 48,
    51, 52, 62, 65, 97, 101, 102,
    103, 105, 117, 134, 143, 145,
    146, 166, 167
  pan-Asian, 132, 155
  philanthropic, 101
  polysemic, 146, 167
  Wing Chun, 13, 33, 45
philanthropy, 84, 85, 86, 87, 88, 89,
    91, 93, 97, 100, 106, 107, 166
  and Buddhism, 99
  as a strategy, 160
  Hollywood, 86
polysemy
  polysemic image, 161
  polysemic personality, 10
post-cinema, 14, 15
publicity, 3, 5, 12, 22, 54, 56, 59,
    61, 63, 68, 69, 70, 73, 74, 75,
    77, 79, 89, 90, 96, 97, 102,
    103, 109, 111, 114, 118, 123,
    154, 160, 166
  celebrity, 95, 106
  offscreen, 45
  star, 82

Reeves, Keanu, 27, 132, 136,
    139, 141
  'Asian Keanu Reeves', 144, 150

reinvention, 45, 170
reputation, 5, 34, 84, 87, 95, 96,
    99, 128
resistance, 41
  icon of, 41
  pan-Asian, 154
  resistance to the West, 153
reworking, 13, 26
  fan, 28
Rouge One, 29, 30, 31, 35, 37,
    49, 50

scandal, 108, 119, 121, 122, 123
  media, 120
  quasi-sex, 27
  sex, 109, 111, 167
scrutiny, 5, 19, 75, 85, 86, 93,
    103, 112, 122
Shaolin Temple, 69, 87, 102, 104
'sick men of Asia', 42
social media, 59, 73, 74
social network, 5, 20, 27, 77, 83,
    89, 90, 95, 99, 101, 106, 159
special effect, 54, 65, 71
  computer-generated, 87
spectator, 22, 23
spectators as a 'manipulated'
    mass, 21
star
  celebrity, 138, 140
  Hollywood, 11, 21, 22, 27
  kung fu, 39
  martial arts, 2, 29, 41, 59, 65,
    67, 69, 86, 88, 101, 105,
    122, 166

transnational Chinese, 11, 13, 32, 55, 78, 84, 145, 160, 169

star image, 6, 8, 12, 14, 21, 24, 27, 74, 77, 78, 82, 85, 88, 89, 90, 96, 106, 111, 122, 130, 132, 147, 149, 163, 164, 165, 166, 168

   'glocalised', 12

   pan-Asian, 156

   polysemic, 132

star persona, 22, 23, 26, 28, 60, 67, 69, 88, 89, 90, 95, 106, 129, 145, 160, 163, 166

Star Wars, 2, 29, 30, 35, 37, 39, 49, 50

stardom, 7, 15, 21, 22, 23, 51, 60, 64, 67, 82, 86, 95, 96, 104, 133, 136, 140, 141, 142, 145, 153, 155, 169

   border-crossing, 10

   Chinese, 6, 12, 15, 19, 28, 78, 170

   Chinese female, 129

   Chinese movie, 26

   cosmopolitan, 103

   cyber, 4

   film, 5

   global, 27, 62, 106

   Hollywood, 65

   Hollywood A-list male, 142

   hybrid, 154

   in cyberspace, 59

   international, 6, 9, 108

   international Chinese, 7

   martial arts, 68, 169

   performance of, 169

   regional, 126

   screen, 4

   transnational, 6, 27, 63

   transnational Chinese, 8, 10, 19, 156

studio

   Hollywood, 66

subjectivity, 72

   Chinese, 36, 37

   erasing of, 65

   in language, 113

   star, 151

substantiality, 18, 31, 44, 168

   absence of, 18

   historical, 165

The Forbidden Kingdom, 54, 68, 69, 70, 71, 72, 87, 88, 166

transgression

   intimate, 120

   moral, 121

transnational cinema, 6, 13

transnational cultural politics, 109

transnational superstardom, 31, 128

transnationality, 10

universality, 12, 130, 156

user-generated content (UGC), 4

video-sharing site, 4, 107, 110, 119, 167

virtuality, 170

Web 2.0, 4, 5, 6, 13, 20, 24, 32,
  59, 106, 131, 169, 170
web users, 12, 13, 14, 20, 23, 30,
  59, 74, 125, 128, 149
Wikipedia, 20
wikis, 20
Wing Chun, 55
  icon of, 34
  master of, 34
Wing Chun personality, 35,
  36, 37
Wong, Hei-fung, 16, 34, 101,
  102, 104
World Wide Web, 3, 4, 20, 23, 31
Wu Xia, 53, 54, 55, 144, 146,
  149, 155

Yen, Donnie, 2, 7, 9, 13, 14, 24,
  26, 29, 30, 31, 32, 33, 34, 35,
  38, 39, 42, 43, 45, 46, 47, 48,
49, 51, 52, 53, 54, 55, 69, 122,
  126, 144, 149, 166
Yeoh, Michelle, 2, 7, 8, 13, 33, 55,
  115, 117
YouTube, 1, 2, 24, 27, 30, 37, 48,
  49, 64, 107, 109, 110, 111,
  112, 119, 122, 125, 131, 144,
  160
  users of, 126
Yuen, Woo-ping, 1, 2, 7, 30, 33,
  47, 55, 71

Zhang, Yimou, 8, 9, 11, 63, 84,
  109, 112, 113, 119, 145, 146
Zhang, Ziyi, 1, 2, 8, 9, 11, 13, 14,
  24, 27, 32, 46, 63, 69, 107,
  108, 109, 110, 111, 112, 113,
  114, 115, 117, 118, 119, 120,
  121, 122, 123, 124, 125, 126,
  127, 128, 144, 145, 167